The
Creation
of a
Serial
Killer

JACK OLSEN

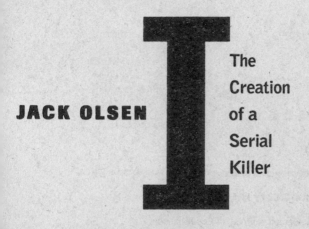

I

The
Creation
of a
Serial
Killer

St. Martin's Paperbacks

I: THE CREATION OF A SERIAL KILLER

Copyright © 2002 by Jack Olsen.

Cover photograph courtesy of Les Jesperson.

Library of Congress Catalog Card Number: 2001058892

ISBN: 0-312-98384-0
EAN: 80312-98384-0

Printed in the United States of America

St. Martin's Press hardcover edition / August 2002
St. Martin's Paperbacks edition / August 2003

St. Martin's Paperbacks are published by St. Martin's Press, 175 Fifth Avenue, New York, NY 10010.

10 9 8 7 6 5 4

Jonathan Rhoades Olsen, "Lefty," beloved son
We always made each other laugh

PROLOGUE A Tawdry Little Murder

On a chilly winter day in Portland, Oregon, Taunja Bennett kissed her mother good-bye and said she was off to meet a boyfriend. She disappeared from sight in the direction of a bus stop, her Walkman plugged into her ears. Lately the twenty-three-year-old high school dropout had been listening over and over to "Back to Life" by Soul II Soul. She carried a small black purse.

Taunja was mildly retarded from oxygen deprivation at birth. She'd been a difficult child. In a cooking class at Cleveland High School, she assaulted a classmate in a quarrel over a piece of cake. Addicted to alcohol and drugs, she was committed to a state hospital for six months. At twenty-one, she frequented northeast Portland bars like the Woodshed, the Copper Penny and Thatcher's. She hustled drinks, shot pool and got into trouble with men. She was petite and pretty—five-five, with glistening dark brown hair, liquid brown eyes, a trim figure, and a naively impulsive manner. She introduced herself to strangers by throwing her arms around them. Recently she'd complained to her mother that a man had taken her home from the B&I Tavern, beaten her and "pimped me out." She said she was afraid to go back to the same bar. But her memory had always been short.

ON JANUARY 22, 1990, the morning after Loretta Bennett said good-bye to her daughter, a bicyclist braked hard at a splash of color on a steep embankment above the Columbia River Gorge, ten miles east of Portland. Wisps of fog drifted up from the water and partly obscured the squat stone edifice known as Vista House, a popular lookout and make-out spot.

Just down the slope from the two-lane road, in a greenish coffin of vine maple, devil's club, poison oak and blackberry tendrils, the biker found a young woman's body, faceup, head pointed downhill, arm splayed backward. Her jeans and panties were around her ankles and her bra was above her breasts. A white nylon rope encircled her neck. The fly front on her jeans had been neatly excised, leaving an oval opening. The woman's face looked as though it had been pounded with a hammer.

The body remained unidentified for eight days, until Loretta Bennett saw a police sketch on the evening news and visited the morgue. Detectives were puzzled by the savagery of the killing. It was unlikely that a random acquaintance would wreak such devastation on a fellow human, even in the frenzy of rape. Investigators believed they were dealing with a highly personal act of retribution or revenge.

TWO MORE weeks passed before police reported their first promising lead. On February 13, Detective Alan Corson of the Oregon State Police interviewed Carol Copeland, the B&I bartender who'd been on duty the afternoon before the body was found. Corson reported:

> *Ms. Copeland stated on this date, Taunja Bennett arrived at the B&I Tavern sometime around noon to 1 P.M. She advised that Taunja came into the tavern alone, and Ms. Copeland noticed she was quite wet and appeared to have walked to the tavern in the rain. She stated that Taunja appeared to be in a happy mood, and she purchased a beer at the bar, paying for it with small change. . . .*
>
> *Ms. Copeland stated Taunja began socializing in the bar, talking to various patrons. She began talking to two men who were playing pool at the east end of the bar. She stated Taunja continued*

talking with the two men playing pool, and at approximately 4–4:30 P.M., Taunja walked over to the bar and asked Carol if she wanted to go out disco-dancing after Carol got off work at 5 P.M. . . .

Carol stated she told Taunja that she should not go with these two men because Taunja did not know them and it was not a safe thing to do. Taunja replied she would be OK and returned to where the men were playing pool.

A night bartender described one of the pool shooters as about thirty, a few inches over six feet tall, with short blond hair. The second player was blond and shorter. She recalled serving them a pitcher of beer. At around 8:00 P.M., she'd noticed that the blond men and Taunja Bennett were gone.

ANOTHER TWO weeks passed before police announced that they'd caught the killers. They weren't the pool shooters but a May-and-December couple, John Sosnovske and Laverne Pavlinac. The fifty-seven-year-old twice-married grandmother, a state hospital worker, confessed in detail and implicated the thirty-nine-year-old Sosnovske, a rough-hewn sawyer who was already on probation for a series of drunken crimes and misdemeanors. The gray-haired woman told police that her besotted boyfriend had picked up Taunja Bennett in a tavern and driven her to a ravine above the Columbia Gorge, where she'd held a rope around the victim's neck while Sosnovske committed acts of rape and murder. The plump, matronly woman produced a cut-out section of fly front from a pair of Levi's jeans and led police to the spot where she and her lover had dumped the body.

John Sosnovske denied involvement but failed two lie-detector tests. After he was arraigned on murder charges, he tried to shift blame for the killing to a fellow alcoholic who proved to be innocent. Police reported finding a scribbled note in Sosnovske's possession: "T. Bennett: A Good Piece." The sawyer's light brown hair matched a strand found on the corpse's arm.

The tawdry little murder case was marked closed.

1

KEITH

HUNTER

JESPERSON 1

1 | Bloody Murder

*The offender typically reports being in an upset
and distressed frame of mind at the time of the offense. His predominant mood state appears to be
a combination of anger, distress, frustration, and
depression, and the offense is typically preceded
by some upsetting event, often, but not invariably,
involving some significant woman in the as-
sailant's life.*
— A. Nicholas Groth with H. Jean Birnbaum,
Men Who Rape

It was the kind of day that always got me down—windy,
gray, boring. I was in a bad mood before I even rolled out
of bed. Everything was going wrong in my life. I thought, *I
can't deal with this spooky old house one more minute. I've
got to get out.* I was tired and depressed. Rape and murder
were the last things on my mind.

Hanging out was always hard on me. I was raised on
work. The whole family tree was like that—work, work
and more work. But I had too many driving violations to
go back to my job as a long-distance trucker, at least for a
while. I was collecting unemployment and sending half to
my ex-wife. Which meant I was usually broke. And bored.

• • •

The whole Christmas season had been a downer. I'd sold everything to buy presents for my kids. Sold my eighteen-speed Twin Voyager for $350, half what it was worth. Sold my graphite fishing pole, my Garcia 5000 reel, lures, sinkers, line, fishing tackle I'd accumulated since I was a kid. Sold everything I owned to bring in cash for Christmas.

I was living in my girlfriend's little ranch house in Portland, just off Interstate 84. I'd left my wife and kids for Peggy Jones (a pseudonym), and now the bitch was out on the road, screwing another trucker. Five days after Christmas she'd gone to a truck stop and started flirting again. Didn't come home that night and didn't call—nothing new for Peg.

Just after New Year's the phone rang and an operator said, "I have a collect call for Keith Jesperson." It was Peggy, telling me she was in Knoxville with her new boyfriend. She ordered me out of her house—"Move! If you're gonna stay there, you're gonna pay me rent." She told me to send her money, called me an asshole and hung up.

I felt like punching somebody, even though it wasn't my nature. I was sitting out front stewing when I spotted an alley cat. I lured it into the house and prodded it into a corner where it couldn't get away. Then I strangled it. I got my dislike of cats from my dad, I guess. I'd killed animals since I was five or six. For a while it was one of my jobs. Killing cats was no big deal to me. It kind of relieved the pressure.

I was never violent with human beings, but at the same time I was nobody's wimp. A few days after Peg ran off with the other trucker, I'd gone to Albertson's Market to do some freelance labor, unloading sixty-pound bags off a truck. Eight of the regular lumpers came after me with clubs and baseball bats. I grabbed the first guy and broke his arm with his own bat. I snapped another guy's leg.

They ran like deer. When you stand six-six and weigh 250 pounds and know how to box, you're already a lethal weapon.

Peggy always tried to make me play the stern daddy with her two kids. I refused. She kicked their ass, but I'd been beaten as a kid and made up my mind I would never hit a child or a woman. I never hit my own kids, never laid a hand on my ex-wife or any other woman. Once I got so mad at my wife I put my fist through a door, but I didn't come close to hitting her.

It was lonely without my girlfriend, and I only wished she'd come back. She was trouble, but we always had great sex. Without her my social life consisted of drinking coffee and talking with other drivers at the truck stops around Portland. Or I'd watch TV, take long walks, and shoot pool in taverns. Usually I stayed out till after midnight, doing nothing. I never felt at home in Peg's spooky house and looked for every excuse to get away.

In the middle of January she'd phoned again and told me she'd made a firm decision to stay with the new boyfriend, and we were finished for good. I got pissed and depressed at the same time. Now all I had for company was the ghosts that hung out in Peg's house. The family story was that they were two men who hanged themselves fifty or sixty years ago. I swear you could feel them in the air. You'd walk down the hallway and brush against something you couldn't see. At night they crawled across Peggy and me in bed. Shadows on the walls would appear and fade out. Sometimes the ghosts would yell and howl and bang on the walls. We just learned to accept it. What else?

On that dismal morning of January 21, 1990, I left the house with only a few bucks so I wouldn't overspend. I was killing time, as usual, but I never thought I'd end up killing a human being.

I decided to shoot some pool. In the bars it was winner stays up and challengers pay, so I could usually play free as long as I wanted. I was good at nine-ball. I called razzle-dazzle shots, two-rail shots, English, massés, trick shots. I was almost good enough to hustle professionally.

About 2:00 P.M. I found myself in the B&I Tavern with a buck or two in my pocket. The B&I was like a half-dozen other joints in the Gresham neighborhood. It was a seedy old place in a blue-collar area of plain wooden houses, bars and liquor stores, small shops. A smelly bluish haze came up from the trucks and cars on Burnside and the other arterials. They call Portland "the Rose City," but there weren't many roses in this part of town.

Three pool tables were open, so I grabbed a cue, put in my quarters, and broke the balls. I went to the bar to order a black coffee—watching my weight. When I turned around, I saw that one gal had started a game with two blond-haired guys. She was about five-six, with dark hair to her shoulders and a petite build—looked a lot like my ex-wife Rose but even prettier. This gal had kind of a round face and a big happy smile like she didn't have a care.

When she noticed me eyeballing her, she ran up and gave me a big hug. The barmaid twirled her index finger around her ear and said, "Why are you hugging this guy? You don't know him. He's not a part of your life." Later the waitress told me the girl was a retard who hung out with losers in bars and pool halls. She was very sweet and nice, but she didn't know enough to come in out of the rain.

After I shot a few racks by myself, the girl asked me to join her and the two guys, said her name was Taunja. A friendly game of pool would have been okay, but I noticed that their tabletop was empty. That meant they were trolling for a beer sponsor. I walked home.

• • •

I moped around and watched TV for an hour or two, but everything still seemed flat and depressing. I kept remembering the pretty girl hugging me and the bartender motioning that she was a little off. My fantasies shifted into high.

I drove my borrowed 74 Nova two-door back to the B&I, thinking, *She must actually like me! Retard or not, how often does* that *happen?* By the time I arrived, I was totally turned on.

As I was walking into the tavern she was walking out. I followed her to the parking lot. I thought, *If I can get her into my car, I'll try to take her home and have sex with her. If she resists, maybe I'll take it anyway.* Four or five years earlier I'd tried to take a gal by force in my truck, but she got away. After that, I cleaned up my act. Now I felt like trying again. My whole life was screwed up and I was on my ass. What did I have to lose?

I walked up to the girl and said, "Hi. How you doing? Remember me? This afternoon I was in the tavern—and you hugged me."

She smiled and said, "Oh, yeah, I remember you. What do you want?"

I said, "I was just going to eat someplace. How'd you like to go have a bite to eat, maybe play pool later?"

I guess that's what she wanted to hear. "Sure sounds good to me," she said.

I led her to my car and she got in. I opened my wallet to show her that I was broke, but I told her I had a twenty in my dresser drawer. "It's only six blocks from here. Do you mind coming with me for a few minutes?" She nodded.

I parked in the driveway next to Peggy's old Ford Pinto. I said, "Why don't you come inside for a few minutes? I could use the bathroom and maybe shave."

"Well, all right," she said. "I'll leave my Walkman and purse in the car."

I thought about actually taking her to dinner, mainly because if I showed her a good time she'd put out for sure.

But I also needed to follow through with my fantasy. I was thinking about what I'd done to the cat.

I guided Taunja to my front door. She asked me who owned the parked Pinto and I told her my roommate was trucking in the East and wouldn't be back for weeks. I closed the door behind us and went into the bedroom to figure out my next move. My mind was spinning. I thought about keeping her as my sex slave. I wanted total possession—no bullshit and no back talk. I would keep her for a couple of weeks and then kick her out. I'd read about Ted Bundy keeping his women for a long time before he killed them. Some women had it coming.

The girl spied Jesus Christ on the wall and said, "Nice picture. What's with the mattress on the floor?"

I said, "I sleep and watch TV there. I feel more comfortable."

I was fascinated at her trust in a total stranger. Maybe it was because she was half-drunk. I realized that I was in full control.

I came up behind her and kissed her neck. She ran straight for the door. I grabbed her and said, "I guess sex is out of the question?"

When she didn't answer I laid her on the mattress and kissed her. The curtains were shut and the windows and doors closed. She was trapped!

She wriggled away and ran to the door again. I was surprised at how strong she was. I dragged her back to the mattress. I could feel her trembling in my grip. But just when I thought she was totally scared, she kissed me and told me to hurry up.

"Kiss me again," I said, "with feeling." When she realized that I was giving the orders, she began to put out a little. After a while I yanked down her jeans and rubbed her crotch. I reached under her top and pushed the bra up over her breasts and felt her up.

We kissed some more and she guided me in. In a few strokes I came in an orgasm. I didn't want to stop. I stayed inside and waited, and pretty soon I was giving it to her again, slow and easy.

She finally got tired of waiting for me. She didn't know I'd already come. She yanked at me and started babbling. "I don't feel a thing. Why don't you get it over with and take me out to dinner! No more kissing! I'm not in love with you, man. Let's go! I'm hungry."

I saw red. It brought back so many nights with other women. *Wham bam thank you Keith.* A lot of women are users. Sex is a means to an end, not a romantic thing. They'll give you a little, but not because they love you.

I pumped in another orgasm and then I looked down at her with my dick still inside and thought, *Now that it's over, she'll expect payment in full.* Well, I'm not giving her a dime. I don't have to put up with that kind of selfish shit anymore. I looked at her face and I could swear my ex-wife looked back.

I decided to knock her out with one punch. She would wake up hog-tied and nowhere to go. Then I could take all the sex I wanted. I would figure out what to do with her after I'd had my fun. I still wasn't thinking about murder.

I put all of my strength into one blow and punched her in the temple. She just stared at me. I hit her again to knock her out, but she stayed awake. I couldn't understand. When I was a boxer I knocked guys out with one punch, wearing twelve-ounce gloves!

I hit her again and again, but she wouldn't go under. I thought, *Why isn't this like the crime shows on TV?* The more I hit her, the more I wanted to hit her. It felt like me and the cat, only better. In all my thirty-four years I'd never hit a female, but I smashed this girl twenty times—rights, lefts, jabs, uppercuts, hooks. I punched her till I couldn't recognize her face and then I punched her some more. It just felt good. I felt like I was paying back the women in my life, the demons in the house, all my troubles. The ghosts would run off—no more noises in the night, waking me up. Now they knew what I could do.

I stopped punching and looked down. Her face was squashed—broken nose, broken jaw, teeth sticking through her lips. But she still wasn't out! She clawed at the blankets and cried, kept saying, "Mommy! Mommy! Make him stop! *Make him stop, Mommy!*" Her eyes were bloody. She clawed at me, but all she caught was air.

After a while I began to feel a little bad about what I'd done. I knew she would die if I didn't do something. *Do I want to keep her in this condition for days? Or should I end her torture quickly?* I couldn't take her to the hospital, I'd go to jail for sure.

I had to put her out of her misery.

I choked her till my knuckles turned white, but every time I let loose, she gasped. This went on for four or five minutes. *Why won't she die?* It was frustrating. I felt like I was losing control. I was trying to do one simple thing, and I couldn't do it—the story of my life.

I squeezed as hard as I could. She peed the floor and stopped moving. I went into the kitchen, poured a cup of coffee and sat down to think out what I should do next—a guy who'd never even slapped a woman, and now I got a dead body on my hands.

2 | Ghosts

After I drank my coffee, I dressed her. There was blood all over the walls and floor. I never realized how much blood could come out of one girl's body. The light shone on the metal buttons on her fly, and I wondered if they would hold fingerprints. I used a steak knife to cut out the fly and threw it in the fireplace.

I washed and dried my clothes and put them back on. I had to be extra sure she didn't wake up, so I went to the garage for a piece of half-inch nylon rope and cinched it as tight as I could around her neck. I heard one of the ghosts rattling around, and I hollered, "Now you got company, you bastards!" I sat with Taunja for a while, halfway enjoying my power over her and halfway wishing I could bring her back to life. But pretty soon I realized I had to get rid of the body and establish an alibi or I could end up at the end of a rope. I was no criminal, but I watched *Perry Mason* every morning and knew how important a good alibi could be. I said good-bye to Taunja and drove straight to the B&I Tavern to start laying the groundwork.

I drank a Bud Lite and talked to the barmaid and some customers till about 9:30 P.M. I made sure they saw me leave alone. Then I drove ten miles east to the Vista House, a tourist attraction with a view of the Columbia River Gorge. I found plenty of good places to hide a body.

By now I was beginning to think a little straighter. On

the way back home I told myself, *Don't make stupid mistakes when you dump her. Don't run out of gas. Don't throw up.* I had a sensitive stomach. Dirty diapers could make me sick.

At the A.M./P.M. Market I filled my tank and checked my lights. I didn't need some cop pulling me over for a dead taillight and finding a dead woman in my car.

I backed into my driveway to block off the neighbors' view when I loaded the body. I switched off the dome light so it wouldn't go on when the doors opened. I was feeling unreal, a little woozy. I went inside to take another look. Was this really happening?

The girl was right where I'd left her on the mattress. I'm still in a state of disbelief. I'm saying to myself, *Why? Why? Now look what I'm in for!*

I decided that I'd just wanted to see what it was like to kill, to see if I could do it. My girlfriend Peggy had wanted me to kill her ex-husband and I told her I couldn't. Now maybe I could do the job and get her back.

The phone rang. My heart jumped. Who would be calling at midnight?

It was Peg. I asked, "Where are you?"

"In the East," she says. "I'm working my way back."

What a relief! For a second I thought she was in town and on her way home. My heart slowed down.

She said, "Nothing's working out here." She asked me to send money for her to come home. She said she hated her codriver because he wouldn't let her drive when he slept. Plus he wanted to jump her at every stop. And he was a "male chauvinist bastard."

I knew the real reason she wanted me back. She was finally seeing long-distance trucking for what it truly is: hard, tough, demanding work. There was no nice-guy Keith to be patient with her and cover up for her mistakes and let her crash in the sleeper most of the time. She said her codriver estimated her true miles, and it was never more than three hundred per day. Substandard. But she'd always been a lousy trucker, even when she was driving with me. Driving trucks is no job for a ninety-eight-pound ditz that doesn't know her ass from her elbow.

I kept her on the phone while I stared at the body on the mattress. I said, "The ghosts are scared of me now. They know I'm badder than they are."

"What are you talking about?" she said. "Are they still keeping you up?"

"No! They aren't making their moves and I don't think they want to. Not now."

She let that pass and told me that she was headed home—promised to call me when she got close. She said she loved me, and I said I loved her too. I wasn't sure if it was true, but I loved our sex life together, that's for sure. Peggy was an Olympic athlete in bed.

That little conversation revived my hard-on. Would I abuse a dead body? I felt the dead girl's skin. Her tits were clammy and turned me off. After a while I masturbated on her to clear my brain. For a lot of years after that, the memory of her dead body spurred on dreams and fantasies, and I could always masturbate at the thought of Taunja. She became my favorite fantasy.

3 | A Word to the Dead

I looked at my watch and it was after midnight—time to dump the body. I turned off the lights and made sure the coast was clear. She'd stiffened up, and I tied a rope around her neck to make her easier to drag. I pulled her out the front door by her feet, squeezed her onto the front seat of the Nova hatchback, folded her legs inside and pushed the door shut so it wouldn't make a loud click.

Her head rested against the window, but there was nothing I could do about that. Other drivers would just think she was drunk. I brought an extra pair of shoes to put on after I finished dumping her body. My triple-E Cannondale bicycling shoes had a flat, ribbed sole with a tread pattern that would be easy to trace. I would miss them—I used to ride forty or fifty miles a day.

I locked the little brown house and drove back out to Crown Point, being careful not to speed or cross over the center line. Vista House is locked in the wintertime, but five or six cars were in the parking lot. I talked to the dead girl as we looked for her final resting place. "Where will you sleep tonight, sweetheart? In that culvert over there? That ditch? Those briers?"

I drove a mile past Vista House to a straight stretch of roadway. Pretty soon my headlights showed a ravine. I grabbed her hand, pulled her out of the car and dragged her down the embankment. It was a steep grade, and I tripped on shrubs and bushes. About sixty feet from the road, I let loose of her and said, "This is it. Your home!" Her head was pointed downhill, and one arm stuck out backward.

I should have covered her with leaves, but I thought I saw some lights below me and rushed toward my car to get the hell out. Scrambling up the slope I saw a big bony hand backlit by the moon. I panicked before I realized it was the silhouette of a dead tree.

I drove off fast. When I reached the first sharp turn, my lights hit the side of an oncoming Multnomah county sheriff's car. I watched in my rearview mirror to see if he stopped. He never slowed down.

I was pissed at myself for leaving the body so close to the road, but it was too late now. I threw my biking shoes in the underbrush along the shoulder. I dropped her Walkman on the Sandy River Bridge deck so cars and trucks would flatten it. Then I took I-84 west to the Burns Brothers Truck Stop in Troutdale, one of my hangouts when I was driving truck.

I'd just ordered coffee when three state-patrol cops headed straight toward my booth. I thought, *These guys know. They know!* And her purse is outside in my car!

They took seats in the next booth, and I recognized a couple of them from my days on the road. After my heart slowed down, I started a conversation to build up my alibi. One of them asked if I was still driving truck, and I told them I was in between rides. We talked for a while and they left.

I stayed at the truck stop till 8:00 A.M., making sure that plenty of people saw me and talked to me. Then I drove three miles up the Sandy River Road, took two dollars from the dead girl's purse and flipped it into a blackberry patch where nobody would ever find it. A smart move, too. It stayed there for five years and finally saved two people's ass.

Back home **again,** I opened up the house windows to get rid of the faint smell of death. I scraped dried blood off the walls and washed the sheets and blankets, vacuumed the floor and cleaned the rugs with a carpet cleaner. Eventually I had to deodorize the carpet twice and steam clean it.

I tried to wash the bloodstains off the ceiling and decided to paint it over with latex as soon as the blood was completely dried. Cops have a spray that makes bloodstains fluoresce like headlights. I'd seen it used on some TV shows. I reminded myself to finish the paint job before Peggy showed up.

Later in the day I went out and looked at some used cars to help my alibi. Would a killer shop for a car the next day?

I tried to forget the details of what I'd done, tried to pretend that someone else did it. That was the only way I could get through the next few nights. I couldn't get her face out of my mind. What kind of animal would pound an innocent young woman's face into mush? I decided I should commit suicide. But then I thought, *No, I won't. I can't do this to the Jesperson name. My kids would be ashamed. Dad would be so angry.*

A few mornings later, after I watched *Perry Mason*, I walked to Albertson's Market for the paper. I read that a biker had found the body of a woman in the Columbia Gorge. The article said the cops were looking for two six-footers who'd been seen shooting pool with her in a bar. It was a relief that nobody was looking for me.

I decided to put suicide out of my mind. But I couldn't shake the feeling that everybody knew I was a murderer, even the people I passed on the street. Ever since I was a kid, I'd always felt guilty about something or other.

I thought about the killing and gave myself some excuses for what I'd done. That I was angry and depressed. That I just snapped. That the girl pushed my buttons by acting cold. That she asked for it by trying to con me out of dinner. Or that she was nothing but a street whore anyway.

After a while I had to confront the truth. Killing that girl came straight from my fantasies. She could have been any woman. In those last few minutes on the mattress on the floor, nothing could have stopped me.

I wondered why I didn't keep her alive for a week or two, take more time to enjoy her. I masturbated at the memory of her skin under mine. My penis remembered how it felt. It was the only sex I was getting.

A month went by and I read in the paper that two suspects were in custody. *Huh?* How could they be guilty of a murder that I committed? I figured the cops had picked up the two blond beer-drinkers from the B&I Tavern and forced them to confess. It bothered me a little that the wrong guys were taking my fall, but I also realized how lucky I was. As long as I stayed out of the B&I, the cops could never lay a glove on me. I'd gotten away with murder.

Then the weird situation turned weirder. The suspects turned out to be a couple of barflies, a man and a woman. The newspaper stories were skimpy, but it looked like the woman had confessed and implicated her boyfriend. She led the police to the exact spot where I dumped the body, out near Vista House. I was going nuts trying to figure out what was going on. It made as much sense as our ghosts.

A few days later I read that the D.A. had charged the barflies with murder. It wasn't my problem anymore.

4 | Mr. Mom

Peggy came home with her two children. Just what I didn't need—another house full of kids. She promised they'd behave. Well, sure! She beat the crap out of them and expected me to do the same. I couldn't. How could anybody beat a kid that was five years old? Or any kid?

She sat around for a while, then took a full-time job waitressing. Now I'm Mr. Mom, dusting the furniture, cleaning the shitter and baby-sitting. It felt bad to take Peggy's kids to the movies when my own divorced kids in Spokane were doing without.

We started having big fights again. Things got so bad, I would walk out the back door as she walked in the front. I just didn't want to confront her anymore, except in bed. We still had good sex, but otherwise it was over. The ghosts would wake me up in the middle of the night and I'd find my hands around her neck. I realized that I got a big rush out of killing that girl and wouldn't mind doing another one. This was crazy thinking and I knew it.

I had to get away from Portland and this house before I lost it completely. I was *already* crazy. A freak. I had nightmares about killing an innocent girl, woke up screaming from guilt and shame, and a few minutes later I would fantasize about doing it again.

• • •

In March, two months after the killing, I headed south on I-5 for a construction job in Sacramento. Approaching Rogue River, Oregon, I was thinking about kidnapping women for sex and maybe even killing again. I tried to push the idea out of my mind, but it jumped right back in. I thought about my old girlfriend Nancy Flowers that lived up in the woods, not far off the interstate. I'd met her at a truck stop at Mile Marker 161 in Oregon and stayed with her a few nights. She was forty-four—nine years older than me—good-looking, divorced, a swinger. She advertised herself to magazines and sold photos of herself in the nude. But I got her for free. She'd showed me where she kept her collection of pictures and her loose cash.

As I drove, my mind ran wild with the possibilities. Maybe she wouldn't make me welcome. What difference did it make? If she gave me trouble, I might grab her and put her away for good. Then I'd take her money. I was pissed at the world anyway. I tried to think straight, but I couldn't. I was starting to be afraid of what I'd become.

The closer I got to her house, the harder my penis got. I thought about enslaving her for a few days. I felt her presence as I approached her door. I felt her softness as if she was already hugging me.

I knocked, and nobody answered. I found her spare key under the rock where she kept it and let myself in.

The place was empty. I smelt something a little off, like a rat died in the walls. I could feel a woman's presence. What the hell happened here?

I drove to the little market at the Y-junction and asked where Nancy was hanging out. They told me her ex-husband and another biker had paid her a little visit. One raped her while the other beat her to death with a crowbar. She died in the living room. A few weeks later the rapist ran his mouth and one of his friends ratted him out. They were in jail awaiting trial.

As I headed south, I thought, *What a bummer. I might have killed Nancy myself if she'd been home. Everybody's dying all around me. I'm seeing death everywhere. Where do I turn? What the hell, I killed Taunja Bennett and got away with it. I could kill anybody. It's up to me.* It was a heavy thought.

5 | Breast-Feeding

I left Rogue River on I-5 and stopped at the Pear Tree Truck Stop in Phoenix, Oregon, to see if any female hitch-hikers were around. For a change there wasn't a lot lizard in sight.

I drove to a shopping area in Shasta, California, and bought myself some celery and peanut butter for dinner. It was all I could afford, and I was watching my weight again. I certainly didn't need to get any bigger. I always thought of myself as a nice-looking extra-extra-large-sized guy with glasses. I had the same blue eyes and brown hair as James Dean, and I combed it straight back like Elvis. I walked with my chest out and my back straight. I wore cowboy boots to add an extra two inches. I never had a problem attracting female attention, but if I put on too much weight they might shy away.

At the Shasta Shopping Center I tried to decide if I wanted to sleep in my car or take a cheap motel room. I had the re-tarded girl on my mind and needed some privacy. While I was thinking, a nice-looking woman strolled up. A baby sucked her breast while she sucked a pint of Jack Daniels. She says, "What're *you* lookin' at? It's only natural."

She took a few steps closer to give me a better look at her tits and sat on a railroad tie. I could see she was half-drunk. She told me her name was Jean (a pseudonym) and her kid was six months old. I told her I was Keith Hunter Jesperson and I was on my way to a temporary job at Copenhagen Utilities in Sacramento. She said she'd just had a big fight with her husband. After we talked a little more, she took the last sip from her pint and asked me to walk her to the Jiffy Mart to buy some beer.

I carried the twelve-pack back to my car and we sat in the front seat and griped about our troubles. Then she had me drive her out in the country to a lookout place where the locals went. She handed me her baby, dropped her jeans, and peed right next to the open door. I couldn't believe a woman would do that. So when she got back, I handed her the baby and did the same thing. She was giving me ideas.

The conversation naturally turned to sex. She claimed to be the best blow job in Shasta County. She was sexy, all right, maybe five-eight, 140 to 150 pounds, comfortable figure. While she was talking, I unzipped my pants and pulled him out. I played with him in the dark in hopes that she'd go down on me.

She laid the baby on the backseat and leaned over my lap. I grabbed her by her hair and shoved her face down—that made me even hotter.

I was about to orgasm when a whimper came from the backseat and she pulled off. She said, "I don't know what I'm doing here. I'm married and I don't need this. Drive me home!" Just like that!

I shoved her back on my cock as hard as I could. A stiff prick has no conscience. When her lips touched him, he shot all over her face.

She started screaming at me, so I put her in a headlock and yanked hard. I was trying to break her neck, but I just couldn't get the leverage. It takes a lot of pressure to break a human neck.

I tried three times before the baby cried in the backseat and she yelled, "Don't hurt my baby!"

I realized that if I killed Jean, I'd have to kill the baby

too. I could never kill a kid, and I came back to my senses. I stepped out of the car, took some deep breaths and counted to twenty. All thoughts of killing went away.

Now Jean grabs her baby and heads for town. After she walked a hundred yards or so, I drove up and said, "Get back in! I'll drive you wherever you want to go. It's too cold to walk. It's not good for the baby." After she got in, I said, "I'm sorry. I don't know what came over me."

I dropped her off at the same place I met her. That was my big mistake. I should have killed her.

Continuing south, I pulled into a rest stop to think about what I'd just done. I'd released a victim that could put me in prison for a long time. And she had my name. But if she went to the cops, it would be her word against mine. I figured I had nothing to worry about. If I'd abandoned her in the cold, it would've been different. But by bringing her and the baby back safely, my story would stand up. If I'd intended to kill her, why the hell would I drive her back to town?

6 | Handcuffed

I threw out the last of the beer and drove to a truck stop in Corning. As I pulled in, I noticed a cop staring at my car. He had hands and arms like a gunfighter's.

I parked and asked one of the desk girls for a shower-room key. I was just walking back to my car when I was surrounded by cops pointing their guns and telling me to lay facedown.

"What's this all about?" I asked.

They handcuffed me and read me my rights. They said I was wanted back in Shasta for assault.

They let me up and asked what happened. I told them about the Jack Daniel's and how Jean asked me to buy beer and peed in front of me and bragged about her blow jobs. I said, "I don't know what's the problem. I had my arm around her neck, but I didn't try to hurt her. The car was cramped. There just wasn't enough room to do it right."

I put all the blame on her. I told them that it pissed her off when I shot my load in her mouth. I told them that she yanked on my arm to pull away, and that made her twist her neck and pissed her off worse. I told them about the baby crying and how she told me she needed to get home. I told them how I drove her back to town and how I didn't do anything wrong except get involved with a half-drunk married woman.

A cop asked, "Why would she claim you attacked her?"

I said, "Maybe she needed to explain why she was out so late with the baby. Maybe she thought her husband would feel sorry for her. Don't ask me to explain women."

Our two versions were close and only took off in opposite directions at the crucial spot where I tried to break her neck. But my story made more sense than hers. I said, "If I was going to assault this woman, why would I tell her my name and who I worked for and where I was headed? All I wanted to do was grab some sleep and keep on driving. She was the one that wanted to make out. How would I find that lover's lane by myself?"

They took off the handcuffs, and I began to get the feeling they were leaning my way. "Hey," I said, "if you had an easy chance to get lucky, wouldn't you?"

One of the cops said, "Well, we kinda believe you, but Shasta wants you to talk to a detective." They photographed and fingerprinted me and told me to check in with the Shasta police. Then they drove me back to my car and took off.

I took the interstate to Shasta and went straight to the sheriff's department and identified myself. They threw me against a wall like a side of beef and handcuffed and patted me down. I went through my story again and offered to prove it with evidence.

We got in a cruiser and they took me to the shopping area where I met Jean. I showed them my tire tracks in the gravel, showed them the empty whisky bottle near the railroad tie where she sat. I still had the receipt for the beer, and a clerk confirmed that I'd bought it. I told the deputies I was on my way to a construction job in Sacramento. I wasn't a bum and I wasn't a sex maniac.

Back at the sheriff's office they took off the cuffs and told me to keep in touch till the matter was taken care of. A deputy warned, "From now on, be careful who you party with."

As I drove away, I began a big argument with my other

self. I've always had two sides to my personality—Mr. Nice Guy and the demon. The demon comes out when I drink. He scares the crap out of me. He breaks the law just for the hell of it. It was him that tried to kill Jean.

I also realized that I should have let the demon kill her to keep her quiet. But NO! When Mr. Nice Guy saw her walking down the road with her baby, he had to soften up and give her a ride to town. *Stupid!* At that point it was a simple assault at worst, not even a sexual assault like she'd told the cops. That should have been the end of it. I didn't know enough about the treachery of women.

7 | Back to Peg

I worked the Sacramento construction job for a couple of months and never got over feeling paranoid. Every day I expected to be arrested for assault. I kept hoping that Shasta would drop the charges. Maybe they had a file on Jean the slut. Maybe the bitch pulled the same stunt on some other poor guy.

To save money I slept in my car and showered on the job. I brooded a lot. I couldn't help but resent my losses—my wife Rose, my kids, Peggy, the jobs I lost, the trucks I wrecked, the whole sad story. I was becoming withdrawn and depressed.

I began to hang out at the Cinch Tavern in Sacramento. Sometimes I'd play pool with the locals, and I joined the horseshoe team, but my heart wasn't in it. I met a girl in a laundromat and dated her a few times till I found out she just wanted to use my car. I attracted these parasites like flies.

It got hard to conceal my feelings. I'd sit at the bar and stare into the water pitcher. A nice old couple watched me for weeks and the woman finally said, "Someone really must of hurt you in your past."

"Why do you say that?" I asked.

"It's written all over your face."

• • •

After a few months I headed north to a new job. On the way I checked out a truck stop that we called Panty Hose Junction, but there was no action. I drove on through to Washougal, Washington, to visit my old friend Billy Smith (pseudonym) and return the car he'd loaned me. I bought a 1969 Chevrolet three-quarter-ton pickup and drove to my next temporary job in Astoria, at the mouth of the Columbia River. The work ran out after two weeks and I headed back to Portland. I wondered, *Does Peggy have another boyfriend? Will she want to get back together?*

I drove past her little brown house. She was on the lawn with her two kids—no signs of a new man. She looked good, and I did miss her, not just her body. I was getting bored with lot lizards and heads. The good side of me wanted to settle down and live a normal married life. But the bad side just wanted sex. My penis decided the vote.

I parked a little ways down the street. Peggy took one look at me and started to shake. She said, "Come on in, Keith! We need to talk." She looked ready to cry.

In the room where I beat Taunja Bennett to death, Peggy and her kids sat across from me. She was shaking. "Why the hell did you leave?" she said.

We talked about our misunderstandings and our lives, and we got as close as ever. I asked if she wanted to try again and she said yes.

After the kids went to bed, we found out that our bodies missed each other. The next morning it was like I never left.

In October 1990, nine months after Taunja, I got bad news about my ten-year-old son Jason. He was living four hundred miles away with my ex-wife and our two daughters. Jason had run into a tree and suffered a bad concussion.

I drove nonstop to Spokane. While I was doctoring my

son I realized that whatever else I did in life, I had to be near my kids. They were the world to me, my only real world. They loved me totally, the way I loved them.

So while I was in Spokane I called a local trucking company and made out an application. They gave me a driving test and found I handled eighteen-wheelers like I was born in one.

Peggy and her kids came from Portland to join me. She hired a nanny so she could go trucking with me again. Back when we were codriving, we'd have sex two or three times a day. I remembered the fun and games, but I'd forgotten about her lousy driving habits.

The first few months, our trucking deal went okay, even though I had to do 90 percent of the driving. My demon quieted a little. I still thought about taking women by force, but not as much as before. Living in Spokane, I saw a lot of my kids.

But in my life things never stayed good for long. Peggy began to piss me off, and I went back to heavy fantasizing. She was as good as ever in the sleeper, but she'd always been better at fucking than trucking. She used every excuse in the world to get out of driving. She'd say, "Oh my God, Keith! Look at those snowflakes! You can't expect me to drive in this."

She confined her driving to straight highways or gently rolling hills. We were supposed to be a team, but this was flatbedding and she couldn't even lift the tarps. I did 100 percent of the loading and unloading. The company didn't mind—we were logging sixty-five-hundred miles a week—but I was exhausted. It pissed me off that Peggy got credit for so many of my driving hours. Too many other people got credit for my work when I was a kid, and I'd had it up to here.

• • •

In January 1991 we were in Portland between hauls when I heard something crazy on TV. The couple that was arrested for my murder had been convicted! They showed a video of the woman leading the cops to the place where I dumped the body. I thought about the ghosts. Could they be behind this? It was *The Twilight Zone* for sure.

I was still relieved that somebody else was taking my heat, but it was annoying, too—the heaviest thing I'd ever done in my life, and others were getting the attention. I was still the Invisible Man.

Just before trial the woman changed her story and claimed she was innocent, but the jury found her guilty anyway. The guy didn't want to risk a death sentence, so he copped a plea. They both got fifteen years to life—for *my* murder.

I tried to figure it out. Either they were crazy or I was crazy. Or the justice system was crazy. All three of us didn't kill this girl. Were there two Taunja Bennetts? I wondered if those two losers had killed another girl and dumped her at the same spot. Or were they railroaded by the cops?

I had to stop thinking about it or flip out. I was already crazy enough.

2

A KILLER'S LIFE 1

1 | A Little like Hell

"We always knew he was different," Keith Jesperson's father admits, "but we never thought he would kill."

The old man sits in an overstuffed chair in his RV, sniffing oxygen through a tube, softly stroking his Yorkshire terrier, wondering if he remembered to take his Paxil, and brooding about a problem he has never solved.

"Looking back on Keith's life, knowing all he's done," Leslie Samuel Jesperson says in a soft rustic accent, "makes me wonder if there was anything that prompted his bizarre behavior. He says it's all my fault—He says, 'Dad, you and your belt made me a killer.' That's bull and he knows it. No kid ever had a better upbringing. He started out as a normal boy, a sweet-natured little bugger."

In his eighty-two-thousand-dollar rig, parked deep in a relative's apple orchard near Yakima, Washington, the father shows off a favorite picture of his son, seated next to a piano. "He's a year and a half old. Look at those beautiful golden locks. He played a recital with his big brother, Bruce, and made us so proud. Till we cut his hair, folks said that Keith was the cutest little girl they ever saw. Of all my five kids he was the most lovable, the most huggable." In a trembling voice the father reads a poem he wrote about his huggable son:

It only seems like yesterday
That you rode upon my back.
I bucked you off on the chesterfield,
Had a birthday cake for a snack.

Then at night when you went to bed,
All snuggled with Duke in your arms,
Mom would come in and give you a hug,
Releasing some of her charms.

Keith Hunter Jesperson, permanent resident of a walled domain, bridled when his father's words were repeated to him later. "I hugged my dog every day," he said, "but I never hugged my mother and father. And they didn't hug me or my brothers and sisters. I never thought about this one way or the other. It's just the way we were. In our family nobody hugged except me and my dog."

Three decades after his pet's death, he still mourned his chocolate Lab. "Duke was my closest friend for fourteen years. When Dad shot Duke, he might as well of shot me."

Jesperson the elder was a strong man from a line of strong men, stolid figures of the north, inured to zero temperatures, gale-force winds and blizzards. They were also inured to empty stomachs. In the 1930s Leslie's blacksmith father migrated eastward from the family homestead in rainy British Columbia to the parched prairies of Saskatchewan. After a few years he was beaten back to B.C. by the dust bowl famine known in Canada as the Dirty Thirties. It was a terrible defeat for Arthur Jesperson, and he remained in a sullen mood for the rest of his life. The Jespersons, descended from warrior Danes, were unaccustomed to losing fights or giving up. They didn't always accomplish what they set out to do, but they kept on trying, even unto death. When one of Arthur's brothers was committed to a mental hospital, he decided to kill himself.

When no other means were available, he pounded a three-and-a-half-inch nail into his skull.

Still sniffing from his oxygen tube, Leslie Jesperson spoke about his Canadian childhood, a mix of Dickens and Dante: "You never saw anybody work as hard as my dad and us six kids. We forge-welded, shod horses, made logging equipment—anything that could be created with a forge, a bellows and muscle. From kindergarten on we kids worked alongside Dad when we weren't in school. We had two forges and two anvils and a trip hammer in between to draw out the red-hot irons. I swung the sledge while my dad held the splitters, punches and other tools to make tongs and bull hooks.

"After a few hours nonstop I'd collapse in a wheelbarrow, but pretty soon Dad would have the forges fired up again and the iron would be sizzling hot, and the place would reek of fire and fumes. If it sounds a little like hell, well, it was! No choice—you just did your job and shut up about it. By the time I left home, I could squeeze 240 pounds, just like my dad. That was as high as our scale would read. If we got out of line, he hit us with his razor strop. There was a worn spot where it hit. Dad's strap was a hell of an educator."

Leslie's imprisoned son Keith remembered his paternal grandfather as a forbidding presence who sat silently in a corner of his living room next to the cribbage board, symbol of the family's favorite indoor sport. "My dad's father was a tough guy—*had* to be to survive. He had a cold business sense. Never said much to us kids, never showed emotion. He treated women like they took up too much space. He raised my dad to be the same."

A female relative by marriage claimed that after old Art Jesperson went broke on the prairies, he established a money-grubbing tone that would taint family life for generations. She said, "Art never got over having to shoot gophers to put meat on the table. It drove him to drink and distorted his viewpoint. From the Dirty Thirties till the day he died, he saw everything in terms of money. At family reunions money was all the Jespersons talked about. It's how they kept score. They even saw Keith's tragedy in terms of money. Everybody was gonna get rich off those poor murdered women."

Les Jesperson, the killer's father, quit school in the tenth grade and scratched out a living welding, plumbing, blacksmithing and working as a whistle punk in a logging camp. He taught himself Morse code, advanced mathematics, electronics, hydraulic and mechanical engineering, industrial design, and the basics of manufacturing. During an epidemic he made coffins for Indian tribes. He designed and built a machine for pulling logs, a splitter for making cedar shakes, a new type of haytedder for working hay, an automated premix cement plant, a device called the Jesperson bin filler and other industrial marvels. He revamped the hops industry with a spreadlock clip that anchored a climbing string in the earth so that the vines could grow tall, then designed a machine that manufactured the clips at the rate of six hundred per minute. At the height of his prosperity, before he sold the rights to his patent, his plant spewed out clips by the ton. Then he invented a harvester that doubled hops production in the field. He was hired to speed up apple processing assembly lines, improvising complex new equipment as needed.

One of the autodidact's hobbies was collecting metal scraps and transforming them into objets d'art; a Saskatchewan museum displayed his creations. He taught himself keyboard and accordion and played Lawrence Welk–type music for neighborhood dances. He carved, painted, sketched, told jokes, photographed, designed, composed, and wrote poetry that included a bawdy poem to his wife:

Roses are red
And some are white
So how about a little bit tonight?

And some mawkish advice to his children:

Even though people say,
How strong the heart can be,
It's the most fragile part of you,
And must be handled tenderly.

In any group the polymath moved in his own force field, commanding attention with humor, wisecracks, backslaps and over-the-top ebullience. Old friends remembered him as well over six feet tall, but he never topped five-eleven. His rural accent made him sound like a patient old grandpa, but his closest relatives knew that there were tightly controlled frustration and anger underneath.

At all stages of his life, Les Jesperson seemed to have limitless energy. At twenty-eight, he won election as the youngest alderman in Chilliwack, British Columbia, a town of forty-thousand just across the border from Washington. He was renowned as the only city official who could mollify the wild-eyed Russian sect called the Doukhabors. When they rode naked into the city, the cry would go out: "Get Les!"

At thirty he was named to the post of Master of the Fraser River Dikes. He started several businesses, moving from one to another when he was bored. He was a founder of the Chilliwack Boxing Club and the Chilliwack Search and Rescue Unit. Sometimes he wondered if he'd spread himself too thin and shorted his family in the process— "Every day I was in the *Chilliwack Progress* for one thing or another. All that attention might've made Keith a little jealous, might've started him on the wrong path."

• • •

As a husband and father Les Jesperson seemed to play out his adult life in two discrete acts. From his marriage at age twenty until he turned forty-seven, he drank heavily, excelled at a dozen different jobs, and dominated his family.

In act two, his late adulthood, he detuned his behavior. "I quit drinking when I realized I was drunk by ten o'clock every morning. I never went to A.A. I quit on my own." The newly sober father renewed his interest in family life and churned out volumes of poetry. By then all but one of his children—his younger daughter, Jill—were raised and gone.

2 | Fallen Idol

". . . The last decade has produced strong data suggesting that genetic factors related to the drinking behavior of biological fathers have a significant effect on the behavioral and intellectual development of their children."

—Robin Karr-Morse and Meredith S. Wiley,
Ghosts from the Nursery:
Tracing the Roots of Violence

Growing up, young Keith saw his father as an icon, an engineering genius, a towering figure of such authority and dominance that no one in his family even thought of challenging him. In discussing the relationship later, Keith would pause to collect his thoughts and memories, choke back tears and sighs, and smile or laugh only rarely. "I love my dad, and I hate my dad. He's so, uh . . . overpowering. Dad is good at *everything*. It only takes him a few minutes to make friends. Sometimes he comes off as a know-it-all, but maybe he *does* know it all!

"When I was growing up, he really didn't pay us kids much attention. He'd work and eat and then drink himself to sleep. He was too pickled to stay up late and read to us or help with our homework. He worked our asses off. Sunday was a work day. If we laid in bed ten minutes too late, we got the belt.

"He liked to put us down with sarcasm and wisecracks, but at the same time he acted proud of us. He'd say, 'You're a Jesperson. Behave like one.' I inherited his sick sense of humor. When I was a little kid I asked him how I could tell if our electrified fence was on. He said, 'Piss on it.' I felt the shock in my balls. He just stood there laughing and said, 'Consider it a learning experience.' He got my sister Sharon to touch our electric fence when she was little. He laughed at her, too.

"Deep down inside, Dad never respected kids. He had no tolerance, no understanding. He'd get mad at us for not knowing something we'd never been taught. He put himself on a pedestal to be admired and respected, and he was so self-involved that he missed everything else about his family. You never saw him at our school plays. It didn't benefit him, didn't bring in any cash. That was solely how he judged things. Mother always wanted to visit Hawaii and Alaska, but he wouldn't take her. There was no benefit to him. Dad did what *Dad* wanted."

The father seemed to go from one serious medical problem to another: prostate cancer, hypoglycemia, vehicle accident injuries, depression, alcoholism. He broke three ribs coughing and quit smoking when a doctor predicted that he would be dead of lung cancer or pneumonia in six months.

No one could recall when he took a day off from work, drunk or sober, except for infrequent excursions with his children and regular summer visits to the family camp in the Blackwater region of British Columbia. He showed little interest in religion and resisted his wife's urgings to send the children to Sunday school. There was no appeal from his decisions. He seemed to look down on females and passed his attitude to his sons. Keith said his father liked to brag, "I stayed with your mom because she was a good cook."

3 | "Dad's Slave"

According to her children Gladys Bellamy Jesperson's culinary skills were the least of her qualities. The Bellamys came from English stock by way of the windswept wide-open spaces of Grande Prairie, Alberta. Her father, Roy, a dairy farmer, went broke during the same Dirty Thirties that defeated the blacksmith Art Jesperson. The Jespersons and Bellamys became acquainted after Roy Bellamy gave up on cows and opened a billiards parlor in Chilliwack, B.C. Unlike the irreligious Les Jesperson, Roy Bellamy and his wife Marjorie were devout Protestants and strict teetotalers. When a friend brought them a bottle of Christmas cheer, they ordered him off the property.

In the passage of time the elder Bellamys made a favorite of their grandson Keith, the future murderer. "Leslie always favored Bruce and Brad," Marjorie Bellamy once explained. "Our daughter Gladys favored Jill and Sharon. I always had a heart for Keith because he's the one that got left out."

Gladys Bellamy Jesperson grew up in a puritanical home in which the slightest mention of sex and sexuality was taboo. She was banished from the barn when the bull serviced the cow and when any of the animals gave birth. No one in the family, including her husband, ever saw Gladys naked. "That was her preference," Les said of his wife years later. "Her parents taught her to be ashamed of her body. I never saw one Bellamy touch another."

Keith and his four siblings remembered their mother as a workhorse and immaculate housekeeper who held the family together. "Dad's whole thing was making money," his daughter Jill recalled. "Mom did everything else."

Gladys Bellamy Jesperson was a large, plain woman, a half-inch shorter than six feet, with rich curly hair that she passed on to her son Keith. Resolute and dignified, she tried to shield her children from their father's harsh discipline, but with indifferent success. She seemed to keep a little distance between herself and others, even her own brood. When Les took them camping each summer, Gladys was happy to stay home. In Keith's memory he saw her posed primly on the couch, glasses reflecting the TV screen, her knitting needles giving off little flashes of light. He thought he knew why his mother stayed home. "She was Dad's slave. She was relieved when he was gone. It gave her a little breathing room."

Gladys was as meticulous about her person as she was about her home. She designed and made her children's clothes, including trousers and suits. As she put on weight through the years, she altered her own dresses and created new wardrobes to conceal her amplitude. She knitted "Indian sweaters" for every member of her extended family. She was sensitive about her appearance and kept her bedroom door firmly shut after chemotherapy forced her into wigs. But she didn't stop knitting. By then her children were grown.

4 | The "Now What?" Brother

When people look at a dangerous violent criminal at the beginning of his developmental process rather than at the very end of it, they will see, perhaps unexpectedly, that the dangerous violent criminal began as a relatively benign human being for whom they would probably have more sympathy than antipathy.

—Richard Rhodes, *Why They Kill:*
The Discoveries of a Maverick Criminologist

Keith was regarded as the slowest of the Jesperson children, "the one who dawdled," as a sister described him. He was born on April 6, 1955, and his earliest memory was of rolling a rock down a slide in a play park. It hit his little brother Brad on the head, drew blood and made him cry. His sister Sharon took the blame, and not for the last time.

Keith was toilet-trained by two, obedient, quiet, but easily distracted. "He couldn't focus on anything for very long," a relative recalled. He took continual ragging about his sluggish ways but didn't seem to mind.

In later years his father liked to screen a home movie of a family hike. Little Keith lagged twenty feet behind the others, staring up at trees, dragging his moccasins. At some point on every outing, he got lost. The family watchword was: "Where's Keith?" Siblings thought of him as the "now what?" brother. He was ungainly, a slow runner, bored by team sports or parlor games except cribbage. He learned how to manipulate the pegs on a cribbage board before he could read.

The Jesperson children grew up in a rural atmosphere, first in Chilliwack, B.C., later 250 miles south in Selah, Washington, an apple-scented orchard community of ten thousand. No one could remember a time when the family didn't own horses, sheep, ducks and/or dogs. His perpetually mobile father built the family's Chilliwack home on land that his ancestors homesteaded in 1909, moved the house from the city to a pastoral area outside of town, cleared five acres with a borrowed bulldozer, built a barn with a loft for his children and a wooden bridge big enough for the family horses to cross the little creek that rose from springs above the property line. Later he dammed the creek and built a waterwheel to trap chinook and silver salmon as they swam up from the Vedder River to spawn. Sometimes the family's anglers were joined by the odd black bear, deer, fox or a nearby farmer's fractious bull. Les attached a rope swing to a maple that reached almost to the far side of the creek, and Tarzan yells resounded all summer.

Gladys Jesperson grew tired of rounding up children who were usually deployed over a compass rose of directions, and so she bought an orange whistle with a unique warble that could be heard for miles. At its sound the children sprinted for home. Years later Keith sometimes jerked awake to the sound of his mother's whistle, blowing down the prison corridors in his dreams.

Even before he started school the boy was unusually shy. He seemed content to play alone, digging tunnels in a mound of dirt, building forts, lofting pebbles at rising trout and salmon. "Keith is such a happy child," his mother told friends. "He can sit in one spot all by himself. You come back an hour later and he's still right there."

The child found comfort in his own company. "I never really felt at home in our house, so I fantasized. In those days we called it daydreaming. I'd pretend to be a miner or a heavy-equipment operator. I would take my bow and arrow and be a great white hunter in Africa. I stood along our creek and fired torpedoes at enemy U-boats, created the ocean in my mind and sent destroyers off to war. When I finally got my own BB gun, I became a sniper shooting at the enemy. I saw myself as an enforcer for good, a war hero, *superboy!* Keith would save the world."

Sitting inside the walls that would enclose him for the rest of his life, the would-be hero remembered his household as "quiet and peaceful when Dad was away and tense when he was home."

It was one of the family's continuing paradoxes that Keith also saw himself as his father's sidekick. "Dad and I hung out a lot, played cribbage, rode horses up in the hills. As long as I stayed in line, he was the best dad a kid could have—generous, smart, funny. He made me his helper on a lot of his projects, made me feel special. But he never relaxed his rules, and he was tough. We'd be riding along in his pickup and I'd be holding his rye and Coke for him, and he'd say something like, 'You spill one goddamn drop, you're no son of mine!' He kept you on edge."

The patriarch's favorite instrument of punishment was his thick leather belt. "All my children got it," Les admitted years later. "When I was a kid, I was strapped harder than any of 'em, and I didn't grow up to be a serial killer. A lot of kids could use a little beating nowadays. I was strict but a good father. I raised my kids like I was raised."

Keith remembered hiding under the kitchen table to avoid his father's discipline. "I was four. Dad was yelling, 'Don't you run away from me!' He threw me down, whipped off his belt and doubled it, held it with both hands at the ends and popped it with a scary slapping sound. Then he hit my butt with the folded end. He told me to stop crying or he'd give me something to cry about.[1] I bit my lip and kept quiet."

Keith remembered getting belted after he killed his father's pet duck with a rock. His mother tried to intervene but finally gave way. "Mom was always on our side, but she couldn't stop Dad if he was drinking. Sometimes she smacked my ass with a big wooden spoon, but never hard. She'd usually say, 'Wait till your father gets home, and then you'll get it.' Dad was our discipline."

Duke, the closest friend of the boy's childhood, came into his life just before his fifth birthday. Keith shared a room with his younger brother, Brad, but the stocky brown Lab always ended up in Keith's bed, burrowing under the covers, growling softly if his sleep was disturbed.

The subject of the dog was one of the few that seemed to animate Keith in belated discussions of his childhood. "Even today I sleep pretty much in a fetal position. I'm still making room for Duke. He trained me good. He was a chaser and a fighter. Chased salmon up our creek and came home smelling like cat food. Chased cars and got hit seven times—he figured that was his job, and since he was a Jesperson, nothing was gonna stop him. When Mr. Hamilton's vicious dogs crossed our yard, Duke ran 'em off. Out of the eleven Hamilton dogs, he killed two and maimed three.

"If I set foot in our pastures, Duke warded off the bulls or heifers. He would herd me like a sheep to keep me out of danger. One day Dad rowed us to the middle of a lake. He looked back and said, 'What the hell is that?' It was Duke, trying to catch up. He'd swum for half a mile and

---

[1] Les Jesperson emphatically denied that the incident took place.

damn near drowned. For the rest of that summer, he wouldn't let me out of his sight.

"I fed him scraps at the dinner table and let him lick my plate. Having a male dog as my constant companion gave me a head start about sex. He'd jump any bitch smaller than a Great Dane. Maybe that's why I always liked it doggy style—it was the first sex I saw."

At six the shy boy sold eels for sturgeon bait. With his equally taciturn friend Joe Smoker, he embarked on a career as a poacher, snagging salmon from the creek and hooking trout in private ponds. "Joe was a half-breed Indian from a large poor family, and all he had to offer was friendship. Well, Dad's idea was that friendship was a waste of time if it didn't offer any capital gain. He warned me to stay away from Joe. But we stayed friends for years."

During spawning runs the good companions killed gravid salmon with spears or arrows. "I was caught breaking the game laws so many times that the wardens stopped chasing me. If they saw me fishing, they'd just drive to our house and wait. They knew I sneaked trout and salmon home under my overcoat. Once I was caught fishing in a stocked pond, and the farmer shot me in the back with a load of rock salt. Mom took out the salt with tweezers. Thank God she never told Dad."

Like most of the other residents of the leafy town of Chilliwack, Les Jesperson wasn't averse to a little poaching on his own. He taught his son to lie facedown on the dock and grab salmon by the tail. It was one of Keith's fondest memories. "We would do it together. Poaching wasn't much of an offense where we lived. Getting caught was the crime. Dad was a city official, and he didn't like to be embarrassed in front of the other politicians."

Sometimes the Jesperson males prowled the creek

banks for muskrats. "I'd yank one out of the water by its
tail and throw it up on the bank. Then Dad or one of my
brothers would club it to death. We also killed gophers,
hundreds of 'em. They were a farm pest, and nobody
missed 'em. Dad has films of us boys blood-spattered from
killing gophers and other varmints. It was our form of
recreation. After we grew up and got married, Dad liked to
show the film to our wives. He would joke, 'Watch my
natural-born killers as they dispense of their victims! You
don't want to run into *them* in a dark alley.' "

To the squeamish Les pointed out, "The farmers wanted
those gophers killed. We were doing them a favor."

Like many other rural fathers, the alpha-male encouraged
his sons to hunt. When they were small, he provided them
with BB guns to sharpen their shooting eyes. He carefully
warned his boys not to shoot at people, but Keith had his
own interpretation of the rule. "To me that meant, Don't
shoot people in the face. Everywhere else was okay. I
would pretend to be a sniper and sting the other kids good.
I shot my neighbor's penis while he was taking a leak. He
pissed all over himself."

Les handcrafted high-powered slingshots with surgical
tubing and warned his sons not to shoot anyone above the
elbows. Keith soon learned that marbles produced a true
trajectory, and he let loose at the rear end of an overweight
neighbor who was bending over to pick raspberries. "I got
caught and she took me straight to Dad. She was limping
and crying, putting it on. Dad tried to keep a straight face.
He told her he couldn't punish me till he got a good look at
the evidence. After he finished laughing at his own joke, he
gave me a light spanking in front of her. This time he used
his hands instead of the belt."

5 | Keith's World

In his early years Keith passed most of his free time with a man sixty years his senior, his maternal grandfather, Roy Bellamy. "He wasn't like my Jesperson grandpa. I could talk to him, and if I did something wrong, he would never tell Dad. Grandpa Bellamy's strongest word was *no*. We used to troll for salmon in his twelve-foot boat, *Little Cotto*. We'd leave at sunup and come back at dark. I still see him steering the boat and drinking coffee from his thermos while I keep my finger on the line to feel for strikes. We were the only ones on either side of the family that had the patience for this kind of fishing.

"Grandpa always made sure I caught the most fish—silver salmon and chinooks up to thirty pounds. We were good company, didn't need anybody else. I wonder how I would've turned out if Grandpa had lived a little longer. He died when I was nine. That's the only funeral I ever cried at. They played 'I Hear a Symphony.' I cried again when I got home and learned that Grandpa had left me his boat and gear. I used to open his tackle box and stick my nose inside to pick up his smell. Dad traded *Little Cotto* for another boat. I kept on fishing, but it was never the same."

For a while Keith had problems with a mischievous boy named Martin. "His parents would bring him over when they visited and he was always getting into trouble and blaming me. Dad would punish me in front of everybody. One day I'd had enough. I cornered Martin behind the garage and yelled, 'I'm gonna kill you, you son of a bitch.' When Dad pulled me off, Martin was unconscious. I would have killed him if I hadn't been stopped—not a doubt in my mind. I wasn't surprised to get the belt. That was one time when I was guilty."

Looking back, Keith considered the incident as a watershed in his early development. "That's when I began to think of myself as two people, one watching the other. When I was kicking Martin's ass, a gentler part of me stood by and watched. Maybe I'm still that way. When I'm taking care of a serious problem, I feel like I'm on the outside looking in. I can honestly say that the person that beat Martin was not the real me. I would never hurt another kid, no matter what he did. It wasn't my nature. But that day I just kind of stepped aside and let the bad side take over. It was the same with the women I killed. My murders happened in slow motion and later I would fantasize about what I *should* have done. I'd be thinking, *If only I could do it all over, I would do it different*. But the girls ended up just as dead."

At seven Keith contracted simultaneous cases of impetigo and pneumonia and was restricted to his room. His mother applied salve to his festering sores while the others stayed as far away as possible. At the end of the long quarantine, Brad, Bruce and Sharon built him a lean-to fort of cedar boughs. In his selective memory it was the only act of sibling camaraderie he could recall from his childhood. The lean-to remained his refuge until he broke into a small abandoned school and created a fort in the dusty attic, coexisting with bats and mice.

For as far back as he could remember, animals large and small had seemed more real to him than his family. He explained that he'd spent his entire childhood in something he thought of as "Keith's World." His brothers and classmates were firmly excluded. "I was always treated different, and this was my solution."

He shared a birthday with his older brother, Bruce, and every year their mother arranged joint parties. Bruce was an outgoing, convivial boy, and to Keith the festivities always seemed focused on the older brother. "I was hurt by that. The only thing good about the parties was the cake that mother always cooked—German chocolate with raspberry filling and chocolate icing and marshmallow rabbits on the side. She made a nest of coconut on top and filled it with jelly beans. Then she wrapped dimes and quarters in waxed paper and hid them in the cake."

In keeping with his dark brown memories, he claimed that other party guests always found the coins.

From his first days at a five-room elementary school a mile down the road, the boy was teased about being oversized. He didn't challenge the name-callers because he was afraid that he would be punished by his teachers and later by his father. He hung back and tried to imitate the other students. "In first grade, I filled up notebooks with 'pretend' writing—scribbles and circles and crooked lines. I couldn't understand my own writing, but I thought the teacher would. That's the way I thought it worked in school. At the end of the first week, she held up my answer book and said, 'This is exactly how *not* to do it.' She put me on display."

In his first years of school, his grades were consistently low, and there was talk of leaving him back. "I was scared to take my report card home. It took a lot of spankings to find out that I was nearsighted. I couldn't see the writing on the blackboard. I would have complained earlier, but I thought every kid had the same problem. That was *my* mistake, not the teachers' or my parents'. When they finally found out, they got me glasses, and my grades improved a little. But I never really caught up."

The boy's coordination seemed to lag his rapid growth, and he developed an ambling, disconnected walk. He never quite learned how to sit a horse. If the family horse Dynamite broke into a trot, he usually fell off.

On a school sports day, he was entered in the hop, skip and jump. At the starting line a teacher called out, "Okay, Keith, go ahead."

He hopped, skipped, and jumped in place.

The other students laughed as he fled the athletic field for home. "I said to myself, *That's fine. I don't need them.*"

In elementary school the boy became so upset by corporal punishment that in later years, when he had little to do except brood about his wrong turnings, he composed an essay on punishment and pain. Written in his usual overwrought style, "The Strop at Unsworth School" included meticulously drawn diagrams:

> When I was introduced to "the beavertail" at elementary school, I was in the first grade. My first introduction was three strikes across the palm. When stropped in school I returned home to get it over my ass with Dad's belt. By the time I got to sixth grade, I had been nailed by the strop at least fifteen times. The standard punishment was three times on each palm and allowed to swell, then repeated three more times and then a waiting period before my hands were forced under cold water which hurt worse than being hit.
>
> One time when my Indian friend Joe Smoker and I got nailed for fighting, Joe held his hand over the mahogany desk of the principal and jerked his hand back on the downswing. The dent

in Joe's desk made the principal angrier, so he hit us harder with the next round.

The beavertail looked like a hasp file, only flexible. It had a wooden handle five inches long with a leather belt two inches wide and eighteen inches long encased in a herringbone patterned stainless steel wire blanket. Holding it out, it was stiff enough to not droop too much. Sometimes the wire braided mesh would wrap around your skin and draw a little blood. I can still hear it hit my palm the day he punished Joe and me.

Asked to hold out our hands with the palms open, the first strike stung like hell. The second strike went deeper and the third strike hit swollen flesh. Red, puffy and tight skin was the trademark of the right hand as it hung down by my side. With tears in my eyes, I would have to hold my left hand out knowing it would be struck by a full grown man swinging as hard as he could. My right hand in pain and now my left hand's pain had my total attention. For three hits the pain increased and then I was forced to watch Joe Smoker get it just as he'd been forced to watch me.

After the principal got done with Joe, then it was back to me and my right hand now tight with swelling was forced to bear three more blasts from the strop. Then my left as blood trickled down my open sores on my right hand. After the punishment, he took us to the bathroom and held our hands under the running cold water to reduce the swelling. The whole process lasted twenty minutes.

At home, Dad would be told that I got in trouble at school. Hence out came the belt and I'd take another beating. The next day I couldn't sit or write. He seldom beat Bruce or Brad, but our

*oldest sister Sharon got it. Once when he was
drunk, I saw him break down the bathroom door
to beat her. It was always worse when he was
drunk.*[2]

---

[2]Les Jesperson emphatically denied that any such incident took place.
His daughter Sharon declined comment on her father or her
childhood.

6 | Animal Friends and Enemies

As he approached adolescence, Keith continued to aggravate his teachers and amuse his classmates, but he tried to live with his own nonconformity. His friendships were few and short-lived. "You become convinced that there's something about you that sets you off. After a while it just seems natural. My brothers were never my friends. My sisters were nice, but they were girls. I learned not to care about friends."

He found companionship in the animal world: his dog, Duke, the family horses, tame rabbits, wild birds. He splinted a raven's broken wing with a popsicle stick and arranged the convalescing bird in a bed of soft rags. "After school my big brother Bruce took Blackie to a neighbor's house. They dumped the orange crate and threw their jackknives at him till he died."

The enraged Keith stomped into Bruce's second-story room. "I threw all his plastic airplane models out the window, little planes that he'd assembled, with decals, controls that worked, wheels. I said, 'Fly, suckers, fly!' *Crash crash crash*. My mother finished the job by driving over them when she came home. I got punished for wrecking the models, but Bruce didn't get punished for killing my crow. Dad just said, 'Get over it, Son. It's just a dumb crow.'"

• • •

In Keith's memory his father abided most dumb animals but hated cats. "He would put them in a gunnysack and drown them. He was easier on dogs. He'd shoo away strays and they'd run off whining. Townspeople dumped their unwanted pets at the end of our road. We had a steady supply."

Sometimes Keith helped his father control invasions of feral cats. "I felt the same as Dad—they were a pain in the ass. They'd get in our garbage, yowl all night and keep everybody awake. We always made sure to kill the kittens. Sharon and Jill didn't approve, but they were girls. Sharon would say, 'That's not nice, Keith!' My sisters would see bloodstains in the barn and start bawling."

The boy also helped rid the family property of garter snakes. "Our place was overrun—hundreds of them. Dad taught me how to take a hoe and chop them in half. I enjoyed watching them fight the blade and sometimes I tortured them with gardening tools. It was one more way to have fun."

7 | Sex for Kids

Keith's first sexual fumblings began at five. He kissed a four-year-old girl in the backseat of his mother's station wagon and enjoyed more-intimate sessions in the hayloft. "We practiced sex for a year or so—not sex as adults think, but sex for kids, kissing, touching a little bit, showing what we had. Mostly we kissed. We would kiss until we thought we had it right."

He met a redheaded beauty at the Unsworth School and felt his first romantic stirrings. "But I only knew kissing, I didn't know romance. We were in the same class from first to sixth grade, and I still think about her. It's part of my fantasizing. When I was grown and living in the States, I would go back to Chilliwack to see her brother, but the real reason was to see her. She developed a rare disease, and the last time I saw her, she was in the hospital. I heard that she died."

Keith's early interest in sex soon led to curiosity and confusion about what went on between his parents. "My first realization was that anytime us kids got the belt, it was in their bedroom. That's where I killed my victims later, in my sleeper with the curtain closed. Maybe there was a connection in my own mind."

Late at night the boy would sit on the staircase trying to

interpret bedroom sounds. "In the daytime I'd hear Dad say, 'Gladys, why don't you try to look sexy for me? Go to the store and buy something sexy.' *Sexy?* I wished I knew what he meant. It was such a loaded word. Our parents expected us to learn sex by watching animals, but it didn't take long to find out that was only a small part of the story. I wanted to ask Mom to explain, but I couldn't get up the nerve."

Keith and some schoolmates were playing at a neighbor's dairy farm when a workman offered to advance their sexual education. "He stripped and made us do the same. He said that sex was touching our peepees together, and he started to play with his pecker until it got larger and erect. Then he asked us to touch him. He was making a move on a boy when I grabbed my clothes and ran. He yelled at me to not tell anyone. I thought, *Don't worry! I won't.*

"Later I asked the boy how he liked it. He said that it hurt and he told his father what happened and his father told him to keep it quiet. The dairyman did it to him doggy style and after it was over he forced him to lick his pecker. I was disgusted and didn't want to hear about it. We never saw that man again. I always wondered how he got that way."

Keith became even more confused about sex during a camping trip with his father and friends. He'd learned a song from an older boy, and he sang it to one of his father's friends en route to the campsite. "He laughed so hard he nearly ran his car off the road. Around the campfire that night everybody was drinking, and he told my dad that Keith knew a cute song. Dad ordered me to sing it. I said, 'Dad, it's got some bad words.' Dad said, 'Sing it, Son!' I said, 'Do you promise not to hit me?' "

Les promised, and Keith sang a long, bawdy song that began:

> Good morning, Mr. Murphy, God bless your
> heart and soul.
> Last night I fucked your daughter, but I couldn't
> find her hole. . . .

And ended:

> I finally got it out, sir. It was red, black, and
> blue.
> Goddamn it, Mr. Murphy, next time I'll buttfuck
> *you*.

Keith feared dire punishment, but his father kept his word. "After that, Dad turned me into his little monkey on a string. He'd haul me out in front of women and everybody else to sing that song. Around the house we couldn't even whisper words like *breast* or *sex*. But in front of company I could use words like 'buttfuck.' I couldn't figure adults out."

8 | Calling a Bitch a Bitch

Throughout his life Keith remained troubled about an incident that happened when he was nine and still living in Chilliwack:

> *I got into a fight with a boy my age. His mother yelled at me to get off her property and quit picking on her kid. She was yelling fuck this and fuck that, and I yelled back that she was a bitch. I was riding my bike home when the boy's sixteen-year-old brother jumped out of his car, slugged me and kicked me twice with his pointy-toe cowboy boots. Then he drove over my bike and wrecked it.*
>
> *My father didn't like getting dragged out of a city council meeting by a constable of the RCMP and told that his son Keith had called a bitch a bitch and a few other names and the bitch was filing a slander suit. Dad was embarrassed and angry. He'd been drinking since noon, and he drove straight home. Before Mother could tell him the whole story, his fist struck me down and he dragged me into his bedroom. He worked me over with his belt till I couldn't scream anymore, kept yelling that I made a fool of him in front of Madame Chairperson.*
>
> *Mom finally pulled him off and said, "Leslie,*

Keith was not at fault." She showed him the bruise where Brian's brother slugged me and this made him call Brian's mother and cuss her out worse than she'd cussed me. He slammed the phone down, turned to me and said, "Let this be a lesson to you."

Mom said, "Don't you want to apologize to Keith?"

Dad said, "He probably had it coming anyway."[3]

I didn't know what to think. More than anything else in the world, I wanted to please my father. I wanted him to accept me for who I was and what I did, and I would do anything to satisfy him. He was the closest thing to God. But even when I was right I was wrong. I'd think, "Yes, Dad, go ahead and blame me. I'll take the responsibility even if I'm not at fault. Just try to love your son, Dad." Maybe he did, but he didn't show it.

To Keith one of his rural acquaintanceships seemed to echo his relationship with his father. A neighbor boy was the same age and in the same class, and the two should have been close friends. But something about Keith seemed to provoke the boy. "I was his punching bag. We were swimming at Cultus Lake when he tried to drown me. He held my head below the surface, let me come up for air, then pushed me down again. After five or ten minutes of this I started to see black. I believe my life was spared by the counselor that jumped in the pool and pulled him off."

Keith realized that he had to stand up to the bully sooner or later. "At the public swimming pool I held him under till a lifeguard pulled me off. I had every intention of drowning him. I guess you could say it was the second murder attempt of my childhood. The other was that little bastard Martin. It was like I only had one way to fight—all-out."

---

[3] Les Jesperson denied that the incident happened.

9 | Alka-Seltzer for Seagulls

Nor is brutalization a process that occurs exclusively within families. Peer groups can brutalize, as gangs do.

—Richard Rhodes, *Why They Kill: The Discoveries of a Maverick Criminologist*

With a shaky balance of power established in the Jesperson neighborhood, a small clique of boys accepted Keith and began to teach him some of their techniques of animal torture. "They would blow up a sparrow with a two-inch firecracker. I can still hear the sound, smell the smell. *Boom!* A puff of feathers would float down. With the robins and jays it just blew their legs off. They nailed crows to a board and threw knives at them. That's how they killed Blackie."

The boys force-fed Alka-Seltzer to seagulls till their stomachs burst, nailed cats and small dogs to a board and stuck them with nails and needles. "Our favorite thing was to crimp a couple of cats' tails together with wire and hang them over a rope. They'd claw each other till one was dead. The winner would yowl and scream till it died from its own wounds while we sat and watched."

Before long Keith had become a participant in the torture games, always leaving his dog Duke home in case the blood lust got out of hand. "We'd take firecrackers and set 'em off in a cat's mouth or up its ass. We'd do this till the cat died. In the winter we used a box and string to catch birds eating our grain. We'd inject them with bleach and watch them shake and die. That's what we did for fun. Pretty soon it felt like a normal thing to do."

Soon Keith added the excitement of arson to the excitement of animal torture. He'd always found an odd comfort in watching fires dwindle down to the last ember. "I'd ask to be the one who lit the burn barrel. I found that aerosol cans blew up in fire. I'd act like it was an accident when I threw in a half can of hair spray. A ball of flame would jump up like a miniature atomic bomb. Butane lighters exploded, too.

"Campfires were so soothing, I'd sit there for hours after everybody else had turned in. Sometimes I'd find bugs and toss 'em in, hear 'em crackle and split their skins. Or I'd throw an old log full of bugs in the flames and watch 'em scramble. When I was ten, Joe Smoker and I got hold of some Roman candles and shot them at each other. One of his grandfather's junker cars caught fire and we spent the next ten minutes putting it out. Nobody found out who did it."

The companions weren't so lucky when they accidentally torched an empty house owned by a neighbor named Webster. "We started a fire in the fireplace and a spark flew into a stack of newspapers. We put it out and ran. A half hour later we heard the fire trucks. That old house burned to the ground. Someone saw me running and told on me, and I had to take the blame.

"I knew better than to argue with Dad about it. In his eyes, denying blame was as bad as being guilty. I was punished and had to pay off my neighbor with my life savings—almost fifty bucks. Later on the neighbor told Dad he collected on the insurance and was glad we'd burnt the place down. He never thought to give me back my money."

In his endless accounting of raw deals and childhood disappointments, Keith claimed that he was forced to take the blame for the bullying of a smaller boy by his younger brother Brad. As in almost all his reminiscences, he cast his father as villain. "Brad came home in a panic and asked me if a grown-up had called. He told me that he got in a fight with a kid and the parent threatened to call Dad. When the phone rang later that afternoon, I answered it. The man accused me of beating up his son. Then he asked me my name and I told him. He said he would call back to talk to Dad that evening.

"When the call came, Dad answered. I saw him stare hard at me. As usual he'd been drinking. When he put down the phone, he punched me with his fist.[4] He said he would teach me what it felt like to be beat up by a bully. I told him it wasn't me and he called me a liar. After he was finished, Brad stepped up and took the blame. Dad taught him a lesson as well. When it was all over, I waited for an apology. As usual Dad told me to consider it a learning experience."

---

[4] Les Jesperson emphatically denied that he ever hit any of his children with a fist. He commented, "My son seems to have a photographic memory of things that never happened."

10 | Church of Hard Work

Keith remembered being impressed into his father's work-force when he was eleven. "Dad had a huge work ethic. He said that if we worked our asses off we would grow up to be big and strong and successful. If we didn't work hard, we'd grow up to be bums. Me, I just wanted to be a kid for a few more years. Mom thought my brothers and I should start Sunday school, but Dad said the Bible was a crutch for the weak and we could make up our minds about religion when we were grown. "Right now," he says, "you're gonna work on Sundays. And you're gonna pay room and board." He said his dad charged him and his brothers room and board, too, and it taught them the value of money.

"He put us to work cleaning nuts and bolts that he'd soaked in barrels of oil as part of a contract for salvaging a Fraser River bridge. We scrubbed them with wire brushes till they gleamed. Sharp little shreds kept getting under our fingernails—hurt like hell.

"When we finally finished with the nuts and bolts, he made us mow and bale our hay. If he didn't have a job for us, he'd create one. Work was his church, and he was the preacher. He put my older sister Sharon out of the house when she was sixteen and told her not to come back till she got a job."

• • •

In addition to working for his father, eleven-year-old Keith began delivering morning newspapers. The *Province* was published daily, and the boy took pride in delivering in the harsh Canadian weather. On the worst days his mother chauffeured him in her Ford Falcon.

Adults on his seven-mile route took a liking to the curly-haired boy, and for the first time he began to feel a slight kinship with adults. On collection day some of his customers would leave exact change on their front porches, and others would put out larger bills and notes and expect him to leave the correct change. He was surprised by the show of trust from strangers. "I liked everybody on my paper route. I even liked the dogs that snapped at me till I got to know them. I gave good service, and I got good tips. Some of my customers would have a cup of hot chocolate waiting when I rode up on my bike. I began to get the idea that people were pretty good at heart—a few, anyway."

In fifth grade Keith began a friendship with a neighborhood boy named Reg Routley. Close personal relationships were still rare in his life, and this one flourished. Every day the boys met after school, fished for salmon and trout, hunted rabbits and squirrels, explored the woods, flirted with girls and enjoyed each other's company. Then the head of the Jesperson clan announced that they were leaving the country.

3

KEITH

HUNTER

JESPERSON 2

1 Roadblock

A month after I found out that two innocent people had been sentenced to prison for my murder, my girlfriend Peggy and I headed east with a truckload of lumber for Illinois. As we pushed through an Iowa storm, the heavy wet snow built up on top of our trailer. At the Rock Island check station, the scale master red-lighted me and made me pull around to the parking area. She said we needed to pay eighty-four dollars for overweight and knock off the snow. Otherwise, we couldn't leave.

I said, "I'm not gonna pay. It's your Iowa snow!" In the back of my mind, I'm thinking, *Goddamn it, whenever I get in trouble, it's always a woman.*

She told me to wait right there while she stepped inside the shack to check something. She ran my name in her N.C.I.C. computer and came up with a warrant from Shasta County, California. She placed me under arrest on a charge of sexual assault.

Peggy yelled that it was a mistake. I gave her a look that told her to shut up. She was pissed, mostly because she knew she would have to deliver the load by herself and con somebody into doing the untarping.

The scale lady let me clean off the snow so Peggy could drive away. We sat together in the cab for a few minutes and I told her that I might be going down for a long time. I was feeling paranoid and I made the mistake of telling her that while she'd been driving with that other guy in Tennessee, I'd killed a girl in Portland, and they might hold me for that, too. I didn't tell her who I killed. I explained that I did the killing to get in practice for the ex-husband she'd asked me to execute.

At first she acted like she didn't believe my story, but when the truth finally sank in, she flipped, called me every name in the book and then started bawling like a baby. I didn't know what to say to calm her down. Before they drove me away in a sheriff's car, I gave Peg all my money. She was still sniffling when she hauled ass with our load of lumber.

At two in the morning I was locked into the county jail. Eight hours later I was arraigned on a charge of first-degree sexual assault and informed I would be extradited to California.

I told the judge that I wouldn't fight the warrant. I said, "I'm innocent, Your Honor, and I want to go back and prove it. But I want you to drop your eighty-four-dollar ticket. It's wrong!" I was sensitive about bum raps. I'd taken too many as a kid. The judge voided the ticket.

I was put in a holding cell with sixteen other guys. It was my first real experience with jailbirds. I got up to change the TV channel, and a big black dude said, "You can't do that. You gotta arm-wrestle me for it."

I pinned him quick. He says, "I wasn't ready."

"Are you ready now?"

I took him down again. He says, "I slipped."

I said, "You slipped, huh? Let's do it one more time." I flung him across the table. I stood up and said, "It's my TV, asshole." I ruled the roost.

After a few days in the tank one of the Rock Island detectives told me that California's felony warrant was too weak and that they'd reduced the charge to a misdemeanor. The cost of extradition wasn't worth it to them. He said that the next time I was in California, I should report to the courthouse in Yreka and clean things up. No big deal. I knew that Shasta County's hottest blow job would never testify about the night she spent with me and her baby— not for a chickenshit misdemeanor.

Rock Island kicked me loose and I walked to the I-80 truck stop to call my trucking office in Spokane. They sent me two hundred dollars for a Greyhound ticket. On the bus ride I told myself, *Dead people tell no lies, and the next time a woman resists like Jean, she will fucking well die. I am not taking any more of this bullshit!*

The long bus ride gave me time to think, and I went over things in my mind. Maybe it was just dumb luck, but I killed the girl in Portland and two innocent people took the fall. I assaulted a woman in California, and the cops turned me loose. I'm arrested in Rock Island, and I wiggle out of that one, too.

I realized that I was making fools out of everybody, but it was still a little annoying that nobody knew it. I had mixed feelings of frustration and power, cockiness. I'd finally reached my father's level—smarter than anybody else. I could get away with murder.

I couldn't resist rolling the dice again. As I sat on the throne at a Greyhound rest stop in Livingston, Montana, I pulled out my pen. Who reads that graffiti shit anyway? I wrote, "I killed Tanya Bennet January 21, 1990 in Portland Oregon. I beat her to death, raped her and loved it. Yes I'm sick, but I enjoy myself too. People took the blame and I'm free."

That summed up my attitude—arrogance, pride, superi-

ority. Why not taunt the cops a little? I was in such a good
mood that I signed my graffiti with one of those silly little
Happy Faces. I was so happy to be free again.

I was disappointed that nothing came of my message—not
a word in the papers or TV or on radio. I waited two
months till I was driving through Umatilla, Oregon, and
wrote another restroom note: "Killed Tanya Bennett in
Portland. Two people got the blame so I can kill again.
(Cut buttons off jeans—proof)." *Let's see them ignore this
one.*

But they did. When would those stupid cops catch on
that they had the wrong people?

2 | A Little Antsy

> *The psychopath never adjudicates the situation with reference to the future. He just plunges ahead. . . . They have to constantly escalate in order to get a kick out of life.*
>
> —Thomas P. Detre, M.D.,
> Yale University professor of psychiatry

My trucking boss in Spokane fired me when he got word about the Shasta case, and Peggy quit the company in protest. In February of '91 I went to Alaska to work on a fish-processing ship, the *Ocean Pride* out of Dutch Harbor. I crewed on that boat for a month and set a new record of 136 boxes an hour, breaking the old record by forty boxes, but the job was a little too dull for my taste. The ocean wasn't for a kid who grew up fishing rivers and streams.

I flew back to Peggy in Portland, caught a few freelance laboring jobs, and then got hired as a trucker out of Yakima, Washington. Peg and her kids stayed at her house in Portland, and I lived in my truck to save money till we could get a place together.

I still fantasized about Taunja and how I should have let her live and used her as my personal sex slave. I tried to keep myself busy and healthy and in good physical shape. I kept an Igloo cooler full of Slim Fast diet drink in a cabinet in my truck. On long hauls I could live on one hundred dollars' worth of Slim Fast for a week. I tried to avoid high-bulk foods that made me sleepy. I could chase a can of Slim Fast with a quart of ruby grapefruit juice, pop a handful of NoDoz, and drive for three or four days without sleeping. More than once I drove from one coast to the other, stopping only for fuel.

I didn't think my diet would hurt me, but I noticed that I was getting a little antsy. Sometimes I would pull off the road and jog till my nerves settled down. Late one night I parked my truck on Highway 97 at Lava Butte, just south of Bend, Oregon. A corkscrew road led up to a lookout tower that was usually unmanned. I'd run up there a few times and once talked with a lady lookout, and I knew they had a portable TV and radio. Just for a little excitement I decided to steal their stuff.

I took a pry bar out of my toolbox and headed up the road. When I got near the top, I saw a parked car. It didn't hit me till I was starting to climb the tower steps that the lookout might be manned—better yet, womanned. I began to think about rape.

I felt strong, confident. I felt sweaty and cunning, almost panting. I fantasized about sliding between the woman's legs without any foreplay and making her take it, ready or not. My ex-wife Rose always said that she hated sex because I forced it on her. Now was my chance to force it on a total stranger. *It has to be tonight, sister, right now! And no back talk!* To me forced sex was a total turn-on.

But as I climbed closer I began to see the downside. I realized that I could get my ass in a crack. Was a midnight jump in a lookout tower worth risking the Shasta County bullshit all over again? Getting bit in the ass months after I had my fun? No way. I decided to climb up to the top and jack off to my fantasies.

On the catwalk I looked out toward Bend like a tourist. I was taking my peter out when I saw a flicker of motion below. A car was pulling alongside my truck.

It had to be a cop, so I ditched the pry bar and climbed down. At the bottom I started running wind sprints on the shoulder. By the time I finished, the trooper was gone.

When I got back to my trucking office, the boss asked me why I was climbing Lava Butte at midnight. I told him I was jogging like I'd done lots of times before. He said the Bend sheriff called to tell me to stay the hell away from Lava Butte. My boss told me to avoid the lookout trail or he'd fire me.

Two weeks later I jogged up Lava Butte and talked to the lookout in broad daylight. I told her I was sorry if I startled her when I made my climb. She said that she was the one who'd reported me. I told her that from now on I'd jog during the day. She said she would tell the other lookouts that I was a regular. I think she liked me. That was the end of another near miss.

The whole incident made me decide that if I had to have forced sex, I'd better stick to hookers. They were in no position to blow the whistle. I figured they deserved whatever they got. Most of them were dopers anyway. I picked up two or three and treated them rough—not beating them, but manhandling them, taking hard sex, getting my money's worth.

One night I delivered at Smith Foods in Phoenix and then picked up a hooker with nice titties and hard nipples. After I got her in my sleeper, I wrestled her down and told her to shut up if she knew what was good for her. She panicked and gave up, and I rode her hard for an hour or so before I told her to get lost.

"What about my money?" she yelled when she was out of the cab.

I said, "You weren't a good-enough fuck. Get outa here!"

She stepped up on the running board and sprayed me in the face with a can of pepper mace. My lungs caught fire and I was coughing and trying not to vomit. The only thing that saved my eyes was my glasses.

I drove away fast with my head out the window to dry the stuff off. Now I wasn't just a killer, I was a rapist. What next? I was good and scared. That pepper spray could have been a gun.

I decided to make sure of what the next hooker brought into my truck. It was a year and a half since Taunja, but the thought of taking a woman by force was stronger than ever. God help the next gal that gave me trouble.

3 | Plum Purple-Blue

When 1992 rolled around, my ex-wife and kids were still living in Spokane, my girlfriend Peggy was at her mother's house in Portland, and I was living out of truck No. 22 of A&G Trucking. It was a 1989 379-Series Peterbilt conventional tractor with a 244-inch wheelbase, low-profile 24.5 tires, and a fifteen-speed transmission. My four-hundred-ATAC Caterpillar engine pulled a loaded forty-eight-foot reefer like it was a toy wagon—no strain at all. My rig always drew stares—plum-purple-blue metallic paint, dual chrome stacks, polished aluminum wheels and all the extra chrome the company could afford. I had Christmas-tree lights and a Vari-shield to push air over the top of the reefer. I loved that truck. I tried to give both of us a wash every day or two. A truck that fine, it was worth the extra money.

It wasn't easy being on the road all the time, missing Peg and my kids, but I made the best of it. I had a forty-eight-inch sleeper with two built-in closets and a mattress seven feet long—six inches longer than me. At night I'd lay in bed and read and listen to the other trucks pulling in and settling down for the night—drivers talking, jacking around, flirting with the lizards. Inside my sleeper I was the king of the road.

I had a standard Uniden forty-channel sidebander, but I pretty much stayed off the air. I tried to avoid that "breaker

breaker" shit, trading inside information and jokes, telling
where the Smokies were hiding. Instead I just listened. My
high-power Cobra 25 radio brought in signals from forty
miles away. I'd hear all the gossip.

There was never a shortage of sex for truckers, but I was
still a little nervous about being alone with women after
taking that blast of pepper spray. Then I got another chance
to get into the same kind of trouble, and I was too stupid to
say no.

4 | Killing Again

Then when he started killing women, he actually breathed life back into a couple of them, because they lost consciousness too quickly. He said, "I wasn't going to let myself be robbed of the experience. I wanted to see in her eyes that she knew she was going to die, and that I was going to take her life. . . ."

—Janet Warren,
Department of Behavioral Medicine and Psychiatry,
University of Virginia, discussing a serial killer

It was a hot summer day in 1992, and I was parked at the brake-check area on I-15 just before it dropped down the hill to San Bernardino, California. I had my coveralls on and I was under the truck, setting my brakes in case the scale-house guard decided to inspect.

I was just about done when I heard a woman's voice, "Hey, can I get a ride?"

I looked around and didn't see anybody.

"Hey, can I get a ride!"

I peeked around a tire and here's this girl looking at me—tight bleached-out blue jeans, a loose white top, big tits. She wasn't beautiful, but pretty enough. I was downwind and she smelt nice. She asked again and I said, "Yeah, sure! Where you going?"

She said, "Well, L.A. Or . . . anywhere we end up."

I said, "Who are you and where in hell did you come from?"

She giggled and said, "Oh, I'm just a throwaway woman. I got a ride with that guy over there."

I saw a parked Albertson's grocery truck. They weren't allowed to pick up riders. That was why the driver dropped her off before the scale house.

I said, "Wait a minute." I crawled out and asked where she really wanted to go. I'd been through this conversation a hundred times.

She said, "Phoenix."

"Somebody meeting you?"

"No. It just sounds like a nice place."

I pulled off my dirty old coveralls. It was broad daylight, hot as a welder's torch in that damn desert town. She waved good-bye to the Albertson trucker and climbed into my cab. I thought, *God, this is the one.*

She told me her name was Claudia. She looked clean, but she had no luggage—a bad sign. It meant she could be a female hobo mooching off drivers. She could be a doper looking for a fix.

She sat back and lit a cigarette while I went into the restaurant to get a couple of ice teas to go. We drove east past the Banning scales to the Burns Brothers truck stop at Coachella. After a brief lunch we walked through the store, and I could see that she expected me to buy her some clothes. When I promised to buy her a new outfit at the mall in Phoenix, we went back to the truck and climbed into the air-conditioned sleeper.

I leaned over and kissed her, but she didn't kiss back. She said, "If you want sex, just ask for it and I'll tell you how much."

I said, "I don't pay for it."

I tried to kiss her again and she pressed her lips together. I readjusted her position on the bed and started yanking off her clothes. When she was naked, I stripped and began to grope her body. I had to force her legs apart to enter her and that made the sex even better. I orgasmed fast.

Not wanting this to end too quick, I waited for my hardness to return. I was thinking, *This bitch is mine. I'll do what I want to her.*

We had more sex and she pretended to get into it. I knew what she was thinking. If she convinced me we were friends, I wouldn't hurt her. I was on to her act.

We stopped at the next truck stop, ate and showered. I wondered why she didn't just take off, but after I bought her some cigarettes I found out what she was really looking for. She asked me for some "crank," and when I told her I didn't fool with drugs, she got agitated. She grabbed my CB microphone and asked the whole damn world if anybody had crank.

I pulled the mike away and told her I didn't allow drugs of any kind in my truck and to stay the hell off my radio. I said, "Calm down! Look, you won't starve if you ride with me. I'll take care of your needs, but—no dope. Forget about it."

She said, "Well, how about some spending money then?"

She took my twenty-dollar bill and whined, "That's all?" She said she'd allowed me to have sex with her and she was worth a lot more than twenty dollars. I reminded her that I didn't pay for pussy.

She said, "Gimme the money I saw in your wallet or I'll blow the whistle on you."

I said, "For what?"

She said, "Gimme the money and I'll walk away. No questions asked. Otherwise I'll tell that security guard how you assaulted me."

My mind was going wild with the possibilities. I said, "Are you *crazy?*"

She said, "What's it gonna be? Your money or jail?"

I reached over and locked the doors. I said, "Neither one, bitch."

I grabbed the roll of duct tape under my pillow and

taped her arms in front of her. Then I taped her ankles together.

I looked out over the parking lot and saw it was empty. I pushed my fist into her neck like I did to Taunja and she went to sleep. Just like that.

I was trying to decide what to do with her body when she opened her mouth and said, "This is bullshit! You can't kill me!"

I taped her arms to the side vent so that she wouldn't fall off the bed. I got dressed and told her to shut up. Now that I was heading toward my second murder I knew I'd be facing the devil someday, and to please him I had to do a better job of killing. That made this murder easier morally because God had nothing to do with it. Neither did right and wrong. It was me and the devil doing our thing. Now I could concentrate on killing.

I'm raping her in the sleeper again when I hear two cars pull up in the shadow of my truck. Cops! One was a K-9 unit with a dog. They were using my shade to cool the dog while they went inside and ate.

I eased away nice and easy and got back on I-10. By the time we reached Indio, she'd worked herself out of the tape and was trying to get dressed. I open the curtain and I see she's ready to pop out and run. She was just waiting for me to stop.

I drove my plum Pete toward a wide graveled area and yanked the maxi air brake. I pushed her down and taped her all over again, this time good and tight. She kept saying, "I'm tired of this, *I'm tired of this*." Well, who the hell wasn't?

At the next truck stop I screwed her till I couldn't get it up anymore. It was supreme, it was total gratification. *I'm running this show, bitch. You're mine!*

I started to play a little death game with her, use her like a toy, an amusement. I choked her, let her wake up, choked her again, let her wake up again. That's the kind of game I should've played with Taunja.

Each time this woman came to, she made threats. "You

bastard, I'm not gonna take this shit. I'll turn you into the cops, you son of a bitch." For somebody who was already half-dead, she was sure cocky.

After I choked her the third time, I waited ten or fifteen minutes till she revived. I said, "Take a deep breath. Count to ten. Now—hold your breath." Then I choked her out again.

When she woke up, I told her to count to nine and squeezed her neck again. I was playing with her like a cat with a mouse. As the game went on I'd tell her to count to eight, then seven, six, five. I was breaking her mind. I wanted her to accept that one of these times she wouldn't wake up. Finally she caught on and just accepted the game.

My adrenaline rushed as I squeezed the breath out of her lungs for the last time. The power in my hands was supernatural, and even though I was wiped out, it gave me another hard-on.

I needed to get rid of her body. But where? I went into the truck stop restaurant and relaxed with an ice tea. I was surprised at how calm I felt. I knew I should feel remorse, but I just wished I could start all over again.

5 | Smoky Bear

I drove east to look for a dumping place. It was late afternoon but still hot. I decided to go to the shady side of the San Bernardino Mountains and wait till dark. Near the Patton War Museum exit I saw a place that looked promising and I parked off to the side. I scouted a deep ravine next to the truck and decided to take a nap before I made my move. With a blanket between me and Claudia, I fell into a light sleep as the afternoon slipped away.

Around 7:00 P.M., I heard some truckers talking on the CB radio about a Smoky Bear parked by a purple truck on the eastbound side. I thought, *A purple truck? My God, that's me!* I climbed into the front and looked out my window. He was sitting twenty feet away.

I glanced back to make sure she was still dead. I touched her, and her body was getting stiff. I sat up and waited for the knock. *What was he doing there?* I thought, *Why don't I step out and ask him?*

I grabbed two Cokes from my cooler and walked over. We socialized for five or ten minutes. He wouldn't accept a drink, but he was friendly. I told him I stopped because my tires got hot. He told me that a spotter plane was working and to be careful about my speed.

I walked back to my truck and acted like I was checking

the tread. I climbed into my cab and pulled out my log-books and wrote down my hours of service in plain sight of the trooper. I didn't need him to check my logbooks and start sniffing around. Cops know dead bodies. They have a smell of their own.

I honked and waved as I eased back on the interstate toward Arizona. I wondered if he made any notes about truck number twenty-two of A&G Trucking on a certain date and time. I decided to put some miles between us before I dumped the body.

I drove two hours to the desert town of Blythe, just east of Palm Springs near the Arizona border. I breathed better when I saw that I wasn't followed.

At Highway 95 I turned south into the foothills and drove six or eight miles to a wide spot where I could park. I waited till the sun went behind the hill so I could have just enough light to do the job but not enough to be observed. I dragged Claudia into a brushy canyon and covered her with tumbleweed.

At the Flying J Truck Stop at Arizona Exit 1, I threw my sleeping bag in the shower to get rid of the death smell and dried it on the way to Phoenix by hanging it over my Vari-shield windjammer. My thoughts were not of remorse. This woman deserved to die for the threats she made against me. I was just keeping another Jean from getting some other poor fool in trouble by giving false testimony to the police. Since I'd gotten away with the Taunja Bennett death, I was beginning to feel immortal. It was a game now. I was boss, and I was invulnerable.

I drove into Phoenix and delivered my load the next morning. I threw away my bedding and bought new sheets and pillow slips. All day long I kept thinking how easy it was to kill. I had everything going for me. I was highly mobile. Nobody questioned a girl riding in a truck, and my sleeper was enclosed. In fact, the truckers' lingo for a sleeper was "coffin." Nobody could see the bed when I closed the curtain. I was in Keith's World again.

6 | Sudden Death

All sexual crime is driven by fantasy. . . .
    —Stephen Michaud, biographer of Ted Bundy

After I killed Claudia, I couldn't fantasize about Taunja without thinking of the two of them at the same time. My fantasies flowed from one to the other. What hadn't happened to Claudia *had* happened to Taunja and vice versa. Claudia's death was an extension of Taunja's death. I fantasized other deaths, too. I was obsessed with rape and killing.

I realized that the reason I got away with my murders was that after I killed I took my time and thought things out. I didn't just dump the bodies. I worried constantly about making a mistake. I did things right.

Once in a while I'd drive past a prison and blow my air horn and look up at the guard towers and yell, "Home sweet home! I'll end up with you guys someday!"

I already had a prisoner's state of mind. I had a premonition that by the time I reached my fortieth birthday, I'd be a retired millionaire or in prison. Deep inside I knew which one. I knew I'd thrown my life away when I started to kill.

•   •   •

About a month after Claudia I had an overnight load of beef going from Ellensburg, Washington, to Fresno, California. I didn't like the truck I was assigned—a 1991 Peterbilt conventional with fifteen-speed transmission and a 3406 ATAC 425-hp Cat engine. It was painted marine blue—nowhere near as cool as my plum Pete—and it was low geared to the point where it got five-and-a-half miles per gallon. I was never at ease behind that wheel.

I was tired when I entered the southbound rest area at Turlock, California, to catch three or four hours of sleep before finishing the run. Just after midnight a pretty blonde in a red sweater jumped up on my running board and asked if I wanted to party.

Reaching down with my left hand, I fondled her breasts. I told her thanks for the feel but I didn't want anything else. She was a small woman in her late twenties or early thirties—it was hard to tell the age of these lot lizards, with the life they led. I think she said her name was Cynthia.

"Are you sure you don't want a little?" she said. "Don't you like what you feel?"

I said, "Yeah, but I'm tired. Go away and let me sleep."

She said, "Why did you feel me if you don't want me?"

I said, "It's a sure way to see if you're a cop. I don't want to be set up. Maybe I'll be in the mood later."

After she walked away, I shut down my truck, lights and all. If I left a light on, she'd think I was interested and wake me up. She sure looked sweet, but I didn't trust her or any other lizard. Probably had a knife or pistol under her shirt. In Florida one hooker turned into a serial killer, murdering innocent truckers that were out on the road sixteen, eighteen hours a day to support their families.

I kicked off my shoes and crawled into bed. I was sound asleep when the passenger door flew open and something came crashing in.

When I saw it was the same girl, I was pissed. I reached over and grabbed her and slammed her on the bed. Before she could open her mouth, I started to squeeze her throat.

After a while she went limp and I realized she'd stopped breathing. I'd killed my third victim and I didn't even know her name. And for what? *Nothing!* I didn't even play the death game with her. Or have sex. What a waste.

I felt I was being watched. I opened the curtain an inch and saw two strange faces at the window on the passenger side. What had they seen? I had to clear out of there fast.

I pushed in the brake-release valves and hit the starter in the same motion. Still barefooted, I switched on the headlights and pushed in the clutch and shifted into fourth double under. The indistinct faces were still at the window—probably her girlfriends, trying to find out what happened.

I hit the gas and they disappeared. It was just before dawn and I headed south. I listened on the radio for anything about the kidnapping of a woman from a rest area. Then it hit me! *What if she wakes up, like Claudia?*

At the next off-ramp I parked and looked at the woman I never should've killed. She still looked dead, but I gagged her and used plastic ties on her wrists and ankles to make sure she didn't cause more trouble.

Then I heard her breathing. *My God, it's hard to kill somebody!* I gave my truck full throttle. I needed to get past the scale house at Livingston, five miles down the road, so I wouldn't be documented in the neighborhood at the time she disappeared.

I slowed down to legal speed when the scale house came into sight. It was closed.

It was still dark when I eased into the Blueberry Hill Café parking lot. The surface was covered with six inches of powder dirt as I circled behind another parked truck. I smelled death. Was she dead? Would I have to kill her again?

I crawled into the sleeper for a look. A fine-looking girl. Nice tits! Petite, five-four maybe, 110 pounds. She'd soiled my bed with her urine, another mess I'd have to clean up. I would never be able to ask her why she jumped into my truck. I could only guess that a cop showed up or somebody chased her. Or maybe she had another motive. *Thanks to me losing my cool, nobody will ever know.*

I laid her next to the sleeper door so I could dump her out without dragging any of my own stuff in the dirt. At the southwest corner of the café parking lot, there was a large tree with garbage and tumbleweeds piled up around it—a perfect place for a body. I had a shovel and thought of digging a hole in the dirt and driving over her a few times to pack it down, but that would take too much time.

There was a faint glow in the east. Other truckers would be waking up, so I had to hurry. I removed the duct tape and plastic ties in case my fingerprints were on them. I carried her body over my shoulders like a sack of potatoes, dumped it facedown, and pushed her head into the powder. I stepped on her neck to make absolutely sure she was dead. Then I slung her on the garbage pile. For a grave marker I gave her a piece of tumbleweed.

Now I had to make tracks before I was spotted. I drove fast toward Fresno. I was paranoid over the killing and the faces in the window.

I pulled into a rest area, cleaned my mattress and threw the covers away. I drove on to Gilroy and parked at the truck stop at the junction of 101 and 152, across the street from the State Patrol office. I figured that was the safest place to be if they were looking for me.

I slept in the front seat the rest of that morning—or tried to sleep. I wondered if I'd reached the point where killing would never bother me again. I argued with myself over what I was doing. Why? When would my conscience kick in? Did I even have one?

I finally decided I wasn't fit to live. I was a monster. All my life I'd been disliked and I'd disliked myself, but now the dislike had turned to contempt and hatred. I had to commit suicide. But I didn't have the guts.

• • •

For the next week I checked out the parking lots for security officers before I got out of my truck. In restaurants I sat
with my back to the wall, scoping everybody who came in.
Suspicious movements made me shake. I was sure everybody knew I was a killer. I monitored the CB Smokey reports day and night to hear my name. I dreaded calling into
the office in case there was a message from the cops.

But after a few more weeks of paranoia, I realized I was
free and clear again. John and Laverne What's-their-names
were in their third year in the penitentiary for killing
Taunja, and I was running around killing more.

It looked like I would never be punished by God or Satan. I decided there *was* no God or Satan, and when we
died our lives just flickered out. The sooner a person un-
derstands that there's no punishment after death and allows
their own inner impulses to take over, the sooner they become an unstoppable serial killer. That's the point I'd
reached. It was scary, but it was exciting, too.

7 | "A Busy Little Whore"

. . . Future antisocials quickly learn that they are viewed as misfits in society, that their misfortunes will be compounded by the deprecatory and close-minded attitude of the larger community. . . . They learn it is better to be predator than prey.

—T. Millon and R. Davis,
Disorders of Personality—DSM-IV and Beyond

In the first week of November 1992, it was pouring rain on the Pacific Coast and I had a load of meat northbound out of Selma, California. My first drop was United Grocery in Medford, my last at Waremart in Salem, the state capital. I was nearing Salem with about eight-thousand pounds left when I felt the urge for female company.

I went to the Burns Brothers Truck Stop on I-5 at Wilsonville to find a hooker I knew named Laurie Pentland. She was twenty-three or twenty-four, not the best-looking girl in the world but a real crowd pleaser. The last three times I used her services, she raised her price every time and I didn't say a word of complaint. Thirty-five dollars for a date with her was a lot better than taking another woman out and pouring fifty or a hundred dollars' worth of whisky down her throat for a good-night kiss.

I parked in back and went on the CB radio—"Breaker breaker commercial!" Nobody answered. It was 9:00 P.M. and still early for action. I locked the truck behind me and went inside for coffee.

By ten I gave up on Laurie and decided to turn in. As I walked back to my truck I saw some lizards pulling in. Two of the truckers were signaling with their parking and clearance lights.

On my CB radio I heard a woman calling for company. I recognized Laurie's voice and told her where to find me. She climbed in and told me her price was now forty dollars. I paid up front and put on a rubber, and she curled into my arms. She took it nice and slow, and by the end of an hour I'd shot my last orgasm.

She started to get dressed and I asked her where she was going. She told me she had to find another trick. It was cold and wet outside. I was thinking how snug it was here in my sleeper. *Behind closed doors.* Ever since I was a kid, that's where the most interesting things happened.

Laurie pulled on her raincoat and told me I owed her an extra forty dollars for the long session. Normally, she said, she would get a guy's nut off in fifteen minutes. I reminded her that our deal was forty bucks. She gave me a line of bullshit that her female pimp took her money and if I didn't pay double she wouldn't see a dime.

After a while the sales pitch got louder and turned into a threat—*"You better pay up or I'll call the cops."*

I warned her fair and square: "You don't know the risk you're taking."

She said, "Oh, yes I do. Now gimme the money!"

I gave her one more chance. "I won't put up with this shit. You've got nothing on me."

She said, "Yes, I do! I know your name and who you drive for and where you're delivering. Now give me what I've got coming!"

I said, "I'll tell you what you got coming, girl. I'm gonna strangle you!"

She said. "Go for it!"

I was thinking, *Does this stupid bitch know the chance she's taking for forty lousy bucks?* I pushed her down in the sleeper and gave her a hard stare. She must have thought I had rape on my mind. She wasn't that lucky.

As my hand brushed against her neck, I said, "For that last extra threat, bitch, you just lost your life."

I don't think she believed me till I had my fist in her throat. Nothing could have stopped me by then.

Just before she passed out, I said, "You're number four that pushed your luck with me, bitch. Now you're dead!" I trembled at the excitement of the kill.

For a minute or two I tried to catch my breath. I thought I saw movement in her eyes. I bent over her and heard her breathing. I laid there next to her till she came around again and I started playing with her. She touched me back, I guess out of fear. The death game begins!

I played for an hour and then decided to put her under for good. As she struggled, I could see her will to live fade like a match going out.

Even after she closed her eyes and went limp, I kept pushing till I was sure she was dead. Then I stretched her out and cleaned the spot where she'd peed her raincoat.

I locked the doors behind me and went into the café. I looked into my cup of coffee and wondered about the mentality of these truck-stop hookers. Why did they put themselves in such dangerous positions? Drugs? *This stupid woman* asked *to be killed. I just helped her out.*

Back in the truck I slid in next to her, opened her blouse, and felt her skin. She had firm tits, a good body. To clear my head I masturbated in my hand. Then I covered her up and went through her pockets. She'd been a busy little whore. I retrieved my forty and two hundred dollars more. This would be a bad night for her pimp.

I thought of putting her body in one of the dropped trailers that were lined up in the back row. Wouldn't that be a surprise for the driver? Then I remembered the GI Joe's parking lot in Salem, next to where I was scheduled to deliver in the morning. There were garbage containers and blackberry vines in the back lot.

8 | A Good Night's Work

I headed south on I-5 and switched to 99 to bypass the I-5 Woodburn Port of Entry. I didn't want to be documented going south and I didn't want a nosy cop to check my load. I approached GI Joe's from the south, off Highway 22.

I saw that the back light wasn't working in the parking lot and a few container trailers were butted against the fence. There were plenty of vines to hide the body and some loose trash blowing around as well. A six-foot fence border obscured the property. *Perfect.*

It was around 2:00 A.M. and really dark. I took a wide sweeping turn so my rig wouldn't scratch the fence and leave a paint stain. With flashlight in hand I looked the place over for security. It was empty.

I opened the sleeper door and pulled the whore out by her hair. She fell on her head with a thud, six feet straight down. I dragged her against the fence and covered her with leaves. A good night's work.

I drove to Waremart, a hundred yards down the street, took a nap and delivered my load in the morning. I called my office from Brooks, Oregon, and stopped in Longview, Washington, to wash my bedroll. I thought, *At one time that dumb bitch could have saved her life, but she wouldn't listen. It's never wise to threaten somebody that outweighs you by 150 pounds.*

After I cooled down and began to think logically, I realized that I had to stop killing, if only because I was bound to get caught sooner or later. It was too easy for a long-haul truck driver. And too exciting. This was three deaths in the last four months. I wondered if I would have to quit trucking to quit killing. Or if I even wanted to quit. I didn't know my own mind. I guess I never had.

9 | Spring Rains

Four months after Laurie Pentland I was headed south on I-5 in the early evening of a cold, rainy March day when I pulled into the Petro Truck Stop in Corning, California. A thick fog was rolling in off the ocean, and I had to clean the droplets off my glasses. I locked the truck but left it idling so I wouldn't lose the heat in the cab.

The café was jammed. It looked like the spring rains had flushed the street people out of their cardboard shelters. Some even sat in the hallway. I had a craving for fruit, so I piled up my plate at the buffet table. I was watching my weight, but I couldn't drink one more container of Slim Fast.

Out of the corner of my eye, I saw a wet-looking gal at the counter, staring at the food that passed under her nose. She sipped her coffee and looked half-starved. She was definitely a street person—reddish complexion, wet stringy hair, no makeup, wide-rimmed glasses. A long dress gave her kind of a motherly look or a schoolmarm down on her luck. I could tell she wanted to score a meal.

I didn't know what clicked in my head, but I decided right then and there that I had to take this woman. Why? Did she remind me of schoolteachers I'd liked—or hated? Did she remind me of my mother or my aunts or some of the neighbor women I knew as a kid? I never gave things like that a second's thought. All I knew was I intended to take this woman. This was one of those perfect opportunities that only came because I was driving truck.

I told my waitress, "See that drowned gal sitting over there? Give her anything she wants and put it on my check. But don't tell her who bought it. I don't need somebody following me around like a lost puppy." I didn't want the waitress to make any connections later.

The woman ate like a famished rat. Then she gave me a sweet look like she'd known all along who bought her dinner. I motioned her over and she joined me in my booth.

"Thanks," she said. I nodded like it was nothing to a big spender like me.

She talked a lot but without really telling me anything except that her name was Cindy and she was curious as hell about the nice truck driver. I tried to avoid the personal stuff and the big question of where I was headed. Some of these just want a warm bed and a roof over their head without the worry of being rolled out of their cardboard box in the middle of the night, but others want money for drugs and would knock you in the head to get it. You can't tell just by talking to them.

It was getting late and I knew she would soon be thrown out along with the other hippies. She seemed like a nice-enough person and quite intelligent. I decided to satisfy her curiosity about me. I said, "I'm headed for Salinas to pick up a load of produce for Seattle."

She said, "Then you'll go through Sacramento?"

"I could. Or I could take 505 and bypass Sacramento to 680 South and then 101 South. Or I could go to Sacramento and go through Stockton and Santa Nella and across 152 to 101 South."

"Please," she said, "take me to Sacramento! I have a sister there, and I can stay with her. You won't be sorry. I'll behave myself. *Please!*"

I hate it when they beg. They do it so well. That's what I mean by asking to be killed.

"I have to be in Salinas in the morning," I said. "So I can't linger in Sacramento. You still want to come?"

"Oh, yes," she said.

I pulled a twenty from my pocket for our meals. I bought a half-gallon of orange juice to wash down my NoDoz. When we got to the truck I saw that everything she owned was on her back. A bad sign. Claudia didn't have anything either.

I made a mental note to watch my ass as I steered my rig onto I-5. I kept the heater on high to dry her hair, also to make her shed her coat so I could get a better look at her tits.

Thirty miles south I stopped at the Shell station to look for other trucks from my company and found none. I was clear to do what I wanted.

Both of us used the bathroom. When she came back, I smelt some perfume and noticed that she'd combed her hair and enhanced her face with makeup. She was smiling and her top three buttons were undone. That was no accident. I could see her small breasts.

The Williams rest area came up in ten miles, and after I got rid of more of my coffee in the restroom I climbed back in the truck and kissed her. She kissed back as if she'd wanted it for a long time. I took off her glasses and touched her cheek. She bent her head into my hand to feel my strength.

In the sleeper she asked if I had a rubber. I did. I helped her out of her clothes and we snuggled under the blankets. After a little foreplay she guided me in. We kept at it for a few hours and then I pushed her away. I'd covered my mattress with a plastic protector to make it easier to keep clean.

She said, "This is so cozy and warm. Let's spend the night back here."

I said, "Oh, we will, we will." I thought, *This woman is mine. I own every inch. I might as well let her in on the secret.* I said, "But you won't be around to enjoy it."

She sat up and said, "What does *that* mean?"

"It means I'm gonna kill you."

She just stared at me in disbelief. The thought of owning and killing this woman made me hard again and I tried to get it back into her, but she fought off my uncovered penis. Seemed like she was more afraid of pregnancy than death.

I pumped my last orgasm into her and began the death game. She came back to life four or five times before I crushed her neck for good.

I thought long and hard on what to do next. I dressed her and placed her body next to the sleeper door. I was still under the false impression that I had to hide their bodies so they didn't get found too soon. Little did I know that it made no difference in the end. When killing strangers, it's only necessary to make a clean getaway. A dead body has no traceable links when you're driving cross-country.

I took her down I-5 to 152 and then west about a mile past the truck scales. I deposited her body behind a pile of rocks in thick brush. Then I drove back to US 101 and the Shell Truck Stop at Gilroy. The rain had stopped and it was a beautiful night. I slept like a baby.

10 | Confession

In the fall of 1993 I dropped in on my old friend Billy Smith again. I hadn't killed in five or six months, ever since Cindy in March, but I was nervous because I wanted to do it again. When the feeling was on me, it was all I cared about.

After Bill helped me adjust my clutch, I couldn't keep my secret another minute. I said, "Billy, I got a problem." We were standing in front of his apartment.

He said, "Man, you *are* a problem." That's the way we talked.

I said, "Billy, I'm killing people, and I can't stop."

He looked at me like I'd just farted.

"I mean it, man. I've already killed five women. What can I do?"

He said, "Wimpy Keith is killing women?"

It took a while to convince him I was serious. "Look," he said, "you used to be a fighter. Take a heavy bag with you and knock the shit out of it. Don't be pounding on any more women."

"You don't get it, Billy. I'm not pounding, I'm *killing*."

He looked exasperated. I could see he wasn't enjoying this conversation. He said, "You should see a shrink."

"Yeah, sure. He's gonna run straight out his back door to the cops."

Billy shrugged, like he wanted to get on another subject. I said, "What can I do to stop? Or am I just gonna keep doing this?"

He shook his head and frowned. He said, "Why do you do this?"

"I enjoy it," I said, "but . . . honest to God, I'm fighting it." I wanted to give him names, times and places, but I could see my friend had heard enough.

11 A Cut Above

A few months later I was having coffee at the Burns Brothers Truck Stop in Troutdale, Oregon, when I spotted a blonde, about five-two and maybe one hundred pounds, blue eyes—looked a little like Maggie in *Northern Exposure,* add ten or fifteen years. She sat with her back to me in the next booth. I said, "Now *there's* a back I'd like to rub." She laughed and motioned me over.

She said her name was Julie Winningham and she couldn't believe her luck to run into me. She said, "Where did *you* come from?" A lot of truck-stop women felt that way about me. There weren't many six-foot-six truckers around, especially ones that kept their weight down and had wavy brown hair and a good profile.

We talked for two hours and found out we were definitely on the same wavelength. We got so close that I asked her to take a trip with me. I promised never to force myself on her and told her she would always have the option of falling in love—her choice, no pressure. I really felt that way about her. She was a cut above most of the lot lizards.

I had a load for Seattle and was scheduled for engine maintenance in Yakima the next day. Then I'd be hauling a load of potatoes to the Lucky Stores Warehouse in Irvine, California. I asked her to come along.

She said it sounded like an interesting ride. In a few minutes she was on the way to the parking lot to put a note in her car window saying she'd be gone for a while. She came back with an overnight bag and said, "Let's go!" I couldn't believe how easy it was.

We pulled into Seattle in plenty of time. After we made out in my sleeper, we headed back to Yakima. In the shop my friend Butch asked if the pretty girl was a true blonde. I hadn't screwed her yet, but that's about all I hadn't done. I told Butch she was blonde all over.

Julie and I took my Mercury Topaz downtown and ate. She was a hit wherever we went. She told everybody she wasn't so sure about me but she'd fallen in love with my '89 Peterbilt. I was in the process of buying it from another trucker. Her ex-husband drove truck and she knew which ones were good and which ones were all chrome and no balls.

After our Friday-night dinner we started our trip together. Irvine is just south of L.A., and I had to deliver by Sunday morning. By driving nonstop I made Irvine just after midnight Saturday. After the potatoes were unloaded at dawn, I had a free day and took Julie to Knott's Berry Farm. We partied on the rides till closing, and I bought her a silver necklace and matching bracelet and had her picture taken on a fake newsmagazine cover. Later she gave that picture to her mother and it ended up splashed in all the papers. There was only one bad sign: she acted annoyed that I didn't do drugs or pot.

That night we parked at Truck Town on Cherry Avenue just north of I-10 in Fontana, halfway between L.A. and San Bernardino. The sex was okay, but she didn't make any extra effort. I thought I deserved better after dropping a couple hundred on her jewelry.

I went to a phone booth to check in with my company, and when I got back to the truck she was trying to score some drugs over the CB. She said that pot made her horny and made her a better lover.

After we kissed a few times, she asked me to marry her because she really loved me and wanted to be mine forever. What I didn't know was that she was on the prowl for some big dumb idiot to buy her things and pay her way, and big dumb Keith had taken the bait.

I told her not to try to buy any pot over my radio. The cops monitored all the frequencies. I bought a joint off the truck-stop guy while he was polishing our wheels. Charged me forty bucks—was I shocked!

Julie and I drank doubles at a motel bar in Bakersfield and retired into a sex orgy. She was drunk and horny and we enjoyed each other a long time—not the best sex I ever had, but good enough.

The next morning we picked up another load and headed back to Oregon. She retrieved her car and drove it home. I spent the night with her and then headed back south.

For a long time after that, I would stop by and see her whenever I got a chance. I introduced her to my friends Billy and Ginny Smith, and the three of them got drunk and friendly and she ended up renting a room in their house.

Every time I was routed near her place, I'd call her on the phone and we'd get together. But after a while I realized that something was wrong. My pal Billy had wanted into her pants and I knew it. He was always looking for outside pussy.

I dropped Julie when I realized she was making it with him and didn't care about me and never had. All she wanted was my car, party money and a steady supply of pot. She'd say, "Don't you want me to have fun while you're gone, Keith? Don't you want me to feel good? You have to get me a better car. Don't you want me to be safe?"

I told her I didn't intend to buy her a car or supply her drug habit. We had sex one more night, but she was like a rag doll. In the morning I took her to breakfast and told her we were finished. We'd dated for almost a year, off and on. We got along great at times, but I didn't smoke, and pot was the biggest event in her life. How could I have hooked up with someone like her?

I said to myself, *If I ever see that money-grubbing pot-head again, I'm gonna run as fast as I can.* It was a good idea. If only I'd carried it out.

4

A
KILLER'S
LIFE 2

1 | A Business Move

From the start young Keith Jesperson was bewildered by his family's sudden emigration to central Washington. The town of Selah was only four hours south of Chilliwack, but to the twelve-year-old it might as well have been Bangladesh. "I didn't want to leave Canada—none of us kids did. I knew every tree in our woods, every ripple in our creek. I knew when the first hummingbirds arrived and the last duck left for the winter. My paper route kept me in spending money. Chilliwack was the greenest place on earth. Selah was green, too, but only where it was irrigated. A mile or two out of town you were in desert. A lot of it was a bombing range."

In later years, Les Jesperson explained the move as a business move, a necessary step upwards: "I was approached by a group of hop growers to migrate to the United States and design machinery for the hop industry. I started an engineering office in Moxee, a little town in the Yakima Valley. It was surrounded by hop fields, and there was a heavy demand for the W-shaped clips that I invented. I could have moved my family to six or eight nice towns in the area, but I selected Selah because of the school system. Selah had that old-fashioned hometown image, and I thought my children would grow up there without so many temptations surrounding them."

• • •

At Eastertime 1967 Les moved Gladys and their three sons
and two daughters into a six-bedroom house with three
bathrooms, a four-car garage, formal dining room, oversized kitchen, pond and bomb shelter. The house was in a
comfortably middle-class neighborhood just outside the
Selah city limits, and Keith soon learned that the neighbors weren't much different from Canadians. "Mr. Hertel
had a 1909 Marlon sportster and a Model T Ford. South of
them were the Joneses—they rode motorcycles and snow-
mobiles and went on hill climbs. Mr. Hall worked for
the electric company, and his son became a sheriff. The
Adamses, the Words, the Williamses—they were all good
people. But I never really felt like Selah was home. I felt
like a visitor. I missed Joe Smoker and Reg Routley and
the other kids. Every time Dad went back to Chilliwack on
business, I begged to go along."

With his unflagging energy Les installed lavish landscap-
ing and erected a barn and other outbuildings. For his children he built a miniature log cabin and decorated it with
seven plywood dwarves teetering across a log.

In the late spring of 1967, just after Keith's twelfth
birthday, his mother enrolled him in the final quarter of the
sixth grade. Canadian schools had high standards, and he
found himself far ahead of his classmates at Sunset Elementary. "I just floated through the rest of the year—didn't
speak up in class, didn't study, didn't take part in anything.
I just showed up so I wouldn't get in trouble."

For a long time he felt detached, unconnected, as
though the Selah kids were a different species. "I felt
closer to cartoon characters like Porky Pig and Superman.
I'd never been tight with my brothers and sisters, and I
started to fall away from Mom, too. I appreciated the good
things she did, but it was always in the back of my mind
that she was sleeping with the enemy. Mom was the only

person on earth that could keep Dad from hitting me with his belt, but she didn't do it often enough. That's the way I saw things at the time we moved to Selah. It was just me and Duke against the world."

Keith had always been considered a little different by his fellow Canadians, but to the Americans he seemed just plain strange. To most of them he was the stereotypical backwoods Canuck, and from his first days in the new country he didn't bother to upgrade his image. "Nobody spoke to me when I walked into my first class. I think they expected to see a big geek in snowshoes. When I spelled my name for the teacher, the kids giggled. I thought, *What the hell's so funny about "Keith Hunter Jesperson"?*

"I was considered an immigrant, a foreigner. Feeling left out wasn't exactly new, so it didn't bother me. The Selah kids made fun of my clothes, my shoes, my accent. 'Hey, Keith, you comin' oat?' They didn't know about Canadian pronunciation. If you didn't talk like them, you were stupid. I went home and told Mom I had a speech defect."

A pretty classmate named Sandra Smith nicknamed him "Tiny" in recognition of his bulky shape and his height, just under six feet. He was still ungainly, and soon he was being called "Sloth," after the slow-moving South American animal, and "Monster Man," as well as generic pejoratives like "Fatty," "Hulk," and "Tubby."

His younger sister, Jill, recalled that the nicknames didn't seem to bother him. "He tried to act cool about it. He didn't get all hurt and cry. He just played along as though it was a game. He'd always been teased, especially by his brothers. But the move from Chilliwack definitely changed him. He began laughing about morbid things, found disgusting things funny. He'd never been that way in Canada."

• • •

Keith tried not to make any complaints to his new school-mates. "If I griped, they would've just thought of something worse to call me. Anyway, everybody had nicknames—I wasn't the only one. Mom told my brothers to stop calling me names, but they wouldn't. Pretty soon everybody in the school was doing it. It was just one more thing to hate my brothers for."

The Washington school year was a month shorter than British Columbia's, and Keith used the bonus time to learn his new territory. "By midsummer my dog and I had checked out five miles in every direction. It was either orchard or desert. I didn't try to make friends. I figured if it happened, it happened. Let them come to me. I met a kid named Tom Haggar (pseudonym), and sometimes I played with a few other kids in my class, but I always had the feeling I didn't fit into their little area of comfort. I was different. I didn't mind. I knew how to play by myself."

During the summer his father assigned irrigation responsibilities to the thirteen-year-old boy, including unplugging the gravity-flow ditches, building earthen dams and maintaining a steady flow of water to keep the pastures green for the family horses. It was hard work, and he negotiated a reward from his father. "Hill-climbing was a big deal, and Dad agreed to buy me a new trail cycle if I did my job right. I worked my ass off for that bike. In the spring of 1969 Dad took me and my brother into Yakima and bought a red Honda 90 Trail Cycle for Brad and a yellow one for me. I was so goddamn mad! I'd worked my ass off to earn mine, and Brad got his for nothing.

"When I complained to Dad, he told me to consider it a learning experience. He said, 'Remember, Son, I can always take your bike back.' Right about then I began to realize that Dad saw me and my brothers different. In some ways Dad and me were the closest, but my brothers were the ones that counted. He was already making plans to send them to college. I was the family drudge."

Despite the tension over the bikes, Keith and his father continued to work closely together. "I loved my dad and it gave me a warm feeling. The previous owner of our house never hauled any metal trash away, so we were constantly yanking wire and steel out of the fields. The fences needed repair. And Dad always had some project up his sleeve. He was a genius with tools, and before long we had workbenches, a welding setup, and a lathe, drill press and cutting torch. He taught me how to weld and fabricate, drive heavy equipment, ditch and trench, install drainage pumps, dig basements, build houses—any job involving wood or steel. He was so gifted! He could be an impatient teacher, but he taught me just about everything I know."

2 | Corrupting Influence

[The psychopath] has a completely defective sense of property.

—Robert Lindner, M.D.

In seventh grade at Selah Middle School, Keith and a dozen other boys were sent to the principal's office for throwing snowballs. "I felt better, knowing that I wasn't alone in the snowball business. Each kid that went into the office came out crying. My turn came and the principal ordered me to bend over. He took a paddle made of plywood with holes drilled in it and hit my ass just once. I looked up and waited for more, but all he said was, 'Go to your next class.' I told him it didn't hurt and if that was the best he could do, I would go outside and throw some more snowballs. I was never punished again in the Selah school system. A year or two later the school board banned all paddling."

One day Keith's new friend Tom Haggar introduced him to shoplifting. "He told me how easy it was at Viking Village—'Just slide the stuff up your sleeve and walk out.'"

On a Friday afternoon Tom loaded up on durable goods like small tools, padlocks and penknives while Keith filled both sleeves with Hershey's Kisses, Life Savers, Juicy

Fruit gum and the Kit Kat bars that were made in Canada. He had the same feeling that would always accompany him in the commission of a crime, petty or otherwise. "I felt like the whole world was onto me, like they knew I was stealing before I even started."

In a sense he was right. On their way out the thieves were intercepted and frisked. Owner Bob Mead told them he'd been watching their operation through one-way glass. All Keith could think of was his father's belt. It was wielded less often now that he was almost as big as Les, but surely this offense would bring back the old-style punishment. He wasn't sure he could take the belt again. He might just run back to Chilliwack.

The police inflicted their own punishment first. "They drove us to the school parking lot and made a display of us in front of the other kids, driving slowly around the lot three or four times—dirty little shoplifters on parade. Then they took us to the station and booked and fingerprinted us. The captain gave us a lecture on how we were headed to the penitentiary. He ordered us to tell our parents what we'd done. If we didn't, he said he'd put us in jail."

The senior Jespersons were visiting friends in Canada for the weekend. When they returned late on Sunday night, Keith blurted out, "I sort of got caught shoplifting at Mead's Thriftway."

Les ordered him to his room and called the Haggar boy's father for details. He was told that the shoplifting had been Keith's idea and that Tom was innocent. "Dad said he wasn't surprised. I expected him to start taking off his belt, but he told me to go to bed and he'd see me in the morning."

After a sleepless night Keith was driven to the store and ordered to apologize. The owner seemed disposed to drop the matter, but Les said, "Give him some work so he can make it up to you."

Mead told him to clean up the back alley. "Fair enough,"

his father said. "He'll work for you every day for two weeks."

On the way home Keith got the clear impression that his father was more upset about the public disgrace than the shoplifting. "I'll never forget and I'll never forgive," he quoted his father later. "You humiliated me in front of the whole damn town."

Keith described the scene that night at the dinner table. "Dad gave me a lecture in front of the others. He told me not to bother calling home for a ride when I was finished each day. He said, 'It's only two miles. When I was a boy, I walked farther than that in ice and snow.' He called me our little thief. For a long time afterwards he would say, 'How's our little thief today? Stolen anything lately?' "

Word traveled around the school that Keith was a corrupting influence on the other children and that Canadians couldn't be trusted—"They said we're all a bunch of thieves." His partner in crime snubbed him on the school bus. "So I was back where I started—no friends. Old stuff to me."

Soon afterward he got into his first fight and knocked out his opponent's front tooth. "It was a fair fight, and the other kid picked it, but I got the blame because I was bigger." Getting in trouble was becoming a habit.

3 | Death Album

By eighth grade Keith had begun to retreat into dreams and fantasies. In Keith's World he was bigger, brighter and handsomer than the other boys, and his slightest smile made girls melt in his arms. He saw himself riding tall as a member of the Royal Canadian Mounted Police, the scarlet jacket and leather boots accenting his buff physique. He wrote to his uncle Russell, veteran Mountie and staff sergeant major, and soon was poring over RCMP literature with his father. The only problem was a requirement that a Mountie had to be able to run ten miles, a feat still beyond the bulky boy's capacity.

A relative by marriage showed up with photo albums of enemy soldiers whom he claimed to have killed in Vietnam. At first Keith was uninterested, but after several viewings he felt a stir. "He told me how he pulled out the gooks' teeth with pliers, and how the troopers used prisoners for target practice. He admitted that hearing Vietnamese women scream in pain gave him a hard-on. His stories brought back memories of the dogs and cats I tortured in Chilliwack, how I threw rocks at ducks and broke their skulls. Some of those Polaroids made me wish I'd been in Vietnam. He explained that it's a real rush to snipe people. He told me about shooting the fingers off gooks at one hundred yards. When I thought about it, I got a hard-on as well."

• • •

Keith set about finding something to kill, but the prospects were leaner than in Canada. The Selah house was only a mile and a half from the center of town, and weeks passed without his sighting a single stray. When he found targets of opportunity, his armament proved weak. "I only remember killing one cat with my BB gun—I cornered this big tom and shot him over and over till he finally just laid there and bawled with each new BB shot into his flesh. I shot BBs up his ass and lower body parts. I used rocks to smash his paws and poked his flesh to make him jump. It took fifty-six BBs before he died."

4 | Blood Brothers

By Keith's fourteenth birthday Les had built a shop on the property and put his three sons to work manufacturing the spread-lock clips that were eagerly sought by hops growers all over the world. The pay was $1.50 an hour, and Keith was happy for the opportunity since he hadn't been able to line up another newspaper route. "Bruce was oldest, so he ran the press. On alternating days Brad and I would change boxes and reels of wire weighing upwards of 250 pounds. I carried them around like matchboxes. Once I straddled a 394 V-8 short block motor and pulled it right out of the car. I was as strong as a weightlifter, but for a long time I didn't realize it. One day I was jacking around with Frankie Williams and broke his wrist. After that I had to back off a little. People warned me I didn't know my own strength.

"Working for Dad wiped out my afterschool activities. There were nights when we worked till ten or eleven o'clock to reach our quotas. We used up a half ton of steel every day. When the operation was smooth, we punched out two thousand clips every 2½ minutes. If Bruce couldn't run the press, Brad took over, even though he was the youngest brother. If there was a job that involved sticking your hands in grease and oil and dirt or getting burnt or gassed or scarred, my brothers made sure I got it. I argued with them, but Dad always took their side.

"One day Brad and I got into it, and he said he wished I

was dead. I yelled, 'You want to kill me?' I went to the gun cabinet and pulled out the twelve-gauge side-by-side. I handed it to him and said, 'Go ahead and kill me, prick!' Bruce separated us. From that day on I considered my brothers dead. I'm sure they felt the same about me."

After a violent disagreement with his father, Keith turned to his mother for help, the standard protocol in the family. "Dad had set us up with checking accounts and taught us to balance our checkbooks. But he was also charging room and board, thirty bucks a week for me, and I had to buy my own clothes. After six months I found out that Bruce and Brad weren't paying. Mom complained to Dad, and he stopped charging me. When I asked him to reimburse me for what I'd paid, he told me to consider it another learning experience."

After each blowup, the boy found comfort in the nightly campfires that he set in a far corner of the pasture. "Fire always fascinated me. There's nothing like piling on old broken boards and sticks till the flames shoot high in the air. When I was a kid in Selah, I didn't see it as an addiction, just something to ease the pressure. But it got a lot more serious later. Maybe it's genetic. I heard that Grandma Jesperson had a strange attitude about fire. But nobody would ever talk about it."

Sometimes Keith came perilously close to being arrested. "I put exploding tips on my arrows. I shot one at the home of one of my teachers, ran like hell, and heard it explode. I used a 30-06 shell casing—pulled out the lead and filled it with gunpowder. I'd ram the staff of the arrow into the mouth of the shell and wrap the casing with baling wire. For a detonator I used a nail in a piece of copper tubing. When I shot those arrows into a piece of half-inch plywood, they blew out a hole the size of your fist. I decided that wasn't big enough."

5 | Pasty White Flesh

Through his middle school years the troubled boy remained in a quandary about women. "I didn't understand them. I was hopeless. When I saw a nice girl, I would tell her I liked her, and then she'd reject me. I never went to a prom or a dance. I liked girls from a distance—some I loved. But mostly I worked."

He still fantasized about the red-haired femme fatale of his grammar-school years in Chilliwack. In high school he kissed a few girls and enjoyed it, but he was too shy to proceed. He stood guard for Bruce and the older boys during make-out parties but learned nothing from the sighs and groans in the shadows. As a Jesperson, he was nervous about female nudity and avoided a nearby home where parents permitted their children to run around half-naked.

In his fourteenth year his attitude began to change. He caught his first close look at the female breast and later wrote about the shock.

> *Dad took us on a ten-week trip across thirty-three states and four provinces, and on the way we visited relatives and old friends. We ended up with his brother on Fogo Island off Newfoundland. Uncle Ivan was the minister to a bunch of fishermen and boatsmiths.*
>
> *On the island I met an eighteen-year-old girl*

looking to find a way off Fogo. There I was at fourteen, alone with a mature girl that kissed great and smelt like a woman. We made out on the grassy bluffs, but even though I had a hard-on I didn't dare do anything about it—not with my uncle being the island minister. For an hour or so I played with her breasts through her sweater— that was good enough for a first time. After a while she pulled the sweater off and out popped these pale white breasts with blue veins. Gross! Her pasty white flesh made me want to throw up.

At a party I met a sixteen-year-old with long brown hair down to her tight little ass. I was comfortable with her and I kissed and felt her through her clothes. I was a little relieved that she didn't expose herself because I didn't want to go too far and piss her off. Later on I found out that fourteen-year-olds were already getting married on Fogo.

Apparently no one on the island could keep a secret, and pretty soon Dad was talking about "Keith's girl troubles." He rubbed it in till everybody was laughing and giggling about the naive Keith, how dumb, how backward. I ran down to the dock and crawled under some fishing nets. For hours I pretended to be the Creature from the Black Lagoon, waiting to ambush the next person who came along. That's how angry I was. Luckily no one showed.

For the rest of our time on Fogo, I resorted back to the monster-under-the-net fantasy whenever I thought somebody was about to mention my sex problems. As time went by, I forgot the sixteen-year-old and could no longer see her face, but I'll always remember those chalky sloppy breasts with the ugly blue veins.

When we got back to Selah I began to read up on sex and what really happens between male and females. I fantasized about returning to Fogo and starting over. I should have played with her big bare breasts instead of being turned off by them. We should have had sex. I wonder if she ever got off the island.

Later in his eventful fourteenth year, Keith discovered sexual intercourse. In his self-designated role as habitual victim, he described it as rape in his later writings:

Dad took me on a fishing trip to the Washington coast and on our last evening I was walking on the beach when I came upon a woman of eighteen sitting next to a campfire. We sat and talked, and she told me how handsome and tall I was. We kissed, and after a while she began to take off my clothes. She grabbed my hand and guided my fingers into her, opened up the blanket and flashed some tit.

I got hard and she said, "That'll do nicely." She laid me on my back and climbed on top and popped my cherry, raped me over and over until I couldn't get it up anymore.

As I walked her to her pickup, she told me she'd be there tomorrow night, but Dad and I had to head back to Selah the next day. That weekend put my sexuality into overdrive. Now I knew how exciting it was to be seduced by a loving and willing woman. Now there was nothing else on my mind.

6 | Enter Igor

In 1969 Keith took his poor academic habits and D average to Selah High School as a freshman and came into immediate conflict with other students. As always he magnified every slight and went out of his way to misconstrue school rituals as personal attacks. "They always pantsed the freshmen in front of the girls, but I didn't know it was a tradition. I walked into the high school and found my brother Bruce and ten other juniors waiting to meet me. I kicked and punched and did some serious damage, but they pulled my pants down to my ankles. Then they giggled and walked away. Right in front of everybody I had to undo my belt and pants and pull them back up. When I became an upperclassman myself, I would never pants the freshmen. I just couldn't see the humor in it."

He soon learned that his established reputation as the Middle School nerd had preceded him. Students began calling him Igor, or Ig for short. "Brad started it, just for a joke. But it caught on. We'd all seen Igor in the Frankenstein movies, but I wasn't short, and I wasn't a cripple with a limp. For a while I thought they might be trying to say that Dad was Dr. Frankenstein and I was his geek, but that didn't make much sense either. So I just swallowed hard and took it—Mr. Nice Guy. That was the only way. After a while I didn't even feel like I was in school. I felt like I was *pretending* to be in school. It was the only way I could get through."

In later years Les Jesperson said of his middle son, "Part of his problem was that he was very gullible. You could talk him out of anything. He was everybody's mark."

Students worked Keith for loans and handouts, seldom repaid. He was a regular victim of practical jokes. Even though he was the biggest boy in the freshman class, he tended to yield rather than fight back. A classmate recalled, "He could be bright when he wanted to, but then he would do something stupid. He'd be too kind or too mean, too generous or too stingy. You never saw the in-between. His parents made him open a checking account, and in a few months he was overdrawn. He'd written too many checks to other students. He did a lot of generous things like that, but then he'd turn around and do something cruel and hateful. I always wondered if he was in control of his own brain, if he might've had brain damage. He sure acted like it."

When Keith noticed that Selah High girls seemed impressed by athletes, he went out for the football team. He looked like a natural—two inches over six feet, two hundred pounds, well muscled. On the Vikings' first day of practice, he ran into trouble. "Coach wanted to play me at tackle and guard, the dumb positions. In the scrimmage, he told me, 'Kill 'em, Keith.' I said, 'Coach, I'm not gonna go out there and try to kill somebody.' He said, 'Well, give me one-hundred percent effort. Hit 'em with everything you got.' I said, 'As big as I am, coach, I'd hurt my own teammates.' He said, 'Son, if you don't do what I say, you won't play.'"

Keith rode the bench for several games before he was sent into a game. "Coach told me to take out the other team's running back. He says, 'If you hit him hard, I'll put you on the squad.' I ran right through a blocker and near broke one guy's leg. Then I rammed my helmet in the quarterback's chest and broke two of his ribs. I was thrown out of the game.

"Coach said, 'Great job, Keith.' I thought, *I nearly killed the guy, I got thrown out, and . . . that's a great job?* I told coach I didn't want to play if he only intended to use me to hurt somebody.

"The next game I sat on the bench. I stayed on the squad for a few more games, but my heart wasn't in it. I never could understand the concept of a bunch of guys working together. It didn't come natural to me, I was a loner. The coach had a way of degrading me. He'd walk into the locker room and holler, 'Hi, men,' and then say, 'Hello, Keith.' When he got mad, he referred to us as women or girls. I guess he thought that was a motivator.

"I dared him to call me 'girl' to my face, and he turned away. After that I knew he wouldn't play me, so I quit to concentrate on wrestling and made the 'B' squad. Dad never came to our meets. Mom came once in a while. They both watched my brothers play sports, but they seemed bored with anything I did."

Friendships didn't last long. A fellow student recalled, "Nobody could take all that bellyaching. He was a nice guy in some ways, but it was like he had a permanent toothache. Most of the kids couldn't be bothered."

7 | Alcohol and Marshmallows

At rare intervals in his dreary childhood reminiscences, Keith would admit to occasional moments of joy. "Yeah, we had some fun when I was growing up. It wasn't all work. Dad allowed us to have horses, and I was in 4-H and the Selah Red Hot Riders. I entered shows at the Yakima County Fair and won some ribbons, but not as many as my sisters, Jill and Sharon. We hunted deer on horseback, but I didn't like that style. It seemed too lazy. I preferred stalking my prey on foot with a bow and arrow.

"On summer weekends Dad would take us camping up the Little Naches River. During the day we'd trail-ride up the mountains on horseback, and at night we'd sing songs around the campfire and roast marshmallows while Dad got drunk with his cronies. Sometimes he'd take us to Goose Prairie in his trailer, and I would fish in the American River."

Keith had long been the family's champion angler. "When it came to fishing," his father admitted later, "he outshone us all. He had the patience and always came home with fish. We had many a delicious meal of salmon or trout, thanks to Keith. Catching fish was one thing he did well."

• • •

The oversized boy was proud of his role as the family's star fisherman, and he boasted about it in later reminiscences. But his tales of happy times always seemed to short-circuit back to his limitless repertoire of misery—slights, insults, injustices, cruelties, misunderstandings, inequities, obligations unmet, favors unreturned, debts unpaid, requests spurned. "Rimrock Lake was one of our favorite spots to go water-skiing. I nearly drowned when I was with Bruce and Sharon. They threw the towline to me and a loop went around my neck. Before I had a chance to get loose, Bruce hit the throttle and dragged me a hundred yards before Sharon got him to stop the boat.

"On another trip Bruce brought along a 'horse' for me to ski on—I guess he thought it would make me ski better. The horse is a chair with skis attached. I fell off when they whipped a sharp turn. They offered to tow me again, but I said no thanks and swam back to shore with the horse. It was like swimming in a wheelchair."

He seemed to reserve his storytelling zest for tales of friction, disturbance and loss. "On one of our hunting trips, Brad was riding my quarter horse Dawn when she reared up, came down on a sharp rock and cut her front tendon. Dad went out to investigate, and when he came back, he was carrying her tack—he'd put her out of her misery. I blamed Brad and we got into a fight. He threw a shovel at me and I had to have stitches in my fingers. Then Bruce beat up Brad for hurting me. I never took any revenge. I just kept it inside. No one paid me for my horse.

"My little sister, Jill, loved horses and she'd ride every day if she got the chance. One winter day she rode Flicka out on an ice patch and the horse rolled on her and broke all the toes on one foot. Mother found me in the clip plant and told me to pick her up in the field. I used a wheelbarrow to haul her to Mom's car. I really felt good about helping out like that. Made me feel like part of the family. But it didn't happen often."

8 | Party-goers

At work and play Keith was constantly exposed to alcohol. He enjoyed the buzz but didn't like the loss of control. "I was brought up in a drinking and partying family. In Canada my father and mother belonged to the 24 Hat Club—twelve couples that met to have a good time and drink. Dad did most of the drinking, but my mom just went along. In Selah Dad had an open-bottle policy. We kids could drink all we wanted as long as it was in our house. Dad felt that the best way to keep us balanced about alcohol was to take the mystery out of it, and in my case he was right.

"He kept a supply of Seagram's rye and other hard liquor in his wet bar and a fridge full of beer on the back porch. He'd buy us beer when he drove to Canada or Idaho to stock up on Coors. I rode around with him a lot and learned how to mix his rye and Coke on bumpy roads. When Bruce was a senior, we had keggers at the house. Everybody in Selah was aware of the Jesperson beer parties. I had too much to drink one night and felt a girl's tits. She turned out to be Bruce's date. He kicked and punched me, and I deserved it."

As relaxed as the Jesperson family was about drinking, Les was apoplectic about drugs. "Dad drove that message home every chance he got. If he found out that one of the kids in school was smoking pot, he'd make us dump 'em. If he saw us together on the street, he'd say, 'Find some new friends. I don't want to see you with that son of a bitch.' Later on, when I began to kill, he decided that I must have been on drugs. That enabled him to rationalize what I did and take the stain off the Jesperson name. But drugs had nothing to do with my killing, and neither did alcohol.

"In high school I just about quit drinking so I could be the Good Samaritan to drive kids home from keggers. I saw some terrible sights—guys pissing themselves, vomiting out the window of my car. One boy passed out and a car backed over him and broke his collarbone. I never missed drinking at all. It brought out the wild man in me. I was actually afraid to get drunk because I would develop an I-don't-care attitude and lose control. I liked the feeling of being the only sober person in the house."

When Keith reached sixteen, in the last semester of his sophomore year at Selah High School, he passed his driver's test and joined in Yakima Valley's preoccupation with the internal-combustion engine. He spent four hundred dollars of his hard-earned money on a 1961 Super 88 Oldsmobile sedan, a red-and-white 398 V-8 that no one else wanted because it spewed blue smoke, yawed on its shock absorbers, and barely made one hundred miles on a tank of gas. "Dad said he would buy the first and last tank for me and I guess he did. I near went broke keeping it full after that. I had to siphon gas from tractors and neighbors' cars. One night the neighbors fired a shot in the air to scare me away. They knew it was a Jesperson stealing their gas because I left the can there and it had Canadian addresses on it." Keith kept the car for a year before the engine seized up and he finished the destruction by trying to make repairs.

● ● ●

His next car was a 1947 Willys Jeep CJ2-A that had belonged to a member of the Yakima Valley Mountaineer Jeep Club, hard drivers who spent weekends lurching up and down the surrounding sand hills. Years later he remembered every detail: "My Jeep had an F-head four-cylinder with three-speed stick. I had to get the seat pushed back four inches and the roll bar heightened by four inches. It was primer gray color till I repainted it sun yellow with black-diamond-plate running boards and corner panels. I drove it two years and sold it for what I paid for it: seven hundred dollars. Then I bought a 1967 Ford Fairlane with a 289 V-8, but that was too tame, so I got a used 750cc motorcycle. I rode that bike to Idaho to watch Evel Knievel jump the Snake River with his rockets. I got so excited I damn near made the jump alongside him. Later on I wished I had."

9 | An Infinite Number of Animals

Now that he had transportation of his own, Keith was able to vent some of his darker impulses in private. He would drive a few miles to the Wenas Valley and plink animals with his twenty-two. "I'd pretty much got rid of the stray cats in our neighborhood, but out in the sagebrush there were still plenty of targets—rats, rabbits, deer, coyotes, the odd dog or cat. I shot everything that moved. I liked watching their guts trail behind as they tried to run away. I perfected my shooting eye by knocking out a leg first, then the next leg. Or I'd shoot 'em in the balls or up the ass. A rabbit will scream and so will a deer. The will to survive is great even in the little sage rats. There was an infinity of dumb animals out there. I would sit behind a rock and look down my telescopic sight, and sometimes it would take three or four rounds to finish one off.

"Playing sniper was fun. My dad was a hunter and I knew he would approve. Higher in the mountains I found new targets—rattlesnakes and squirrels and chipmunks, rockchucks, porcupines. I killed sixty-eight snakes one day while out fishing in a little creek between Ellensburg and Selah. The next week I killed twelve. I didn't feel guilty. It was the all-American pastime to go out in the country and blast away. I shot a cow, watched it fall and listened to it bawl for help. I exploded gopher mounds with long, accurate shots and pretended I was firing mortar shells.

"When no one was home, I experimented with dampening the noise of gunfire. Sometimes I'd fire a couple of rounds out our windows and see who jumped. I set up a target and a bullet ricocheted off a piece of steel and caught me in the meat part of the thigh. I could see the end of the slug, and I dug it out with a pocketknife so Dad wouldn't punish me for being careless with weapons.

"I experimented with pipe bombs and cannons, machined the shells on Dad's lathe in the basement and filled them with Red Dot smokeless powder that I bought by the pound. I would drive six or eight miles into the country for firing tests. One of my projectiles carried to a house. The owner chased me down, confiscated my cannon and told me if he ever saw me around again, he'd call the sheriff. Luckily he didn't tell Dad."

The boy's passion for high-speed driving soon brought him to the edge of a manslaughter charge. "On one of our trips back to Chilliwack, I took Brad and Jill and two other kids to a drive-in movie in Dad's 1969 Chevrolet three-quarter-ton pickup. They sat in the truck bed to keep away from me. I paid for the movie because they said Dad forgot to leave them any money. They had to have pop and popcorn, and I had to buy that, too. I thought they'd pay me back later. I was so furious, I could barely see the screen.

"When the show ended, the brats insisted that I take them to the A&W drive-in, where they ran up a big bill with food and shakes. Paying for their food was the last straw, and I decided to get even. With the five of them in the back of the pickup, I drove all over the road, jerked the wheel, floored the gas and hit the brakes till I could hear them rattling around and yelling.

"Just before the Keith Wilson crossroad there were some elevated railroad tracks. With Iron Butterfly at full volume on the radio, I crossed the track at top speed. The pickup flew through the air and landed hard. There was dead silence in the back. They were all scared shitless. A few minutes later I pulled into the lodge parking lot and got out.

"The truck bed was empty. My heart began to pound. In my mind I saw four bodies laying by the road. I was a mass murderer! I wanted to shake the brats up, but I never dreamed they'd go airborne.

"I drove to the track to search for bodies. Everything was quiet. No blood, no patrol cars, no ambulances, nothing. I got back to the lodge just as Dad and Mom and their friends pulled in. They'd been drinking and wanted to know where their kids were. I couldn't say I'd lost them. I couldn't say I flipped them into outer space. I didn't know *what* to say. Then two police cruisers pulled into the parking area with the kids in back, yelling and crying, and the cops explained what they'd just been told about the mad driver, Keith Jesperson.

"Turned out that the kids had jumped out of the pickup at a stop sign two blocks before the railroad crossing. They were already terrified about my driving. The cops had picked them up for curfew violation.

"Dad sobered up fast. The cops wanted to book me for reckless driving and endangerment, but Dad told them that he was a former Chilliwack council member and he could handle the problem himself. That was me: the Problem. *His son*. The cops read me the riot act and left.

"I tried to explain, but whatever I said, Dad called me a liar. He clenched his fists and said he intended to teach me a lesson right there in the parking lot. I was two inches taller, but I could never swing on him, so I kept backing up till I came to a steel pole under an awning. He took a wild swing and *ping!* He hit the pole. He cussed, and I ran for the cedar groves and hid behind a log.[5]

"I woke up around 9:00 A.M., snuck down to the lot next to the lodge and waited for everyone to go out boating for the day. Then I grabbed my bag and stuffed it with my

---

[5]Les Jesperson said he had no memory of the incident. "I certainly never swung at any of my sons."

clothes. I was sixteen and it was time to leave for good, but I didn't have the guts. Just then I saw Mom and learned that the kids had had plenty of money the night before. They just wanted to pull my chain. Nothing was said about it again. That was the last time Dad ever tried to hit me."

10 | Death of Duke

By Keith's junior year at Selah High, Duke's life was nearing its end. When the boy came home from school, the listless brown Lab would be at the front door. At night Duke would shuffle to the bedside and wait to be lifted by his arthritic front legs so that he could crawl under the covers with Keith. When the boy watched TV, he pulled his pet up on the couch. At table Duke had always begged scraps, and he'd become too big for his favorite ottoman. On camping trips the two old friends shared Keith's sleeping bag.

Father and son seldom took the old dog hunting. "Duke wasn't a trained hunter, so he had no idea what to do. Dad would get annoyed. One day I took Duke back to the truck, and Dad chewed me out for giving up on the hunt. I said I didn't like the way he treated my dog. He just said that Duke was stupid. Later he apologized and said it was the alcohol talking. He used that excuse for years."

A few weeks later Keith came home from school to learn from a hired hand that Duke was dead. Years later he recalled his father's explanation: "He must've got in some coyote poison, Keith. He was dragging ass—didn't look good. I had to shoot him."

The news sent the boy reeling. "I went nuts. Duke was a member of the family. To me killing him was murder."

• • •

He tried to get even by mistreating his father's part-poodle. He was happy when she began to fail. "Gypsy developed tumors. Dad gave me seventy-five dollars to have the vet put her to sleep. I drove out to High Valley Ranch, dug a hole and shot her in the head with my twenty-two."

When his father brought home other dogs, Keith tormented them. "If they tried to get into my lap, I'd slap them off. Or I'd flick my finger hard on their nose. They knew I hated their guts, and they'd cock their heads and look at me funny. One of our dogs pissed the floor whenever she saw me. If I spoke to her, she'd run off and disappear for hours. Dad accused me of beating his pets, but he was wrong. They just knew I wouldn't tolerate them.

"Coming back from a camping trip I stared so hard at Dad's German shorthair Pepsi that she jumped out of our pickup at thirty miles an hour. One day I yelled at her and she ran in front of a passing car. Dad asked me to bury her, but she was his dog. I let him take care of it."

Still in his junior year, Keith began to feel intense sexual urges, but his only relief was masturbation. He had grown into a handsome boy, with chiseled features, deep brown eyes and a Byronic swatch of hair that bisected his forehead at a forty-five-degree angle. But he still slouched as he walked, and his muscles and coordination didn't seem to match his looks. A favorite teacher described him as "a big man whose feet never fit under the desk."

He remained baffled by girls. "I didn't know how to talk to them or ask them out. I knew what couples did in cars, but I couldn't bring myself to do it. The few girls I approached always ended up using me. 'Keith, will you drive me to Yakima?' 'Keith, could you lend me five bucks?' Some of the guys said I was pussy-whipped. I didn't know what that meant. In the boys' locker rooms I never learned anything about girls because I was out of the loop. My parents didn't tell me about the birds and bees. My brothers didn't clue me in, because we barely spoke. Being alone with a girl was a big fear for me. How would I unhook her bra? How would I even get started? *What would I say?*

"I thought about making out with girls all the time. I never really fell in love—I just imagined I was in love out of my physical needs. When I saw a hot-looking girl I wanted to jump her bones. I had the finesse of a barnyard bull.

"A friend hooked me up with a girl that asked if she could be my sex kitten. He left us in the backseat of the car and said he'd be back in an hour. It took me that long to get up the nerve to kiss her. When she steered my hand to her crotch, I'm like, *What?* My friend came back and I thought, *What am I doing here? What's going on?*

"Somebody told me that you had to be going steady to make out with a girl. So I asked one of my classmates to be my girlfriend, and she says, 'We haven't gone out yet!' I said, 'Oh, I didn't know you had to go out first.' Pretty soon every kid in the school was repeating that line. I would pass them in the hall, and they'd look away and giggle.

"At a high school dance I liked another girl and she liked me, but I didn't know how to follow through and she faded out of my life. At a party I told a girl, 'I wouldn't mind marrying you someday.' She said, 'Well, we just met an hour ago.' I said, 'I just meant someday.' She blabbed to everyone that I was a creep. I was so backward, I guess she was right.

"I decided I might have a chance with the younger set. I approached a petite girl about five feet tall and ninety pounds, and she looked like she was gonna faint. Later she told one of my friends that I put her in fear of her life. She said that if a giant like me ever wanted sex, she wouldn't be able to fend me off. I thought, *Where does she get off with that assumption? What am I supposed to do? Shrink?*

"I decided I would never have sex with her or any other girl unless she wanted it. But her words made me dream of rape and kidnapping. In the middle of my fantasy, just when I was overpowering this tiny girl, I would lose the thread. What happens after the rape? Would it make her fall for me? At that stage of my life, I was just confused. Murder wasn't part of my dream. Sex, yes. Control, yes. But I couldn't imagine killing a living person. And I kept my fantasies in my head, where they belonged."

In later years Keith realized that his work schedule had been one of the inhibiting factors in his social life. He worked as a laborer, punch-press operator and welder in his father's clip factory, and he took outside jobs for extra spending money. He pumped gas, made apple bins for a fruit company at $2.35 an hour, cut wood, operated a back-hoe, dug ditches, ran errands and even ran heavy equipment. From his earliest years Les Jesperson had taught him by words and example that work was the essence of life.

By his senior year Keith had all but given up on dating. Women remained as mysterious and unapproachable as they'd been in middle school. His sex life was confined to his bed or bathroom.

Then he met a junior named Clarice (pseudonym). "She was a living doll. Pretty face, dark brown hair, cute round glasses, great personality. I met her when I was dragging the Av on a Friday night, when us kids showed off our cars. We went to the drag races at Renegade Raceway and had a great time. I was a little too dumb about sex and she held me off, but I figured she'd be worth the wait. We went out six or seven times, double-dated with my friend Billy Smith, went to movies, had a lot of fun without sex. I missed her when we weren't together. I thought, *If this is love, it doesn't feel too bad.*"

At last Keith Jesperson had a steady girlfriend.

11 | Our Ape Man

As a senior Keith doggedly stuck to wrestling, alternating between the varsity and the Selah Vikings "B" team. He made up in strength what he lacked in finesse, won a few matches, and earned his letter. Teammates proudly wore the big "S" on their hundred-dollar blue-and-gold lettermen's jackets, but he saved his money. His girlfriend knew he was a letterman, and he didn't care what the other kids thought.

At practice the coach lined up the team for the rope climb. Keith had never made it to the top and was tired of being teased about it. This time he hauled his two hundred pounds all the way. At the top the rope pulled loose from the bracket and he fell twenty-five feet to the hardwood floor.

His feet hit first and he slammed hard on his side and head. Witnesses said he bounced three feet. "I was out for a few seconds. I cried in pain and the coach told me to stop acting like a baby. Some of the other kids thought it was funny. I could hold back the crying but not the pain. After Coach told me to get up and quit faking, somebody helped me to my feet and I found I could hop on one leg.

"I wriggled out of my wrestling gear, showered and dressed. All this time I was in terrible pain on my left side, and I felt dizzy. I heard one of my teammates say, 'He didn't even make it to the top!' I was too groggy to argue.

"Coach called my mom, and she rushed me to the emergency room in Yakima Memorial Hospital. My big sister, Sharon, was working there as a nurse at the time. They X-rayed and diagnosed severe sprain. They told me I would be wrestling again in two weeks."

A few days after the injury, Keith tried to pull on his Red Wing hightop logging boots and found that his left foot was too swollen. The pain kept him off his feet for a week, and he wondered why the love of his life had stopped returning his phone calls. He slashed the side of his shoe to fit his swollen foot and drove to Clarice's house. "I limped up to the door and her mother met me. She said, 'She don't wanna see you no more.' I said, 'Why?' As she was shutting the door, she said, 'She just don't.' Clarice didn't even tell me herself. *She didn't even tell me herself.*"

Back home he thought about the breakup and blamed himself. "Clarice enjoyed my company and my car, but the gimpy foot was a little too much. Who would want to be seen with the school freak? I limped for months. Brad and the other kids had called me Igor since middle school. Now I was *really* Igor."

He returned to the wrestling team and tried to work out. At meets, competitors went for his foot. Doctors promised that the swelling would subside. He widened the cut in his left boot and returned to class, but his sagebrush killing sprees, motorcycle and bicycle hill-climbs and trout-fishing expeditions had to be put on hold. He had a few impromptu dates, swore off girls again for the rest of the school year, and worked in the family's punch-press room with his brother Brad.

At the wrestling banquet he was introduced as "Tarzan, our apeman." Everybody else laughed.

12 | Locked Out

Some of his teachers considered Keith brighter than his mediocre academic record and were baffled by his poor showing despite near-perfect attendance. In six years in the Selah school system, he'd won a succession of Cs and Ds, a few Fs, hardly any Bs, and no As. "In my senior year my English teacher accused me of slacking. Well, he was right. I skimmed textbooks. I borrowed homework and cheated on tests just to get Ds. I hated books, especially novels. Poetry was a joke. Walt Whitman? Who gives a shit? Robert Frost? Boring. My English teacher got so mad at me, he locked me out of his class. I heard him telling the kids that I didn't measure up to the other Jespersons. He said that I was just coasting through and that he intended to flunk me. I ran to the principal's office and demanded to know what was going on. He banged on the classroom door and got me back in. The teacher still gave me an F."

At graduation Keith ranked 161 in a class of 174. His GPA was 1.72, his I.Q. 102. With his poor showing and his bad foot, the RCMP seemed like a lost dream.

In the dim light of memory, the Jesperson family had conflicting memories of the middle son's plans after high school. Les recalled that Keith wasn't college material, and no one had known it better than Keith. "The subject never came up. The whole idea would have been ridiculous. Keith barely made it through high school."

In younger daughter Jill's memory "Keith never mentioned college. I think he always wanted to be dad's helper. It was his choice." Other family members weren't so sure.

Keith's version featured his father in his accustomed role of villain. "My sisters knew I resented Dad and asked why I didn't leave home for good. I considered the military, but Dad said I'd end up in Vietnam. I said, 'Dad, I want to go. I'll learn.' He kept saying, *'You can't do it. . . .'* When you hear that often enough, you believe it yourself.

"I applied to Western Washington College for a wrestling scholarship so I could study to become a game warden. They said they would accept me but not on scholarship. When I asked Dad if he would pay my tuition, he said, 'Game warden? There's no money in that, Keith.'

"At the time Bruce was majoring in mechanical engineering and Brad was taking precollege courses. They both went to the University of Washington. Sharon took her nursing degree at Yakima Valley Community College. Jill studied electronics at Edmonds Community College near Seattle. Dad said he might send me to college later. Then he forgot about it.

"In those days he was still drinking heavily. By ten every morning he'd start on the rye and Coke. By suppertime he'd be looped. He kept a bottle in his pickup and another in our car. If anybody complained, he always said, 'I can quit any time I want to.' He kept on drinking till it nearly killed him. Maybe that's why he forgot all about sending me to college."

Keith moved into an apartment in town with a classmate and got a job pumping gas. When his foot pain persisted, his mother took him to a specialist. "I was diagnosed with torn ligaments in the arch and given a cortisone shot directly into my foot. When I left the doctor's office, I fainted in the middle of the street. I had to go back inside and wait till my head cleared.

"I had to wear an arch support, and in the fall I had the first of three operations on my foot. The surgeon fused the joints of my arch with pieces of bone from my hip. After the first procedure I was on crutches for three months. Dad gave me a light job in the basement, working with wood tools. Then he got the idea of suing the Selah school board, and that occupied a lot of our time, running back and forth to the lawyer and the courts.

"Dad had started a construction business with a John Deere 310 backhoe and a beat-up old twelve-yard dump truck, and he got the idea of turning some of our acreage into a trailer park and building some small units for rent. After I was off crutches, I took over the truck. It was a re-conditioned Wittenburg that the Canadian Army had worked to death—rusty red finish, dual drive axles, and front-wheel drive as well. The gearbox was a five-speed with a two-speed splitter, sort of a manual super ten-speed with all-wheel drive. When I drove it down Wenas Road, everybody stared. I felt like I was driving a racing Corvette.

"I had a lot to learn, like keeping the weight to 12,500 pounds on the steering axle and 34,000 on the drivers, to avoid overweight tickets. On my way to a job on Sixteenth Avenue, a state patrolman instructed me to drive my truck to the Bekins Moving and Storage Building so he could weigh it. He drove on ahead to set up the scales.

"I watched him make a U-turn to head back to First Street. I drove quick to my delivery site and laid down a spread of rock and brought the empty truck to the Bekins Building. He asked me where my load was and I told him I'd laid it down at the job site. I said, 'I'm sorry, Officer, but you said you wanted to weigh my truck. If you wanted to weigh the load, you should've told me.' He had to let me go. That was the kind of trick you couldn't be taught.

"Pretty soon that truck became my passion. I'd have

driven it all day for nothing. But Dad found other work for me."

His father taught him how to use a backhoe to dig up compressed rock, sandstone, and loam to provide foundations for the new trailer court. At first Les kept a careful watch, but after a while he left Keith on his own. "That made me feel good. I always prided myself on being a quick learner. Dad decided on a Western theme and said we would name the place Silver Spur Mobile Home Park. He said, 'We're gonna have a hundred units. Eventually I'll retire and you'll take over.'

"It made me proud that he had so much confidence in me. Maybe it wasn't so bad to miss college. I'd always enjoyed working with my dad. It didn't occur to me till later that nobody else could've done that job the way I did it. I was carefully trained."

One weekend Les asked to borrow Keith's Honda 750 motorcycle. "I'd promised Mom not to let Dad drive it because she was afraid he'd kill himself. Right in front of Mom, he said, 'What's the matter, Keith? Don't you trust your old man with your bike?' I said, 'Okay, Dad, but promise me you won't drink and drive.' "

When Keith returned from a weekend hunting trip, his mother said, "I told you not to leave that damn motorcycle here!" Les was in critical condition with internal injuries. He'd lost control on a curve and wiped out in a ditch.

In the odd push-pull of their relationship, Keith couldn't imagine a world without his father's presence, and he sped to the hospital in a panic. "Dad was bandaged and hooked up to tubes. He could barely talk. He whispered, 'Keith, I'm worried about the bike.' I said, 'Hey, Dad, worry about yourself. Bikes can be fixed.' He says, 'That isn't what I'm worried about. Go back and get rid of the bottle before the insurance company gets there.'

"I drove to the farmer's barn where the wrecked bike had been taken and found a bottle of Seagram's rye with an inch left in the bottle and a six-pack of Pepsi with one bottle half-empty. I took a whiff and it was rye and Pepsi—I knew *that* combination. I removed the fairing and swished gasoline around the side boxes to cover the smell.

"Twenty minutes later the cops arrived, inspected the bike and released it to me. The farmer helped me put it in our pickup with his front-end loader. I went back to see Dad and asked him why he'd broken his promise. He said, 'I wasn't drinking, Keith! And don't bring this up again! I was run off the road by a hit-and-run driver in a green sixty-eight Thunderbird. I was *not* drinking!'

"I knew it was bullshit, but I let him talk. He said he wouldn't be able to work for a while and I'd have to run our operation. He promised to make it up to me. When I got home Mom said she really needed me around the house, so I moved back in. When Dad came home with a patch on his eye, he made me sell my bike. Said he couldn't stand the sight of it. My equity went into the family bills.

"Nowadays he tells people I didn't have the balls to make it on my own and came running back to Mom and Dad. Not true—they begged me to come back. He had to wear the eye patch for a long time, and his doctor told him if he didn't stop drinking, he would be dead in a year. He said he quit for Mom and us kids, but he really did it to stay alive.

"With Dad out of action I worked seven days a week, dawn to dark and sometimes later. That was my life for almost a year. It gave me a funny feeling, as though I wasn't really somebody—just one of my father's tools, an accessory. Dad couldn't operate any of our equipment because of his eyes.

"When more surgery was scheduled for my foot, we had to sell the backhoe business. Dad said he wasn't worried. He said the Silver Spur Mobile Home Park would eventually make us rich."

13 | A Kiss for the Maid

By the fall of 1974 Keith had just about given up on women and made a bet with his friend Billy Smith that neither would marry before age thirty. He resigned himself to his lack of charm and finesse and confined his romantic activities to a little lighthearted flirting. At nineteen, he considered a long-term relationship to be out of the question.

A careless mistake by a short-order cook changed his outlook in less than a week. At the Lariat Barbecue in North Yakima, he met Rose Pernick, a seventeen-year-old high school senior, dark haired, pretty, ninety-nine pounds of personality and charm. She'd been raised in the steel town of East Chicago, Indiana, and retained her Midwestern accent.

The meeting was an accident. "I went to the Lariat about midnight and ordered the large Lariatburger and a chocolate shake. I flirted with Pam, a waitress who would never let me take her out, and then I headed home to Selah. When I bit into the burger I noticed they'd forgotten the meat, so I drove back, but Pam was gone. I asked Pam's best friend Rose, 'Hey, could I have a little beef on my burger?'

"She laughed and we talked a while and she seemed interested. I asked her out to a Bighorn concert at the Capitol Theater. At first she said no, but after I came back and asked her a couple more times, she accepted. I couldn't believe I was going on a real date and it was my own idea.

"Dad lent me his Blazer for the date, and I almost got killed crossing Twin Bridges when a car nearly sideswiped me twice and I ended up in a 360. It gave me a gut feeling that this date might be a mistake. I parked off First Street for about twenty minutes while I tried to decide whether to go through with it, but I went ahead and picked her up because I'd already bought the tickets. I kissed her at the concert and again when I dropped her off.

"I wasn't allowed to come inside her house for our first five or six dates. Her mother didn't trust me at all. Mom told me to put off marriage as long as I could, but Dad kept saying that I needed to settle down with a wife. I think he figured that if I married a local girl, I'd be available to work with him.

"Everybody in the family said I was lucky to be engaged. Why couldn't they tell me the truth? That I was too young, too immature. Why hurry? Why didn't they tell me to check out other women first? Nobody gave me any advice. I just blundered ahead like I always did. But something kept telling me I was making a mistake.

"Two weeks before the wedding, I said, 'Dad, I can't marry Rose. I don't really love her.' He says, 'I've already invited the relatives. Don't disgrace your family, Son.'

"Rose wanted out of her house in the worst way. I was her ticket to freedom from her mother and three brothers. She said we'd be married on her eighteenth birthday. I still didn't know how to say no. It almost didn't happen. At the rehearsal at Denny's restaurant, I was thinking how much I would like to run off with the maid of honor, Rose's friend Pam, and I gave her a friendly kiss.

"Rose said, 'Why'd you do that?' I said, 'She kisses better than you.' I felt penned in and wanted to get out of there. But it was too late—I was smothered by Rose and my relatives.

"I got pissed off at the rehearsal. Dad had talked me into buying a travel trailer and putting it in our Silver Spur Mobile Park, right behind his house. I thought that Rose and I should sneak over there for a few hours, but her mother took her home. I didn't expect a bachelor party, and I didn't get one. That was okay. What was there to celebrate?"

14 | Steady Sex

Rose Pernick and Keith Jesperson were married on August 2, 1975, at the Catholic church in the little hops-growing community of Moxee, just southeast of Yakima. Keith was twenty, and Rose was eighteen. When he stood up straight, the groom towered a foot over his bride. Keith's brother Bruce, a handsome six-footer, was best man.

Keith paid for the reception, but Rose was put off by the drinking and insisted that they leave early. Keith didn't mind. "For our honeymoon we stayed in the Starlite Motel on the Trans-Canada Highway near Chilliwack. It rained, and one of the bed legs was broken, and the faucet dripped. We argued all night. Rose was learning that getting away from mother wasn't so great after all. I was still thinking about Pam.

"It was nice to have steady sex, but I knew the thrill would wear off. I also knew I needed more than what Rose offered, but I wasn't exactly sure what. I wasn't experienced about pleasing women. That first night I pulled out to avoid getting her pregnant. She appreciated that. A baby was the last thing we needed."

Keith took a job with a Yakima lumber company, operating a 780 Case backhoe and hauling prefab housing sections in a GMC Low Boy truck, but after another operation on his foot he went back to work for his father. "I still needed to get away from him. It just seemed that no matter what I did in life, he would persuade me to come back. If it wasn't him, then it was Mother telling me that I was needed around the house. I was twenty-one when Rose and I traded in our travel trailer and bought a 1976 Bendix mobile home. Our address was Space 56, Silver Spur Mobile Park. That turned out to be a little too close to home."

With his brothers in college, Keith and his father worked closely together, occasionally in harmony. He learned to hold his own with the ultimate authority figure. "I was driving down a dirt road with chuckholes, and Dad said, 'Hey, you missed one!' I backed up and drove over it again, only faster. I said, 'That'll teach ya to keep your mouth shut, won't it?' Dad didn't say a word. After that I made sure I hit every goddamn hole on the road."

A developing competition between the middle son and the alpha-male became a problem. "As backhoe operators we learned together. Several times he dug himself into a corner with no escape. He finally got it through his head that he might be our family's engineering genius but I was a better equipment operator. After that, he let me do more work on my own. But he was like my shadow. When I finally moved on to other businesses, he followed to stick his nose into every company I worked for. He was a pain in the ass."

The father's memories of their work together were more generous than the son's, as usual. "Keith helped me build a 105-unit mobile court, doing the ditching, water and buildings. He ran the backhoe, the dump truck and everything else. There wasn't an earth-moving machine he couldn't handle expertly. He plumbed, graded and installed sewer systems. He was a quick study. He learned how to weld, use a torch, fabricate metal, install electrical outlets. He learned how to run a crew. When tenants started to move in, he was patient and helpful and became very popular. I couldn't have made it without Keith."

Years later everyday events that Les recalled as minor were described by Keith as trials, ordeals, tests of will. "Dad decided to add on a solarium, with waterfalls and fish ponds and palm trees. I was doing some wiring on an aluminum ladder when he turns on the electricity. *Boom!* It knocks me on my ass. Dad's laughing. He says, 'Did that hurt?' He says, 'I'm sorry, I forgot you were up there.'

"I always had to watch out for his sick sense of humor. He liked to tell kids to piss on the electric fence to see if it was on. I'd yell, 'Don't tell them that! They're *kids*. They'll believe you.' Once I was too late and I heard a yelp. That was Dad's idea of a joke.

"Another day I came out with a cup of coffee, and he says, 'Keith, stand over there.' He had an X marked in the dirt. I said, 'Why, Dad?' He said, 'Just do it.' I stand on the X, and he walks to the breaker box and turns it on. I jump three feet from the 220 volts. Coffee flew all over. He shuts down the breaker and laughs. I says, 'What'd you do that for?' He said, 'I couldn't get the dog to stand over the conduit.'

"I said, 'You mean I'm dumber than a dog?' 'No,' he said. 'You're not dumber, Keith. You're just more obedient. I needed to find the short.' I took my coffee cup into the kitchen to get away from the prick."

Les had a different take on the incident. "I might've sparked him a few times. I always enjoyed practical jokes, especially the ones played on me. But it wasn't 220 volts. It was 12. Keith always had a tendency to exaggerate."

• • •

Despite the jousting the middle son usually enjoyed working with his father. "When a job was done well, he praised my work. I'd always wanted to be accepted by him. We worked fine together as long as I followed his rules. Dad said, 'You have to be strict with the tenants, Keith, or they'll run right over you!' He referred to himself as 'Nasty Landlord' and used it as his handle over the citizens' band radio."

Sometimes Keith felt burdened by the rules. "Dad said, 'Remember, the boss is always right! Even if he's wrong, he's right—especially in front of customers. If something goes wrong, it's your job to take the blame.' Once he cracked a wall with the backhoe. Later that night he knocked on the tenants' door and said he was sorry about his clumsy son. They laughed about it. They'd been home when he did it."

The Silver Spur workday began at daylight when Keith would pick up windblown trash. "After I took the garbage to the dump, I'd start on my daily list of things to do, like replacing heater elements in hot-water tanks and fixing leaks in the rentals. On warm days I poured concrete for new units and hauled in the sand and dirt. I plowed the snow, built fences, planted trees. Dad always had some little criticism—my work lists were in the wrong order or I'd missed some of the trash or I was spending too much time talking to the tenants. One of the women offered to trade me sex for rent, but I wasn't into that. At night I'd watch the women undressing, and I'd fantasize about them when I was in bed with Rose."

Les wondered later if there might have been more to the story. "Keith was popular, maybe a little too popular. One day when I had to evict a woman, she remarked, 'If you don't watch out, I'm gonna charge your son with statutory rape.' She had a teenage girl. I thought it was a joke, and Keith denied everything. He said, 'When would I have time to bother a little girl? I'm always working.' I took him at his word."

15 | Hating Cats

After six months of working with his father, Keith felt a renewed urge to drive out to the badlands and slaughter animals. Les thought he knew how it started. "We couldn't permit strays. That was in our bylaws. Dogs had to be on a leash. Keith got rid of some stray cats and I didn't stop him. In fact I almost persuaded him to do it. But I never taught him to kill. Never! My way was to drown 'em in a gunnysack. Once I saw him take a kitten and smash it down. Killed instantly! It made me shudder."

For once, the father-and-son memories almost meshed. In Keith's version: "One of our tenants had a problem cat, and I warned her to get rid of it. One day Dad and I went to her place to fix a leak, and the cat was still around. Dad said, 'What do you intend to do about this, Keith? You're too soft!' I threw the cat on the pavement to stun it. Then I wrung its neck like a chicken. I said, 'Is that what you wanted?' I drove a few miles and threw it out the window. That night I told the owner, 'Fluffy ran away. Live with it.' She moved out the next day."

Following his customary practice, Keith blamed his harsh attitude on his father. "Dad said, 'You're gonna control the area, Keith. If an animal becomes a pest, shoot it.' I got real good at hitting dogs on the run. I bought a CO_2 pistol and accidentally shot a neighbor's dog and had to pay the vet to dig out the pellet. After that I took a few strays to the pound, but they found their way back.

"I decided to take no prisoners. I killed the pests with whatever I had at hand—hammer, sickle, scythe, screwdriver, shovel, or my bare hands. I'd take a dog into the sagebrush, give him a good kick, then open fire with my thirty-thirty. I tossed the suckers out the window at fifty miles an hour.

"I baited trash cans with poisoned meat and collected bodies in the mornings before anybody got up. One night I killed seven cats and kittens. I caught a dog in our garbage and used a hook scythe to cut off his head, but the blade only went halfway and he ran into the woods. I threw cats in the incinerator. I set one on fire and it ran for the barn. Flames everywhere! Another cat got into our burn barrel. I put a piece of plywood over the top, poured in gasoline and threw in a match. The cat howled till it was cooked. It made me hot and hard.

"I enjoyed the feeling of power. I liked taking a cat or a dog into my room and poking it with a stick. There was no running away from Keith the Avenger. I knew it was wrong to hurt dumb animals, but I did it anyway. It was just . . . an urge."

Keith's little sister made frequent complaints about his cruelty, but she was ignored. "Dad and Keith both hated cats," Jill recalled. "Keith bragged about wringing their necks and throwing them in the garbage. I was taken aback by this. You don't do that to animals. We never dreamed he would do it to people."

5

KEITH

HUNTER

JESPERSON 3

1 | Ignored Again

After I dumped the pothead Julie Winningham, I came across another article about the two losers who were serving time for Taunja Bennett's murder. Something about it pissed me off. I wondered why nobody noticed the graffiti I'd left on the restroom walls. Did they think I was lying?

I decided I needed to give up a little more information to make people believe me. I sent another Happy Face note to the Washington County Courthouse:

> *I killed Miss Bennett Jan 20, 1990 and left her 1½ miles east of Lateral Falls on the switchback. I used a ½" soft nylon rope burnt on one end—frayed cut on the other—and tied it around her neck. Her face her teeth protruded from her mouth. Death was caused by my right fist pushed into her throat until she quit moving. Threw her Walkman away. Her purse $2.00—I threw into the Sandy River. I cut the buttons off her jeans. I had raped her before and after her death. I left her facing downhill and her jeans down by her ankles. I did not know any of them.*

I checked the papers for a month and didn't see a word. I wondered what I had to do to get noticed. The only thing I could accomplish with another note was my own arrest and conviction, but I was dying of curiosity about what was happening. My gut told me to butt out, but I couldn't help myself.

I thought, *Maybe if I gave the cops enough information, I could get those two people out of prison without me coming forward.* At the time I didn't know what police and prosecutors will do to keep from admitting their mistakes. Innocent people can die of old age in prison if their case has been marked "solved." It's just the way law enforcement works.

In April 1994, four years after I killed Taunja, I composed another note on pale blue paper. At the top of page one, I drew a circle with two smaller circles for eyes and a little arc for a mouth. I sent it to the biggest paper in the Northwest, the *Oregonian:*

> *I would like to tell my story! I am a good person at times. I always wanted to be liked. I have been married and divorced with children—I didn't really want to be married but it happened. I have read your paper and enjoyed it a lot. I always have wanted to be noticed like Paul Harvey, Front Page, etc. So I started something I don't know how to stop. On or around January 20th 1990 I picked up Sonya Bennett and took her home. I raped her and beat her real bad. Her face was all broke up. Then I ended her life by pushing my fist into her throat. This turned me on. I got a high. Then panic set in. Where to put the body? I drove out to the Sandy River and threw her purse and Walkman away and I drove the scenic road past the falls. I went back home and dragged her out to the car. I want to know that it was my crime. So I tied a ½" soft white rope cut on end and burned on the other—around her neck. I drove her to switch-back on the scenic road about 1½ miles east of*

Lateral Falls. Dragged her downhill. Her pants were around her knees because I had cut her buttons off. They found her the next day. I wanted her to be found. I felt real bad and afraid that I would be caught. But a man and a woman got blamed for it. My conscience is getting to me now. She was my first and I thought I would not do it again, but I was wrong.

Once again there was no reaction, so I scribbled more details for the *Oregonian:*

My last victim was a street person. It was raining in Corning, California. She was wet and I offered a ride to Sacramento, California. I stopped at a rest area near Williams and had her. I put her body on or near a pile of rocks about 50 yds. North of highway 152 westbound about 20 miles from Santa Nella.

It was getting hard to trust my inner self. I kept arguing with my conscience. I had to get away from long haul trucking. Victims are too easily found. So I quit and found a good job driving where I am in the public eye and out of harms way. The truck has a bold name on the side so it is easily recognized. I got away from what became easy. I do not want to kill again and I want to protect my family from grief. I would tear it apart.

I feel bad but I will not turn myself in. I am not stupid. I do know what would happen to me if I did. In a lot of opinions I should be killed and I feel I deserve it. My responsibility is mine and God will be my judge when I die. I am telling you this because I will be responsible for these crimes and no one else. It all started when I wondered what it would be like to kill someone. And I found out. What a nightmare it has been. I had sent a letter to Washington county judges criminal court

> *taking responsibility, to #1 [the Bennett murder].*
> *But nothing has been in your paper. This freedom*
> *of press you have the ball. I will be reading to find*
> *out. I used gloves and same paper as last letter*
> *"no prints." Look over your shoulder. I may be*
> *closer than you think.*

I didn't sign any of the letters or reread them for errors, but I made a little Happy Face so the paper would know it was the same guy. I figured if the Portland authorities were too stupid to recognize that somebody else did the Bennett murder, maybe the California cops would get to work on the murder in Corning and confirm that I was legitimate.

2 | Firecracker Bandit

> *"Oh, what ecstasy setting fires brings to my body!*
> *What power I feel at the thought of fire! . . . Oh,*
> *what pleasure, what heavenly pleasure!"*
> —serial killer Joseph Kallinger to his biographer,
> Flora Rheta Schreiber

In the second half of 1994, with five or six murders and a couple of assaults and a screwed-up life behind me, I was getting desperate to understand what was going on in my head, and I began reading magazines and paperbacks about serial killers. Passing through Denton, Texas, I picked up a copy of a true-detective magazine and saw an article called "Does Oregon Have Another Serial Killer?" It was about me.

I wrote the author a letter correcting a few of his points and told him where another body could be found. I kept buying the magazine but never saw any mention of my letter later. Everybody was taking me for a liar.

I went to libraries and looked at books on psychology. Why do we kill and hate ourselves for it and swear we'll change our ways—and then kill again? *And enjoy it?* I found a book by an ex-FBI man that was 90 percent horseshit, but it included something about a trio of symptoms. Apparently you could spot a violent criminal in childhood because they wet their beds, abused animals, and set fires. I thought, *Well, two out of three ain't bad.* Sure, I had a few problems with animals and I set some fires. What kid didn't? But I was toilet-trained at two and never wet my bed after that.

I thought this over and asked myself a serious question: *If I set grass fires in the middle of nowhere, will that relax me? Will it curb my appetite for death?*

I decided to give it a try. I invented a simple fuse—you split a book of matches down the middle and set a lit cigarette between the two halves like a little tepee. That gives you eight or ten minutes before the heads flare up.

It was a thrill watching the firefighters and cops from the distance. My arsons probably saved the lives of a few women I'd have killed otherwise. I set fires in different areas of California, Oregon and Washington, and some in Nevada and Arizona. Only once did a police officer check me out. It happened right after I set a 365-acre brushfire on I-97 north of Satus Pass. The traffic was heavy and I was slow getting back to the interstate after I lit the fuse. By the time I got past the Wacky Base Station that monitors CB traffic, I heard fire trucks. The Unicorn Base Station also called in the firemen.

A cop pulled alongside of me while I was parked at the mini-mart off of Simcoe Road, watching the smoke. He asked me a few questions about the fire and I told him I'd heard about it on my radio. He asked if I smoked. I said no and told him a story about my dad breaking his ribs from coughing too hard over cigarettes. The cop left me alone. Later I heard that someone had reported over the CB that a semi-truck had been parked near where the fire started.

Pretty soon my arsons were giving me a regular adrenaline rush. I guess it was partly from seeing the flames and partly from the excitement of almost getting caught. It became as addictive as killing. I'd start fires in tall dry grass and drive to a point where I could call in the alarms myself. I set most of my fires at night. I started a small fire above

Prosser, Washington, on the incline just above town where Horse Heaven Road starts down the hill. I parked on the shoulder of I-82 west and waited to see how long it took to get put out. Not long enough.

I set three more fires on Satus Pass and then a big one at Biggs Junction in the I-97 canyon. It felt good to drive past later and see the damage. That big scar lasted for months. I set small fires along Highway 14 west of the Dalles, Oregon, on the Washington side and south of the scale houses on I-5 in California, and south of Westley, California, at the I-5 exits. One of my fires burned off 2,000 acres in the Columbia Gorge. I set off 365 acres on top of Snoqualmie Pass in the Cascades. What a rush!

In a restaurant in western Washington I overheard two farmers complaining about the low price of wheat. One said he wished a lightning storm would just burn them out. I followed in my semi as they drove out of town. A week or so later I set fire to their fields and about 2,500 acres burned up. It made me feel good to help them collect insurance money.

From fires I naturally got into firecrackers, and they helped me to solve a problem for us truckers. We were always pissed at the old snowbirds like my dad for taking up too much space at rest stops on their way to Arizona and southern California. Three or four of those old farts would park their recreational vehicles in our spots, sitting there with their butane tanks having a barbecue. Well, that wasn't the purpose of the truckers' rest areas. Some of the snowbirds would trailer a car, unhook it, and park it in the next space, taking two of our truck spaces! I decided to do something about it.

Driving through an Indian reservation in Nevada, I bought grosses of fireworks—black cats, 2½-inch crackers, 1,000 to a package. They'd go off like a machine gun. I'd break off a block of 250, put a little hole in the bottom of the package, stick a lit cigarette inside and slide it under some snowbird's motor home. Then I'd lay another block with a two-minute fuse and head for the restroom. The first round goes off, and the people are thinking, *Oh my God, what's that?* They settle down and the second set goes off and they run like rabbits.

I'd sit in the stall and listen to the noise. Then I'd come out all innocent and unsuspected.

One night in California I followed four RVs in a convoy all the way from Williams to the truck stop south of Bakersfield. They got parked and settled in for the night, and— *bang, bang, bang.* They came running out of their RVs and took off. I'm sure they drove all night to get away from me.

It wasn't long before snowbirds up and down I-5 were talking about the firecracker bandit that chased RVers. What fun! I figured it was Dad's nasty sense of humor coming out in me. But the funny thing was, I was doing it to Dad's kind of people!

I visited him at the Happy Wanderer RV Park in Yuma, Arizona, and he said, "Say, Keith, have you heard about this I-5 firecracker bandit?"

I started to laugh.

He gave me a shit-eating grin and said, "You're the son of a bitch doing it!" He'd guessed just from the way I laughed. And from knowing me since I was a kid.

"Yeah," I said. "I keep a supply of two-inchers in my cab."

Dad said, "Did you know you gave one guy a heart attack? He almost died."

I said, "He shouldn't park in a rest area then."

"You better stop that, Keith." He was still telling me what to do.

I said, "I'll stop it when you RVers stop taking our parking places."

3 | Road Rage

The way I figured, arson kept me from killing for over a year, from March of '93, when I killed Cindy in Corning, till the fall of '94, when I started to get restless again. By that time fire wasn't working for me anymore. I looked around for something else exciting.

I went to work driving a flatbed truck across forty-eight states for Systems Transport, and it wasn't long before I started taking out my boredom on other drivers. In Sacramento this guy in a pickup loaded with windshield glass flips me the bird because I kept him from passing. He gets out ahead and lays in the passing lane, blocking the whole damn freeway. I pull even, shake my fist out the window, and yell, "You son of a bitch! Nobody flips me off."

I nudged him off the road. Last I saw, he was losing his load of glass. I figure I did a public service.

On an icy night near Bellingham, Washington, up near the Canadian border, a woman pulls up behind me to pass, but I'm stuck behind another car in the passing lane. She finally gets around my truck and flips me off. Then she slams on her brakes and almost wrecks us both. I think, *You're gonna teach me a lesson, bitch? You got another think coming.*

I drove up on her bumper to spin her out from behind.

She stepped on the gas, but I caught her. Now she's laying on her horn at seventy-five miles an hour. I says, "You wanna fuck with me, bitch?" I ran her into an exit and she swerved off the roadway. I figured she learned her lesson, if she survived.

I was still fantasizing about raping and killing, but I pretty much confined my real-life sex to a few girlfriends, an occasional rider, and my hand. I limited my hitchhikers to women who looked like they were really going somewhere, had extra clothes, and told me in front where they were headed. Girls without baggage were out. They were almost always predators and I didn't trust myself to hold my temper when they showed their true colors. That's what killed Claudia, Cynthia and Laurie.

Sometimes I would have sex with my riders and sometimes I wouldn't. I tried to treat them fair and square—even carried cigarettes for them even though I hated the smell. I would stop and feed them as well because most hadn't eaten for a while. If they liked rough sex, I'd give it to them, but within reason.

As the months went by, it got harder to suppress the killing impulse. But a few seconds' rush wasn't worth months and months of worrying about being caught, jumping at shadows, never getting a good night's sleep.

One day I just decided to park my truck in Yakima and drive to Spokane to visit my ex-wife and kids. I wanted to give Jason, Melissa and Carrie the trampoline they'd always talked about.

I parked outside their house till they caught sight of me, then went inside to hug and kiss them. The hugs hit home. I missed my kids so much. They didn't know I was a serial killer. To them I was just their father.

I told them I didn't have time to wrap their present. They didn't care. It took me an hour to put the damn thing together, and I dollied it into the yard sideways so they couldn't tell what it was. When they finally saw it, they were on cloud nine. They'd wanted a trampoline ever since they'd played on somebody else's a year earlier.

Rose and I watched them bounce for an hour. My own kids. Except for the worries on my mind, it was one of my best days ever.

Later that night I took everybody to the truck stop on Broadway so they could have a big meal and no dirty dishes to clean up. When we got home, the kids bounced for two more hours. I told Rose how glad I was that she was happily remarried and that everything was going good for her now that we'd been divorced six years. Rose deserved the best.

Driving back to Yakima, I thought about how I was lying to my kids, making them think that everything would be all right when I knew good and well I would end up in prison. I worried about what would happen to them with me locked up. What would they think of the dad they loved? When I came to town it was party time for them, and when I left they went back in the dumps. I was a part-time dad that enjoyed calling them on their birthdays and sending money.

I had to watch my temper whenever I was around them because a lot of the time I was in the killing mode. I couldn't trust myself with my own kids. I was afraid to allow them to get into an argument, afraid of what I might do.

My kids deserved a full-time father. At least Dad and Mom had stayed married. I was gone from my kids almost all the time. It was the worst crime of all.

4 Tarot Cards and Bark

Toward the end of 1994 I was driving a navy blue 359 series Peterbilt with ten speeds and a 325-horsepower Cat engine—strictly a work truck, no chrome, no Vari-shield, nothing fancy. When I had my plum Pete I used to wash it all the time—this old heap was lucky to get a bath once a month. The air conditioner never worked right and I kept agitating to get it fixed, but the company didn't care about little things like that.

I was hauling a load of Tread Brite aluminum coils to Florida and sleeping in the truck at night for the cooler air. On the night before delivery time I was at a 76 Unocal truck stop near Tampa when a cute black girl with light complexion came to my truck wearing a Spandex jumpsuit and short hair. I allowed her to sit with me to wait out the security patrols that were cruising. It was around midnight.

She said, "For twenty dollars I could be yours for awhile." I said okay and she went into the sleeper. She said, "You're not one of those serial killers, are you?"

I thought she said it as a joke. But I looked at her face and saw that she was serious. I tried to laugh, but I was too pissed. I said, "You should never ask stupid questions. Do you want me to tell the truth, or lie? If you had your doubts, you should've stayed the hell out."

She pulled the twenty from my fingertips and smiled and said, "It was kind of a stupid question at that."

After some good sex I delivered to the warehouse a couple of miles away and headed back to the same truck stop to wait for 9:00 A.M. to call my dispatcher for a load out of Florida. Walking into the store, I noticed a tall blonde woman in an ankle-length dress toting a cart with three bags. She had a slight Slavic look like Taunja.

As I walked by, she asked if I was headed north. Looking into her baby blues, I pointed to my truck and said, "If you want to ride with me, put your baggage by the passenger door and wait. I don't know for sure where I'm headed. Ask me in about an hour."

She said okay. I said, "Where do you want to end up?"

"Lake Tahoe, Nevada." She said her name was Susanna, Sue Shannon, Sue Anna, something like that. She was about thirty. She had tarot cards and some moss-covered bark. I thought maybe she was a fortune-teller.

I said, "I can probably put you in Reno or at least get you to Nevada. Most of my loads take me to the Northwest. I'll be calling my boss in a while."

Dispatch didn't have a reload yet and told me to call later. The girl came back and asked if I really wanted to take her with me. I told her it didn't matter one way or the other. "If you don't feel safe with me, then find someone else."

It took two phone calls for me to be ordered to Cairo, Georgia, to pick up tubing for the Northwest. Boise would be my first drop. I told her I was ready to leave and she got in and asked if we could swing down to Miami to pick up some of her stuff. A typical truck-stop dingbat! Miami was a four-hundred-mile round-trip and I told her I had to get loaded tonight in the opposite direction. I guess she thought I was a taxi. You try to be nice to these crazy sluts and pretty soon they're breaking your chops.

"Okay," she said. "It doesn't matter." She said that Boise would be close enough for her—anything to get away from Florida.

•   •   •

About eighty miles north of Tampa, we stopped for fuel and got two shower keys. After we washed up, we sat down to dinner. She ordered all-you-can-eat spaghetti and ate three plates. We reached Cairo at midnight and pulled into the pipe yard north of town. Not needing tarps, it was a good load to haul, just forty-five-thousand pounds of electrical conduit, evenly placed. By 1:00 A.M. we were loaded and strapped down. I doubled back to the Florida panhandle to pick up I-10 so we could grab a little rest and head west by daylight. She said it would be okay with her if we shared the sleeper if we stayed dressed.

At 3:00 A.M. we pulled off I-10 for a sleep break. We passed three cop cars parked at a mini-mart and took the last parking spot, right behind a security officer's pickup. He looked like he was asleep, and I didn't give a damn anyway.

I slid in behind Susanna and closed my eyes. I felt her warm body against mine as I dozed off. The death game was far from my mind.

The air conditioner wasn't working and I woke up in my own sweat to roll down the windows. The temperature was still close to the nineties. I turned the dome light on and noticed a very nicely shaped ass right next to my crotch. I imagined her body under her dress-and-pants outfit, fresh and clean from our showers.

I got hard as I pulled off my pants and shirt and slid my arm around her waist. She stirred and sat up, rubbing her eyes.

When she saw me she screamed—not just a short abrupt scream but a high-pitched terrified scream you could hear all over the lot.

I covered her mouth to shut her up. As she wiggled under my hand, I tried to figure how I would explain this to the police and the security. Who would they believe? What lies would this bitch tell? I already knew the answer. No matter what happened, security would file a report and my company would fire me for taking a rider. I was screwed either way.

She tried to pull away and I pushed my hips against her ass and told her that we were parked where no one would hear her if she screamed again. "Do what you're told and you won't get hurt."

She turned and faced me in the dark. "If you let me go," she said, "I won't say anything."

"I'm sorry," I told her, "you just do as I ask and everything will go easy on you. Now make love to me like we're lovers."

At first she fought, but then she realized she was caught and got into the lovemaking. She really seemed to enjoy herself as I screwed her for the next few hours. She surely knew how to please a man—or was it to just please me so I wouldn't hurt her?

After a while she was quiet and seemed to doze off, but I was worried that she might be playing possum till she figured out how to get away. I knew the cops were somewhere around, but they weren't in sight.

I got hard again and pulled up her skirt, and she let out another scream. When she wouldn't shut up, I freaked and choked her to death.

With her body still quivering I drove to an exit in Okaloosa County and hid her in some brush away from the roadway. After I made sure she was dead, I spread the soiled sleeping bag in a puddle and drove back and forth over it. Five women had died in that bedroll. I thought I might have to prove later that she was my kill and not somebody else's, so I grabbed two fourteen-inch white plastic ties from the truck and cinched them around her neck for ID.

I drove fast so I could get by the next scale house before it opened for the day and documented me in the area. I headed north, caught up on my logbook, and got documented in Georgia. That way it looked like I hadn't been in Florida after I left Cairo. Then I pulled off the road for a nap.

• • •

After I woke up, I drove at top speed straight to Alabama and then across Mississippi and up to Shreveport without stopping so I could fuel at the Unocal 76 Truck Stop and get a receipt that showed I was too far from Florida to be connected to Susanna's body.

I went through her things looking for my usual trophies, but all that was worth stealing was a boom box that I ended up giving away. The rest was garbage. The bitch didn't have an ounce of taste.

5 | Truck Afire

Four months later, on Friday the thirteenth of January 1995, I ran into some bad luck. Not my fault—just one of those things. I was driving a plain old work truck—a dark blue 359 series Pete with a four-hundred-horsepower Cat engine—but at least the air conditioner worked. It had oversized stacks that were ten inches over thirteen feet and gave me some hard times under bridges till I hacked off five inches.

This night I was headed down Highway 76 towards Denver with a flat load of extruded aluminum under tarp. I'd just passed the Sterling exit when I heard a big "Boom!" Slabs of rubber flew through the air in all directions.

I turned off cruise control, pulled onto the shoulder and jumped out. The inside rear driver's side tire was burning like a Roman candle. I got the extinguisher and put it out three times, but it kept relighting like those trick candles at birthday parties. The brake drum glowed orange hot and I knew I was in trouble.

I pulled the pin on the fifth wheel and removed the hoses and connecting lines. Then I went to the landing gear and cranked it down so I could drive the truck out from under the load.

By the time I got into the cab, flames were licking at the underside of the trailer. I released the brakes, moved the truck a hundred feet away, parked it and set out warning triangles. As I waited for the fire department, other truckers stopped to see if they could help. I told them that there was nothing to do but enjoy the fire. After fifteen minutes the firefighters sprayed enough water on the drum to cool it off.

Now all my tires were flat and the wiring and hoses were burnt off. The seals in the wheels were burnt and leaking. I took a close look but couldn't determine the cause of the fire. Was it something I did wrong? I considered myself a great truck driver, at the top of my skills, and I didn't want any "driver error" entries on my record.

A wrecker hauled me and the burnt truck to Sterling. It took me a few days to work my way to our Fontana yard near San Bernardino, where I picked up another old Peterbilt for a load to Spokane.

6 | A Plan for the Night

A week later, on the night of January 20, the company put me up at the Ridpath, a great old hotel in downtown Spokane. I was in the lounge flirting with the barmaid when a woman walked in carrying three bags and a large purse. She was about five-six—long dark hair, pale blue-gray wolfish eyes, good figure, nice face, maybe in her midtwenties. She sat at a table about ten feet away and ordered a beer.

While she drank it slowly, I smelt her perfume and watched her as she looked the place over. She was in no hurry to check in. Motel 6 was more her style, it seemed to me.

When our eyes met I smiled and said, "Mind if I join you?" She nodded a yes and I glanced over at a table of other Systems truck drivers watching me make my move. They looked like they had a bet going to see if I would be shot down. The girl and I talked some small talk and I learned that she had just arrived in town and didn't know anybody. I took it she was broke.

The trap was set and I laid plans for the night. I was learning to be more forward with these barroom cowgirls. What was the worst thing that could happen? They could say no and walk away? So what?

After we got to know each other a little better, I said, "My company has put me up for the night and if you haven't checked in already, why don't you share my room? Maybe we'll behave ourselves and maybe not. That's up to you. I never force myself on anybody. Hell, we could start with some dinner. It's on me."

She blinked at me like she was a little surprised and said, "Best offer I had all night! Who do you drive for anyway? What's your name?"

I told her the truth, and after she finished her beer I helped her pick up her bags. At the elevator door she took my arm like we were engaged.

In the room I turned on the TV and she went into the bathroom while I ordered pizza and a six-pack from room service. While we were eating, she told me that she was a strip dancer and wouldn't mind showing me how good she was. She took one of her bags into the bathroom and came out in a leather miniskirt. That was some tease! She had a tattoo of Tweety Bird on her ankle, giving the world the finger. She sat on my penis and we did it for the rest of the night.

She was asleep when I got up in the morning, so I left her thirty dollars and directions on how to reach me through the company. Then I caught the shuttle for the systems yard.

I had a little talk with the owner about my tire fire. I told him that I'd driven eighty miles at cruising speed when it blew. I'd felt no drag, and the truck was on cruise. He read a report from the mechanics and told me that the automatic slack adjuster had ratcheted up against the brake shoes and stuck. The friction caused the drum to get hot and melt a hole in the tire, and the tread burst into flames when I stopped. So it wasn't driver error. What a relief!

I hauled some freight to Cheyenne and made another delivery at Denver. I called our office from there and was assigned to pick up a load of railroad iron for Seattle—twenty-seven

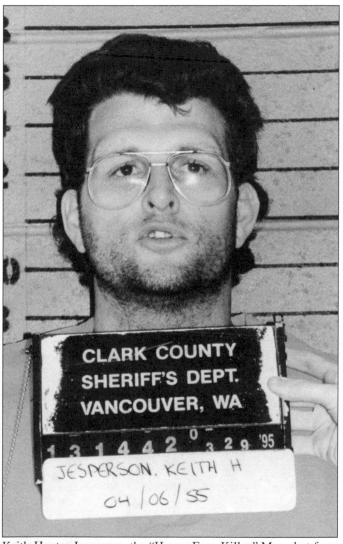

Keith Hunter Jesperson, the "Happy Face Killer." Mug shot from the Clark County, Washington, Sheriff's Department. (*The Oregonian*)

Keith's father, Les, cooking on an open fire. (Courtesy of Les Jesperson)

FAMILY

His mother, Gladys, with Keith's son in 1981. (Courtesy of Les Jesperson)

Keith Hunter Jesperson in 1991. He was already a murderer. (Courtesy of Les Jesperson)

Narcissist.
Jesperson's note reads:
The Right Hand of the Killer
Keith Hunter Jesperson
The Happy Face Killer
Killer of 8 Women
From 1990 to 1995

The meticulous killer: Maps he sketched of his crime scenes. (Courtesy of Les Jesperson)

Jesperson with defense attorney Tom Phelan.
(Dana E. Olsen/*The Oregonian*)

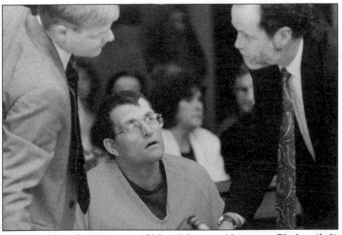

And awaiting the outcome of his trial, seated between Phelan (*left*) and Multnomah County prosecutor Jim McIntyre (*right*). (Michael Lloyd/*The Oregonian*)

While in prison, Jesperson wrote to his father often and attempted to develop his artistic skill. (Courtesy of Les Jesperson)

JESPERSON, THE INMATE

Posing in the prison yard. (Courtesy of Les Jesperson)

And posing with the author. (Courtesy of Jack Olsen)

pieces, forty-four thousand pounds' dead weight. From Seattle I would take a load of cedar boards to Pennsylvania. The dispatcher said a woman named Angela Subrize had left a Spokane phone number.

I called and she asked me if I could figure out a way to help her visit her dad in a little town near Denver. I told her that I was in Denver right now but I was coming back through Spokane on my way to Seattle to drop off a load. She could stay with me in the truck for a day or two, and I'd take her to Denver on my way to Pennsylvania. She gave me directions to where she was staying.

We rendezvoused at her place and she acted thrilled to see me. As I carried her bags to the truck, she clung to my arm in gratitude. Our one night together had been good and I was looking forward to more of the same, but not tonight. I still had to drive 290 miles to Seattle, unload the railroad iron, load the cedar and turn around and head back east.

The cedar was loaded and tarped by 10:00 A.M., and Angela and I drove to North Bend and showered at Ken's Truck Town at Exit 34 on I-90. It was starting to rain when we finished dinner with Lady Rose, a nice lady who ran a CB station that relays weather reports to truckers. She predicted there'd be snow and ice up on Snoqualmie Pass.

That meant no sleep for me. I had to get over the mountains before the state patrol made me put on chains—a bitch of a job. We cleared the pass in light snow and finally reached the Idaho border at 2:00 A.M. Sunday. I caught my first sleep in three days.

Eight A.M. came early as my alarm sounded and Angela stirred in my arms. With her hand she made my penis jump. She aroused me fast and we played till we needed showers again.

It was after ten when we pulled out. The roads were bad and it was slow going. We reached Fort Bridger, Wyoming, at 4:00 A.M. Sunday. At a phone booth I overheard Angela arguing with somebody on my telephone credit card. When she hung up, she said her dad didn't want to see her. Now she wanted to go to Indiana to connect with an old boyfriend.

I listened as she dialed another number and made up with the boyfriend right over the phone. Was she faking all this for my benefit? Why? You never know what these lot lizards and hitchhikers are up to, no matter how much they pretend to like you.

I told her I didn't want her anymore. "Stick with your boyfriend."

Out in the truck she fell into my arms and enticed me with her fresh-smelling body. After an hour of sex she began to act like a boss instead of a piece of ass. "Let's get going," she ordered. "My new husband's waiting in Indianapolis."

"What's the big hurry?" I said. "I have to go through Indiana with this load of cedar. Don't worry. We'll get there."

She started a long story about all the guys that took advantage of her and she thought she was pregnant and didn't know who the father was and blah blah blah. . . .

I said, "How do you know you're pregnant?"

She said, "I missed my last two periods and I been feeling sick in the morning. Now that my boyfriend in Indiana wants me back, we'll make love over and over and then it'll be his baby."

I can be a little slow-witted with women, but I finally saw through her shuck. "So that's it," I said. "I guess if your boyfriend told you to get lost, you'd claim the baby was mine."

"The thought crossed my mind," she said. "But you're a romantic and you'd want to marry me. I never want to be a boring old married lady with a baby."

"Basically you saw me as a free ride and a pocket full of money?"

"Hey, you enjoyed screwing me, and I enjoyed screwing you! I can't deny it, Keith. You really know how to make a woman feel great." She started pulling up her panties and said, "We're off to Indiana!" She acted like I should be all thrilled and excited.

Women! The whole world revolves around what they want. Sure we were good in bed together, but I could say the same about thirty others. Most of them just used sex to get their way. When my wife Rose wasn't in the mood or my old girlfriend Julie Winningham didn't want it, they'd say, "Just hurry up and get it over with." The cruelest words! A woman is the only person that knows whether there will be sex that night. A man can only hope. I thought Angela might be different. *Wrong again, Keith.*

I began to get ideas. I put the truck into gear and headed east on Interstate 80.

7 | Blizzard

As we neared the Nebraska line, Angela was napping in the coffin. I kept thinking about the what-ifs. *What if I get her to Indianapolis and she doesn't want her old boyfriend? What if he doesn't want her? What if she doesn't even have a boyfriend and faked the call?* Was this just one more tactic to stay in my sleeper? Free meals, free showers and all expenses?

I groped in her purse and found pepper mace. I hid it where she wouldn't find it.

The storm had overtaken us during the night and Interstate 80 was getting slower. It was dark when I hit Laramie and started grinding up the Elk Mountain grade. Snowflakes caught in my headlights like sparks, and visibility dropped to a few feet.

I worked my way over the top and down toward Cheyenne. I saw several trucks jackknifed into piles of twisted metal. I was so tired that I thought about parking for the night. Indiana was still over two days away and at least three days in my logbook. If I got stopped by a cop or checked at a weigh station, the book would show that I'd driven too far and too fast, and I'd risk a citation.

It seemed like forever, but we finally made it to the first rest area on Interstate 80 in Nebraska. At 7:00 P.M. I checked the tarps. I had to sleep till I stopped seeing white streaks in my eyeballs—at least four hours. I reminded Angela that I didn't have the luxury of napping while some-one else drove.

I was exhausted, but she didn't want to understand. She was in a hurry to get into her boyfriend's bed. I told her that Indiana could wait for one more sleep period—"If you need to get there quicker, get on the CB radio and find an-other ride. I'm shutting down for a while."

She changed tactics again. Sex, of course. I stroked into her over and over, but that only made me more tired. I was half-asleep while I was still inside her.

I pulled out and said, "Wake me in four or five hours." She looked angry. At this point I really didn't care. I saw right through her. I was mad at her for the very thought of blaming me for her child. That's about as low as a woman can get.

After twenty minutes she yanked me awake and said, "I won't sit here one more minute!"

I rolled over and told her to shut up, but she rattled on. I'd just started to get back to sleep when she shoved against my shoulders and told me we had to leave—*right fucking now!* I kept trying to doze, and she kept waking me up.

This went on for an hour till I sat up and shoved her away. She was already dead. She just didn't know it yet.

I drove east to the first rest area in Nebraska and parked at the very end. I let the truck idle down and told Angela I needed to use the restroom. I stepped out to make sure we weren't being watched. Traffic was light. I got back inside. *Party time!*

I ordered her to shut up and arrange the bed. When she got into the sleeper I pushed her facedown and rolled on top of her. "Get off me!" she said, thinking it was just one more stupidity by the clumsy-ass trucker.

"No," I told her. "It's about time I get a little something for allowing you all the comforts of home."

She whined that Lady Rose had told her I was a nice

man. I said, "You're about to meet the Keith that Lady Rose doesn't know."

I got out my duct tape and started to wrap it around her mouth. "You don't have to do that," she said.

"Oh, yes I do."

She said, "Listen, baby, I'll do what you want." When I didn't respond, she said, "Just let me pray first." She clasped her palms together and prayed to Jesus Christ loud enough for me to hear. Then she said, "You won't hurt me, will you?"

"No, I won't hurt you," I lied.

She told me she never gave head, but I could screw her again. I nodded in approval, and she began to get into the sexual experience like we were lifelong lovers. She kissed me like she loved me and guided me in. Afterwards she climbed on top and rode me till I was half-crazy.

After my second orgasm she claimed to be hungry and asked to stop at a restaurant. I knew this trick. When we stopped, she would yell rape. It wasn't going to happen. I screwed her a third time and held her close till I came again.

She grabbed for her purse and I jerked her hand back. I said, "You were reaching for your pepper mace, weren't you?"

She yelped, "No, I wasn't! *No, I wasn't!*"

I said, "It doesn't matter. I took it out.'

She said, "Oh, no!"

I told her we were going to play the death game and there was nothing she could do about it. After the way she'd treated me, she had it coming.

I shoved her on the floor of the sleeper and began to choke her. I kept up a steady pressure till she was out, then waited for her to breathe again. After the fourth or fifth time, she stopped breathing for good. It was tiring work, and I slept for three or four hours.

When I woke up, I put her body in a plastic garbage bag and set it on the mattress with her head pointing towards the driver's-side sleeper door. I wasn't sure what to do with her because she'd been seen hanging out with me for over a week off and on and she'd used my credit card to call her dad and boyfriend. She probably had a rap sheet. Her fingerprints might even be on file. I decided that I had to make her disappear completely.

I drove to a McDonald's and ordered for two. I sat in the truck and talked to her. "If you just played straight with me, bitch, you could be eating right now." I laughed. I didn't feel remorseful at all. To me she was just another bitchy woman, better off dead.

I felt her breasts as they stiffened up. I started to get hard, but I'd had my fun already. Now that I had a full stomach, it was time to make her invisible.

I needed to be on the far side of the scale house in the morning so I wouldn't be documented. In a few hours I drove by, and the scales were closed. At Mile Marker 198 I pulled into a spot that looked dark—no other parking lights or headlights. If there was anybody else there, I didn't see them. I was going to do a magic trick and I didn't want to give away my secrets.

It was 3:00 A.M. on January 23, 1995, just ten days after my truck caught fire. Angela was already starting to stink. A bad smell comes off dead skin. Not putrefaction, just a skin smell. It's unique, comes from chemicals in the body. Dead deer don't smell like that. Just humans.

I retaped her hands in front so her fingerprints would disappear first. With the truck dark I laid her stiff body on the pavement. I tied a length of black nylon rope to a cross member under my trailer, just long enough to allow her body to drag between the dual rear wheels so she wouldn't be seen from passing vehicles. I connected the rope to her ankles and placed her nose-down under the trailer. That way I could drag her backward and grind off her face and prints. I did all this in about three minutes. A few clusters of traffic passed me but didn't slow down.

I waited for another group to pass before I reentered the

highway. It was a good three miles between me and the drivers in front of me. Traffic was running at about seventy-five, and the top speed of my truck was sixty-four, so I had to allow ample time to grind her to hamburger before the next cluster caught up. I did the math, and my timing was perfect. I ended up dragging her twelve miles before I slowed down to check what was left.

As I pulled over, the next cluster of trucks started to pass, and one of the drivers asked me on the CB, "You okay?"

"Yeah," I said. "I'm just stopping to get rid of some coffee. Do you want to help me?"

He laughed and said, "No, thanks."

The cluster disappeared down the highway. With the road dark again I crawled under the trailer to see what was left of Angela. One shoulder was gone, a thigh gone, her chest was broken, guts gone, arms and hands gone up to her shoulders.

I figured that other drivers would see her body parts in their headlights and think they were roadkill. A two-legged deer! Her face was ground off to the ears—no dental work to worry about.

I dragged what was left down the bank and dumped her in twelve-inch grass about fifty feet from the freeway and ten feet inside the fence. Lights were coming my way as I got back in my cab. Another trucker checked to see if I was okay, and I stuck to my story that I stopped to wet down a tire. A cluster courteously moved over to the left as I entered the interstate.

At Exit 305 near Grand Island, I pulled into the back of the Union 76 station and took a short nap. When I woke up, I phoned in my hours and lied about my location so it would match my logbook and throw the cops off. Then I went outside and cleaned the rest of Angela off the truck.

I drove to Lincoln, crossed over to I-29S and down to I-70 and headed east to match what I'd recorded in my logbook. I made it look like I'd gone through Denver in case they found the body right away. *Hell, officer, I wasn't even in Nebraska.* Who could prove otherwise?

I got rid of her clothes at the Ohio Turnpike, unloaded in Pennsylvania, and picked up a new trailer with a load of frames for Denton, Texas. I'd gotten away with another murder—maybe. I was on edge again because I'd been seen with the victim. I thought, *It won't be long before I'm caught. What made me kill her? Just because I was tired and she was bugging me? What the hell kind of reaction was that?*

I made me sick.

8 | In the Dark

The first few weeks after Angela, I thought about suicide again. I imagined myself slamming into a concrete overpass support at sixty and wrapping around the steering column. But then I thought—with my luck I'll survive as a cripple. I wanted to die before I was caught so my family and my kids wouldn't know me as a murderer. People would wonder why I'd lost control of my truck, but they would assume it was fatigue and sleep deprivation. My children would be sad, but they would never have the torture of knowing their dad killed a bunch of women. Or having their classmates tease them for my crimes. And they wouldn't have to read stories that connected their father with Ted Bundy and John Wayne Gacy and other serial killers. Driving into an overpass support seemed like a good option.

Now that I knew the end was near, I was free to let out some of the emotions I'd been holding back. I would get pissed off at another truck driver, follow him into a truck stop and cut an air line or fuel line or slash a tire. I chained two trucks together and watched them try to drive away. I laughed when they finally realized they were tied together. It felt good to do things like that.

• • •

At night I drove without lights, just for the hell of it. Surprisingly I was able to stay awake longer that way. In the full moon with no traffic, I drove for hours without lights except when I saw other vehicles approaching. Allowing my eyes to become adjusted to the darkness, I'd sneak up on a truck and warn him on the CB that I was about to pass. I told him I was "the voice from nowhere." I would blink my lights after I passed and then switch them back off. The other drivers thought I'd flipped out. I was playing the last game of my life.

I passed a radar trap on Highway 93 while driving blind just north of Las Vegas. My radar detector went off and Smoky's voice came over the CB: "I don't care who you are or where you're going. Just slow it down and turn on some lights!"

About five miles up the road I switched them on. Only a couple of times did I ever come across another driver crazy enough to play this Russian roulette with me. Once I passed a phantom driver as he was in his stealth mode, and I know it scared him because he turned on his lights after I passed him like he was sitting still. I decided that I was having too much fun to kill myself.

9 | Julie Again

On a Sunday morning two months after I turned Angela Subrize into roadkill, I pulled into the Burns Brothers Truck Stop at Troutdale, Oregon, to rest up for a day or two so my logbook and my actual miles would match. I'd dropped my trailer and was driving bobtail. I showered and headed for the bathroom when I saw my old girlfriend Julie Winningham. I wasn't sure if she saw me, so I ducked into the restroom and didn't acknowledge her.

I sat there thinking about what to do. Did I want to deal with her problems again? *Gimme money, buy me clothes, find me some marijuana. . . .* The answer was no. I'd had it with the bitch. But then I remembered some of the dreams I'd had about her, some of the fantasies as I was driving cross-country on NoDoz and coffee and Jolt and Dr. Pepper. I thought, *My logbook won't match my miles for another twenty-four hours, and a good lay is a good lay. Who knows? Maybe she's changed in a year and a half.* In the end Mr. Penis and Miss Pussy won out.

I caught up with her and said, "Hi, Julie."

She said, "Keith!" She gave me a big hug. "Are you married yet?"

"No," I said as we hugged. "Want to have coffee?"

"Sure."

She sat across from me in the restaurant. We were both

shaking. She laughed when I reminded her of the first time we met: *"Now there's a back I'd like to rub."* We talked of what we'd done since our parting. I told her I tried to find her through her mother, but she hadn't called me back. Julie seemed pissed at her mother for that.

After an hour or so she asked forgiveness and so did I. What she didn't tell me was that she was broke again and still saw me as a mark. She claimed that she'd never stopped loving me. I picked up on the same old Julie in her voice. She was a scammer and a damn good one. I decided to play along.

She said she was out of cigarettes and I told her I always carried her brand in the truck just in case I ran into her. We walked out to the truck, and I followed her. She was the same pretty woman as before—same attitude. A bitch who could be fun at times.

She wiggled her ass as we climbed into the bobtail. She didn't even wait for me to sit. She planted a long tongue kiss on me and grabbed at my pants. I figured she missed me or wanted something or both. I was hot, but she said she needed a few drinks first. I knew I was set for at least one night.

After we agreed to go out, she laid down the ground rules. The punch line was that she'd lost her license and had to pay off a fine for DWI. Her court date was coming up on Thursday, and she needed seven hundred dollars. Could I help?

I thought, *She must think her ass is made of platinum!* I decided to go along for the sex. "Sure, Julie," I said. "I'll help." I wouldn't mind her company for a while, and I knew that as long as she expected me to pay up, she'd come across. Otherwise it would be like screwing a dead sturgeon.

We played pool in a bar till 11:00 P.M. and she drank herself drunk, like always. She could easily drink a hundred dollars' worth of liquor a night at bar prices. We drove around so she could introduce me to her local friends, a bunch of boozers and druggies.

When we got back to the parking lot, she proposed to me. I thought, *I'll go along and see what happens.* I was toying with another fantasy—the one where I take sex from a woman and keep her as a slave.

We drove to her mother's house and told her we were getting married. Her mom acted shocked, so we left. Back at the truck stop, Julie laid down and put my hand on her tits. I figured she must really have missed me. The sex was great, unlike her normal sex. She told me she remembered how sexually active I was and she said that from now on she wanted me to save it all for her. Maybe she was just trying to please, but any thought of kidnapping her or killing her went right out the window. By the next morning I was in love again. How could I tell? My dick told me so! She was in love with me, too. I was sure.

When we woke up to the morning sun, I went to the phone booth and called the company and told them where I was if they wanted me. They said it looked like I would have three or four days off. I knew what to do with them.

I bought Julie a carton of cigarettes and coffee and woke her up at 11:00 A.M. She was back to her old bitchy mood. I think she felt that now that I'd gotten sex twice in twenty-four hours, she owned me. So she laid down the law again. Her car had been wrecked. That would cost a thousand dollars. Her drunk-driving trial was coming up, and she'd have to pay fifteen hundred dollars in fines and costs or go to jail. She had lawyers' bills. She was selling her car to a friend and needed me to sign the contract as a witness. I didn't want to put my signature on anything because of those Happy Face letters out there. What if I killed Julie and they found this contract and matched the handwriting?

• • •

That afternoon we drove to the house of one of her scroungy friends and drugs were on the table. I was about ready to leave her there when I heard her ask for pot. They didn't have any, but they knew where she could get some— for a price. Julie said she would buy the first round if someone else would keep it going. I knew she had no money and intended to hustle me for the money, so I walked to my truck.

She came running out and opened the cab door. She was steamed! She said, "You *got* to give me the pot money. My reputation's on the line. You remember the wild times we've had, don't you? You want more, don't you?"

I asked myself if she was worth all the headaches. The answer was no. Before I knew it, she had my wallet out and the money was in her hands. Two twenties. I didn't know what to do about it without making a scene.

They bought the pot and I stayed in my truck until they smoked it up. Then Julie came out to me and we drove over to the back of the lumberyard. We rocked the antenna for four hours of sex—pot made her horny when nothing else did. After I couldn't get it up anymore, she lit her pipe and got a buzz to make her sleep better. Then she cuddled in my arms all night.

10 | The Blame Game

We were supposed to go back to her mother's house for dinner the next day, but I made up a few personal errands so I could get off by myself for a while. Julie could be overbearing at times, smothering me with her closeness.

I drove over to Beacon Rock and hiked for a couple of hours. When I got back to the house, Julie and her mother were screaming at each other. We skipped the dinner and took off in the truck. Those two drunks could never get along.

Julie and I stayed together for a couple more days and then I took off to play a cribbage tournament. When that was over, we hung out for a few more days, but then she got to be too hard to handle. It was one aggravation after another. *Somebody stole my car keys, my mother called the cops on me, I'm worried about the DWI thing, I got no money for food, I gotta depend on you, blah blah blah. . . .* When she said she needed thirty dollars for a flagger's license so she could pick up some easy money in road construction, I thought, *What a switch. She'll earn some money of her own.* So I gave her a fifty-dollar bill. Of course I got no change.

That night I dropped her off at a tavern and gave her another forty dollars to get drunk on while I played crib at the

Round Table Pizza Parlor in Sandy. It was rainy and stormy when I got back to my truck. It was parked along old Highway 14 just east of Washougal.

I was asleep when she climbed in. She helped me out of my jeans and I helped her out of her boots and clothes. She tasted like a pot plant and couldn't wait for me to get inside her.

After an hour and a half of multiple orgasms she lit a cigarette, leaned back against the wall and started bitching. "It was your fault I lost my car. My friends agree. So you owe me six hundred dollars for that. The court hearing is tomorrow. I didn't tell you, but I got two DWIs in one day, and the judge will fine me big-time. I need two thousand dollars."

I said, "Will that about cover it?"

"Engaged couples are supposed to help each other out," she said. "You *will* give me the money, Keith." She sounded confident, maybe because we'd just had sex. But I was on to that game and I'd had it.

Now I realized why she was so happy that I had agreed to marry her. It had nothing to do with loving me. It had to do with cash.

"First thing, Julie," I said. "I don't have two thousand dollars. And if I did, I wouldn't give it to you now. Not with your attitude. When you look at me, you don't see a fiancé. You see dollar bills."

"You'll give me the money all right!" she said. "I just had sex with you, Keith. I've been telling all my friends that you always want it but I never give it to you. Never! That's what they all believe. So if you don't give me the money, I'll tell 'em you raped me for it. Who'll they believe? Little me, or big you?"

I tried to give her a warning. "You don't know what you're saying, Julie. You don't know what you're getting yourself into."

"I know *exactly* what I'm saying! So what's it gonna be, boyfriend? The money or the cops?"

By now she'd scrunched herself against the wall and

was yelling so loud I was afraid she could be heard a block away. I couldn't believe that my sweetheart just backed me into the same corner as some of the other girls had. She pointed at my crotch. My penis was getting hard again. She said, "Keep that ugly thing away from me! Come up with the money first."

It didn't take a genius to figure out what I had to do to her. Was somebody watching my truck, or was she running her scam alone? I decided to take a chance.

I pushed her toward the back of the bed and said, "If I'm gonna pay, then it better be for a good reason."

Maybe she saw what was coming. She went from fighting me to loving me again. Or was she just accepting reality? She seemed to put a lot into the sex. I guess it was because she still believed that Sugar Daddy would come across with the cash. She always screwed better when there was something in it for her.

After the sex I pulled her to the center of the bed and started to strangle her. Her shocked eyes showed surprise. I guess she figured she could hustle me forever.

I choked her till she passed out and then I taped her arms behind her back, taped her ankles, and gagged her good with tape. I was wearing just my shoes and a shirt when I headed east. I knew she would wake up soon and then she'd really know terror.

I braked hard at a stop sign and heard her grunt. She tried to get into the front passenger's seat but fell to the floor and cut her forehead on the seat pedestal. A little pool of blood formed.

I reached down, patted her on her back and said, "Nice of you to join me, Julie. Now just stay there until I stop up ahead, and then you'll find out what's gonna happen to you."

She looked up at me and tried to talk through the duct tape. I said, "You should have never backed me into a corner. Now you're mine."

She was so scared that she lost control of herself. I was talking to the bitch and then she did it all over the floor.

She was just trying to aggravate me. I had to use Carpet Fresh later.

I picked her up and put her on the bed. She stared at me while I wiped the blood off her face with a clean sheet. I rubbed her tits and felt her all over. Then I yanked the tape off her mouth and said, "Now, Julie, we're going to have a kissing lesson. Show me what your life is worth."

That bitch could kiss when she wanted to. She asked me to fuck her again, so I did. She said, "Sweetheart, I was only kidding about the money. I wouldn't really say that to you. I *love* you. Can't you see that?"

I said, "You don't love me, Julie. You never have. Now you're gonna die."

She sniffled and said, "What about your children? I was gonna look after your kids."

I laughed. I said, "You can't even look after yourself! How could I trust you with my kids?" I was thinking, *How do I keep running into these kind of women?*

All this time she's staring at me with tears in her eyes. I removed the tape around her ankles, but I left the tape on her arms so she couldn't go after my eyes with her long fingernails.

When I closed the curtain, she said she felt sick. I blindfolded her with a shirt and waited a couple of minutes. She yelled, "Keith, I want to see you. *Keith!*"

While she was blinded, I touched my fingers to every spot that makes a woman a woman. I did it softly and with care. Pretty soon she went back to her old tricks. "Keith, make love to me again! I want you inside me again. Please! Don't let us end like this."

I entered her, and she put some feeling into it to regain control. "Sweetheart," she whined, "I would never hurt you! I promise that I'll never tell anyone about this night. As far as I'm concerned, it didn't happen. We can start fresh. How about it, sweetheart?"

I said, "You shouldn't have ordered me around. You should never have threatened to yell rape."

"I didn't mean it! Really I didn't."

I let her beg while I orgasmed again. I stayed inside and decided to clue her in on a few things to take to the grave.

"In January nineteen-ninety," I said, "I killed a woman named Taunja Bennett. In nineteen-ninety-two, I killed three more women in Oregon and California."

The muscles in her pussy began working overtime. I felt myself getting hard as she tried to buy some time. She said, "Fuck me, Keith, or cut me into a thousand pieces."

"Okay, Julie, I'll fuck you."

"Fuck me and let me get away from this damn truck!"

As I started again, I told her how I'd dragged a woman under my trailer till a thousand pieces flew off. When she heard that, she went limp. She laid there quiet and docile waiting for the end.

I played the death game three or four times. I thought about saving her for the next night as well but didn't want to push my luck. She could put me in prison. I'd already had a dream about killing her and being hanged.

Dawn was coming, and pretty soon the traffic would be too heavy for me to unload her on the shoulder. I thought back to when I first met her and loved her and wanted her for all time. I needed to do one more killing and then end this murder machine for good.

"Time to go, Julie," I said. "Say bye-bye!"

I ground my fist into her throat. My knuckles went white. When she passed out I sat with her for a few minutes before stepping outside to take a leak. As I was pissing, a sheriff's car drove by. He kept on toward town.

I got back in my truck just in time to hear her whisper, "I love you, Keith. Please let me go. I won't say anything. I promise."

I said, "Everything will be all right, Julie." I kissed her face and decided to let her prove her love. She always told me that she never gave blow jobs, but she broke her rule for me.

After that, I looked down at her face and smiled. I said, "Now you're gonna die."

I put my fist against her throat for the last time. Just before she passed out, I told her, "You're number eight. And, yes, I *will* get away with it." She didn't breathe again.

I drove to a spot on the downhill side of Highway 14 on the Washington State side of the Columbia Gorge, right across the river from where I threw Taunja Bennett's body in Oregon. I carried her over past a guardrail and some garbage sacks and pitched her down a fifteen-foot embankment. I stared at her crumpled body in the weeds and thought how she'd only lasted five days with me. What a waste.

I thought, *You shouldn't have treated me like that, Julie.* I climbed into the driver's seat and leaned my head against the steering wheel and cried. *I love you, Julie! I really do! Why were you like all the rest?*

Then I thought, *Too many people saw us together. This time I'll get caught for sure. Julie and me—we're both dead meat.*

Later that night I decided to drag her body further down the hill, out of sight. But I changed my mind. Part of me wanted to get this nightmare over with, and the best way to get caught was to leave her where she was. I was tired of being a killer. But I would never hand myself over. *Let the cops catch me, do a little work, treat me and my murders with respect, instead of waiting for me to make all the moves. With so many witnesses that had seen Julie and me together, it shouldn't take long.* My life was over anyway. I thought, *Catch me! Convict me! Throw me away! What's the difference? I'm just a piece of shit!*

6

A KILLER'S LIFE 3

1 | A Box Full of Bills

In midsummer 1976, when Keith was twenty-one, the lawsuit over his injured foot was settled on the courthouse steps. His share was thirty-three thousand dollars. "In the back of my mind I wanted to use the money to relocate in Chilliwack. My body might be in Washington, but my heart never left B.C. Ever since the sixth grade I wanted to go back. But Dad came to me with a proposal to make me full-time manager of the Silver Spur and 10-percent owner of all our family property, including the house and the trailer court.

"He said he would borrow money from the bank and Rose and I could throw in my settlement. That way we could add forty-six more lots. He said the park would pay our expenses, gas for our car, all insurance and house payments and utilities, and he would buy me a new pickup equipped with a winch, a four-wheel drive and a snowplow. Dad and Mom would get a thousand dollars per month, and Rose and I would get six hundred. Rose would do the bookkeeping.

"It sounded good, so I signed over my money and went to work. I poured a twenty-by-twenty-foot concrete driveway every day, sometimes two. At night I'd go to Biggs Junction to fish for sturgeon to relax from the pressure, then go back to work at dawn. Within six weeks I finished all the new lots and people were putting houses on them."

• • •

Rose Jesperson had always admired her father-in-law, but now that they were involved in business together, she learned that he could be difficult. She wasn't a trained bookkeeper, but she was good at math, and she kept the trailer park accounts in good order. The paterfamilias was free with his suggestions and advice.

Keith saw storm clouds and considered interceding, but he didn't want to offend either party. "Rose seemed kind of put out, being on the receiving end of Dad's control. She'd get really nervous when he approached our trailer. Now Dad is no dummy. He sees how he affects people and he believes money will fix all. So at Christmas that first year he gave Rose a box full of crinkled-up green papers—five hundred of them.

"Rose dug into the paper looking for her present before she realized it was all dollar bills. Dad said, 'Rose, that's kind of a payment for putting up with me. I'll try to mend my ways.' It smoothed over a few corners. They got along after that. It was a sign that we could all work together. Too bad the pipe dream couldn't last."

With the addition of the new units and the family future secure, Rose announced that she wanted children. The idea unnerved Keith. "I couldn't get in the mood. What if I had kids as screwed up as me? Kids that nobody liked. Kids called Igor."

He was still attracted to other women and coveted a highly respectable member of his bowling team. "Arliss was married to the guy who owned Skookum Bowl. She looked great and was nice and friendly, easy to talk to. I used to have sex with Rose and imagine it was Arliss. I fantasized about making it with her on one of the bowling lanes after she shut the place for the night. I had that dream for years."

• • •

Rose knew nothing about the fantasy affairs, and she remained satisfied though puzzled by her new husband. A friend quoted her: "Keith protects me and he's a great provider. He has an artistic side—he draws beautiful scenes: deer, wild birds, all kinds of outdoor settings. He makes intricate designs, buildings, complex plans, like his father. He solves complicated problems in a few seconds. But he lacks common sense. He'll stand outside in a storm. People walk all over him. He forgets his car keys. He seems passive, but I'm not so sure."

Rose told a few close friends that sometimes she suspected brain damage.

When six months passed and she hadn't conceived, doctors determined that Keith's sperm count was too low. Characteristically, he blamed his father. "The doctor asked if I was under stress. I told him what it was like to work with Dad, and he told me my sperm levels would never recover if I didn't break the connection. By then Rose seemed almost desperate for children and signed us on a waiting list for adoption. I didn't want somebody else's children. I was hoping for a long wait."

2 | Independent Driver

The Silver Spur Mobile Home Park remained in Jesperson hands for two more years before financial problems and family disagreements forced a sale. Keith reluctantly approved. "The palm trees were dying in the solarium. The sewage system was failing, and we had to borrow money for that. We borrowed twenty thousand dollars to put in a new well and pay off some of Dad's creditors. Rose and I were at our wits' end and wanted out. I told Dad to unload the park because he couldn't handle the problems and we didn't want to. He sold out."

In his familiar pattern Keith blamed his father for the demise. He recovered his original thirty-three-thousand-dollar investment but soon lost it on cars, vans, motorcycles, bad loans to friends and usurious credit-card interest. When he was close to bankruptcy, he took on a series of low-paying jobs: hauling wood, plumbing, operating a lathe and drill press, working security at night. After three or four hours of sleep, he would rush back to work. He seemed to have less time for Rose.

"Keith became obsessed with money," a friend recalled. "Every time I saw him he had another part-time job. It wouldn't have surprised me to see him shining shoes on Yakima Avenue."

• • •

Ever since his days behind the wheel of the ancient Wittenburg dump truck, Keith had wanted to learn how to drive big semi-trucks and become an independent driver. He found his opportunity at Muffett and Sons of nearby Buena. "My first job with Muffett was truck driver, equipment operator, welder and mechanic at five bucks an hour and sixty hours a week. I rode my bicycle to work so Rose could have the car. I covered twenty-two miles in just over an hour.

"Now that I was away from the mobile-home park, my stress eased and I started thinking of living in Canada with Rose. But then Melissa was born. I was kinda relieved it was a girl. I like girls. They're not as much trouble. Jason was born a year later. How I loved my babies!"

Finances remained an issue in the young household, especially when Keith discovered that the travel expenses of a long-haul trucker were higher than expected. "Rose kept me on the same tight budget as when we were first married—forty dollars a week for food. Driving truck, my morning coffee was costing me a dollar. With three or four coffee breaks a day, I would've been out of money by Thursday if I didn't lump my own loads and pocket the sixty or eighty dollars. Rose would have sent me out with nothing."

3 | Adventuring with Rose

To friends and relatives the first few years of the Jesperson marriage seemed smooth and uneventful. Despite his early doubts Keith realized that he was in love with Rose. After Jason Roy was born in September 1980 and named after his great-grandfather Roy Bellamy, the young husband tried to spend every free moment with his family.

Later Rose told a friend: "He adored our kids. He always had one in his lap. He made a plastic carrier on the back of his bike so he could carry them around wherever he went. At Christmastime he gave piles of gifts. He was always generous to a fault. He bought an expensive mountain bike for a friend just so they could ride together. He gave gifts that we couldn't afford. That's what he substituted for love. He could only show love to little kids. I called him the Disneyland Dad.

"He took me to a jeweler and said, 'Pick out the diamond ring you want.' I said, 'Why?' He said, 'Just because.' He walked out of the shop and said he'd be back in a while. He couldn't be there when I put on the ring. That would have been too emotional."

Keith started taking his wife "adventuring," as they called it, with his father often coming along for the ride while Gladys stayed home and knitted sweaters—her customary preference. After the trailer-court issues faded, father and son began to enjoy each other's company. On weekends they climbed steep hills in Les's pickup truck. "Dad and I would pick the highest hill and try to go straight up. If the angle got too steep, I'd yell, 'Jump, Rose, *jump!*' She'd fly through the air laughing.

"We explored back roads and made some roads of our own. Dad would say, 'Hey, let's go to Chilliwack.' He'd get us up at 4:00 A.M., and off we'd go in his pickup. He hung out with old friends, and Rose and I toured British Columbia on a motorcycle. Dad and I were always drawn to Chilliwack. It was in our bones."

The conflict between father and son simmered below the surface. "No matter how much fun we had together, I could never forget how he belted me. Once when he baby-sat our kids, I told him, 'Don't hit them. *You do not touch them!* I've never touched my kids and neither will you.'

"Dad said, 'They're *my* grandkids.' I said, 'Well, they're *my* kids!' "

To friends and relatives Keith still seemed to revel in stories that cast his father as a fool or a weakling—a skewed characterization that he seemed to find comforting. He described an ocean fishing trip: "I caught two salmon and Dad got seasick." He liked to tell about the roll of pictures his father shot without film. He tended to put a negative interpretation on Les's activities and routinely referred to him as "the prick."

As always father and son seemed to have little insight about each other's needs and feelings. "Dad still treated me like the runt of the litter, daddy's little helper. He dragged me to a nursing home to visit one of his hunting buddies. He said, 'My friend Smitty's not doing too good with his lung cancer, Keith. I'm going out in the hall. Talk to him, Son. Nobody likes to die alone.' I'm sitting there, listening to the rattly breathing, watching his life drain out. After a while Smitty goes limp. I'm holding his hand for ten or fifteen minutes before I realize he's dead.

"I guess you could say Dad helped me get used to people dying. Was he saying he wanted me with him when he died? Was he afraid of dying alone? Was that why he had me sit with that old guy?

"On our way home he said, 'Keith, someday you'll thank me for putting you through this.' I never feared a dead person after that. When I was killing, I'd talk to my victims as if they were still alive. It was something to thank Dad for."

4 | Escape to Canada

When Keith was assigned to longer hauls and began to spend more time behind the wheel, he managed to be home only five or six days a month. His marriage showed strain. Running on caffeine, he became short-tempered and sharp-tongued. He told Rose that he preferred thin women and criticized her for every extra pound, even during pregnancy. Their sex drives had never been in phase, and they squabbled over his need to rush her into the bedroom whenever he returned from a trip.

The steady trucking job made him feel more in control of his life, but a few of his old urges remained. He set the occasional wildfire. One day he attacked a stray cat in front of his children. He didn't understand their shocked reaction. "Whenever a cat came near me after that, Rose and the kids would holler, 'Don't kill it! *Don't kill it!*' "

He continued to suffer from a feeling of not belonging, of not being accepted by his fellow truckers and friends. "When I was in Canada, I was an American. When I was in the States, I was a Canadian. I even began to lose my accent. So what the hell *was* I? Where did I belong? My best memories were of Chilliwack: Grandpa Bellamy and *Little*

Cotto, catching trout, delivering papers, stuff like that. That's why I never applied for U.S. citizenship. My dream was to go home."

In April 1981, his sixth year of marriage, Keith learned that jobs were open at Fording Coal Company in Elkford, B.C., on the western slope of the Continental Divide. After a short exchange of correspondence, he was hired. The pregnant Rose was less optimistic about the migration but agreed to follow with the children as soon as he was settled in.

Now twenty-six, Keith felt as though he had shaken off shackles. "I couldn't wait to get away from the Yakima Valley and leave Dad and his head games and all the guys that called me Igor. I knew I would find my true self in Canada, and Rose and I would have a great marriage. I would even stop fantasizing about other women.

"On my drive north in the family Plymouth, I was put to the test. I stopped for a pretty hitchhiker with car trouble. She popped her hood and I quizzed her on how the motor died. I saw that the plastic lobe on the points that ride on the shift cam had broken off. After I replaced them, she insisted on buying me dinner and gave me her phone number in Spokane. She was so beautiful, but I resisted temptation. As her car drove out of sight, I parked on the shoulder and masturbated over what might have been."

At the coal mine Keith was put to work as a flagger at nine dollars an hour and soon won a five-dollar raise as driver of the coal-carrying trucks. "Those overgrown Tonka toys were a trip. High up in the cab I was king of the road. Those Wabco dump trucks and Electrohaul 120s weighed 170 tons loaded. They ran on locomotive motors. The tires were taller than me. I could hardly stretch my arms across the tread.

"Driving those babies was like being in the eye of an

electric storm. The diesels generated enough electricity to run two-thousand-horsepower motors. Some of the downhill grades at the mine were 10 percent. If the dynamic disc brakes failed, we were taught to scrape against the rock wall. That saved my ass a few times. It made it easy for me to drive eighteen-wheelers in the mountains later."

After three weeks on the job, he drove his Plymouth back to Yakima for a short visit with his family. Rose was still cleaning up financial odds and ends and told him it would be another month before she could join him.

He was only too glad to return to Elkford without his family. He felt at home with his fellow Canadians and had made new friends. He rode his Honda 750 with a motorcycle touring club called "Gauntlet and Silk." He went on a Saturday night drinking binge with his fellow mine workers but decided not to repeat the experience. "I found that I developed a 'don't give a shit' attitude in the bars. I didn't like myself drunk any more than I liked Dad when he was drunk.

"My schedule changed to four days on and four days off. That meant more time to party. I went out with the single guys and played pool, snooker and darts. I got into some good cribbage games. I met women and had plenty of chances at sex, but I stayed true to Rose. I went home on visits, but each time I hurried back. I missed the bachelor life in Canada.

"At a Sunday parade in Yakima, one of the roaming clowns ran up and kissed Rose. Dad said, 'That'll teach you to pay more attention to your wife.' I didn't give a damn. I couldn't wait to head back north. I didn't care what Dad said anymore.

"Rose and the kids joined me in Canada on the fourth of July, 1981. By now I was out of the young-husband mode, the good-daddy mode, and into the good-times mode. I wanted to come and go as I pleased. That first weekend I went biking with a new friend named Lou Lewis and left my family in Elkford. The next weekend a group of us camped out at Radium Hot Springs. When I got home, Rose was mad—'What about me and the kids? How come you don't take us anywhere?' I barely heard her. I figured I worked hard and I deserved a little fun."

Bachelor playtime ended after the family moved into a two-bedroom apartment. "Rose just wouldn't put up with me playing, and I didn't want to risk losing my kids. I might've been a little detached from everybody else in the world, but I was always tight with Jason, Melissa and Carrie. I remembered how cold Mom had been, and I tried not to repeat my parents' mistakes.

"After Rose said she didn't intend to sit home and knit Indian sweaters like Mom, I got back in the swing of married life, crawling on the floor with my babies, picnicking along the Mackenzie River, hiking in the mountains. It helped that Dad wasn't there to tell me what to do. Everything went great except the sex. Once a week was plenty for Rose, but my style was once a night. Sometimes I got so frustrated that I went into the bathroom and locked the door—a married man, masturbating."

The monthly rent on the new apartment was $983, and other expenses were high, so Keith bid into the welding department as an apprentice. "That's where the money was. Pretty soon my wages were $16 per hour and I was working six, seven days a week, twelve hours a day. Rose and I had a lot of back bills, and I worked all the overtime I could get. In my first two months of welding I made almost $10,000. I bought gifts for everybody. I bought my brother's old truck and drove it back to Canada, and I bought an expensive Jennings Compound Bow and a new set of arrows for myself. Rose and I settled down to raising our family. I was finally getting into married life. Then the walls fell in."

5 | Leather Theft

As usual Keith found a convoluted way to blame his father for the latest downturn in his life. "I'd always been easily swayed, especially if I thought I could get away with something. The mine workers stole tools and resold them. I witnessed thousands of dollars in thefts. One of my bosses smuggled out automobile engine parts in crates. Pretty soon he was driving around with a new Chevy motor! Everybody stole bulk batteries and flashlights, rain gear and boots, and pretty soon I did too.

"My father was scheduled for a visit, and I wanted to please him, like always. Every month or so he'd expect us to treat him royally. Nothing new—he was always around the corner watching. He couldn't control my brothers and sisters, so he did his number on me. This time he changed my life."

Years later Les Jesperson recalled the preliminaries. "I had opened a welding shop in Yakima, and one day when I was working overhead, hot sparks went down my neck and burned me. Talking to Keith on the phone, I said, 'Sure would be nice to have a set of those expensive leather coveralls you guys wear, to protect me from those damn hot sparks.'

"I never blamed my son for what he did. He was just

trying to please his dad. I always wondered if it had something to do with the murders later. Was he trying to impress
me in some sick way? Ever since he was little, that boy did
strange things."

Keith looked around for coveralls in Les's size. "Dad
should have told me not to bother, but all he said was,
'Don't get yourself in trouble, Son.' My leathers were too
big for him, but a friend got me a smaller set. I decided to
smuggle them out in a box along with a set of my own dirty
leathers that were going to the cleaner's.

"As I walked past the security shack, the guard yelled,
'Stop!' I ran around the corner, stashed the leathers and
walked back. The guard followed my trail and found the
goods. He took down my ID number 901680 and said he
had to report me.

"Riding into town on the bus I had that same scary feeling that I always had when I did something wrong, like the
whole universe was watching. That went all the way back
to shoplifting candy at Mead's Thriftway in Selah.

"When I told Dad that I got caught smuggling out his
leathers, he told me I'd made a mistake but to never admit
it. 'Deny everything,' he said, 'Just walk away. You can always get another job.' "

The mining company offered Keith a deal. If he admitted
his guilt and maintained a perfect record, his record would
be wiped clean in a year. "Dad said, 'Don't do it. Come
home. If you stay at Fording, you'll always be known as a
thief.' I think he was just trying to get me back to Selah. If
I had ignored his advice, I probably would've stayed out of
trouble for the rest of my life. But I used his judgment instead of my own. I stuck my nose in the air and denied
everything. Now I was out of a job."

6 | Adrift

For two years Keith rattled around Canada from job to job, none as good as the one he'd lost by theft. To escape the stigma he moved his family one hundred miles east to Lethbridge, Alberta, and went to work for Big Horn Transport, driving night runs to Calgary in a Mack truck with flatbeds, working days as a welder at a low salary that was made even lower by the weak Canadian dollar.

Then he landed a dream job driving a massive Peterbilt that had a four-hundred-horsepower Cat engine, a twelve-ton cherry picker for loading heavy equipment, and a draw winch that could pull a house. He enjoyed the power pulsing into his hands through the twin stick shifts with their nine forward speeds. Truck and trailer had twenty-six tires and hauled loads up to 210,000 pounds. "I was back on top again—the job of a lifetime. My work was like play."

He was laid off after eight months.

A daughter, Carrie Marie, was born on March 17, 1983, bringing the family to five. The breadwinner caught on with a construction company, then drifted to two other jobs while managing an apartment complex in exchange for 50 percent off his $425 monthly rent. "I was spinning my wheels, and I knew why. I'd lost my self-respect. I'd lied to so many people about how I lost the Elkford job that I almost believed my own lies.

"Then somebody talked me into trying out for a local boxing team. I'd boxed a little in Selah, but Dad told me to forget about it—I was too slow. With him out of the picture, I boxed in the Alberta Golden Gloves and on a provincial fight card and enjoyed it even though I usually lost. I did roadwork like a heavyweight champion and dropped from 260 pounds to around 220. I began to feel better about myself. Girls hit on me again, even when Rose was with me. She didn't like it, but I did. It was nice to be the center of attention, even if it was just in taverns. I didn't think about abusing animals. I didn't think about setting fires. I told myself I'd never leave Canada again.

"But the better things got for me, the more Rose complained. Alberta was too cold, the people were backward, she missed her mama, school was too tough for the kids, blah blah blah. When she was at her lowest ebb, Dad shows up and says, 'Mom's got lymph-node cancer, Son. She might live a little longer if you moved our grandkids where she can see 'em.'

"That was all Rose needed to hear. She was taking the kids back to Washington, with or without me. I argued for a few days but finally caved in. By this time I'd pretty much fallen out of love with Rose, but I sure as hell loved my kids.

"In July 1983 I drove Rose, Melissa, Carrie and Jason down to Yakima and put them in a little apartment. Everything we owned fit into the U-Haul trailer behind our 1978 Dodge Monaco. I didn't even have a motorcycle.

"I caught a welding job at eight bucks an hour, a $4.00 cut for moving back to the States. This lasted for five weeks, and then I drove a flatbed trailer for Jerry's Steel in Yakima, hauling metal scrap and returning with finished products. Sometimes I hauled copper, brass and aluminum, and every weekend I drove a van full of old newspapers to a recycling center in Oregon City, Oregon. Some nights I didn't get two hours' sleep. We needed the money.

"When I got my gross income up to $850 a week, Rose started talking about moving out of our apartment. She'd always had the infatuation of owning a home. I tried to tell her to wait till the trucking job proved itself, but she went out and looked at mobile homes every chance she got. I'd get back home on Friday night or Saturday morning and she'd make me help her to look. She'd say, 'We can do this, Keith! We can do it!' When I told her we didn't have enough money saved up, here comes old Dad again, offering to front us the down payment. Control, always control! What could I say?

"A small mobile home would've been enough, but Rose picked out a four-bedroom double-wide. She said, 'We can handle it, Keith. You're making enough money now.' I said, 'Yeah, *now*. But what happens if I lose my job?' I thought, *There's only a few jobs in the Yakima Valley that would allow me to keep up those payments if I was laid off.*

"Rose wouldn't listen and neither would Dad. With his help we paid $30,000 and moved to the High Valley Mobile Home Park in Selah. We were back where we started, but with one difference. Now we owed Dad money."

From the day the family moved in, Keith was hardly ever home. "I practically lived in my truck. I was damn near in love with it. It was an orange-and-white 1964 Kenworth needle-nose conventional with a 350 Cummins, five-and-four transmission, and torsion-bar suspension. Once in a while I also drove an all-white cab-over GMC Astro with a 318 Detroit engine and thirteen-speed Ranger transmission. It screamed when it ran, and we used it to haul sixty foot rebar.

"I began to feel more at home in those trucks than I did with Rose and the kids. Driving truck was the perfect job for me—out on the open road, living on Slim Fast and coffee and NoDoz, nobody telling you what to do or criticizing you—master of your own life. I took crap from nobody!

"One day an old guy in a green mini pickup tried to block me from passing on the canyon road between Ellensburg and Yakima. I pulled out ahead of him and blocked both lanes, grabbed a wrench, and walked back to his truck. He put his pickup in reverse and slammed into the car behind him. I lit out for Jerry's truck yard. I never heard a word about it.

"Sometimes other drivers would flip me off and try to keep me from following too close. Generally I didn't retaliate unless they jammed on the brakes. Then I'd push them out of the lane and they'd freak and motion to me that they got my license plate. I'd just flip them the bird and go on my way. I never heard anything about those complaints either. I was getting away with murder."

7 | Trouble in Bed

The prodigal trucker quickly discovered a side benefit of his nomadic profession. "There were plenty of available women, and not just hookers or lot lizards. I stayed true to Rose, but there was no law against looking. The truck-stop girls always seemed so friendly and flirty. I was a big good-looking guy and every eye turned my way when I walked into a restaurant.

"I would usually head out from Yakima to Seattle around 3:00 A.M. and stop for a quick coffee and flirt with the girls at the Husky Truck Stop in Ellensburg. Those girls sent my heart into overdrive. They would sit at my table and brush against my thigh. My hard-on always told me to get the hell out of there.

"Driving over Snoqualmie Pass on I-90, 1 would talk to Lady Rose and Cherokee at North Bend—more harmless flirting. Usually I would make ten or twelve stops, drive home, and start the cycle all over again the next day. Rose and I were deep in debt and needed every nickel I could earn. Days and nights ran together. I hardly saw my kids at all.

"I was still having bed problems with Rose. It was like she was getting bored with it. Or maybe I didn't know how to do it right. She'd act like sex was a duty, not fun. She would say some of the things that my mom said when I was listening outside the bedroom. Why did the Jesperson men always have to argue their wives into sex?

"Sometimes we had loud fights. Rose would yell, 'Put it away! Stick it in a keyhole!' The only time she showed any interest was when she wanted to get pregnant. If I asked for a blow job, she acted like I was a pervert. Yet I knew that oral sex was a regular thing with other couples. This was the 1980s, not the 1950s. It finally reached the point where I had to take care of my own cock.

"But nobody could masturbate twenty-four hours a day, so I took off on long bike rides or jogs to relieve my sexual energy. On trips to Seattle I would pull the truck off the road and climb seven miles to the tower on top of Tiger Mountain near Issaquah. Whenever I was near the Columbia River Gorge, I would park on I-84 and run a few laps between Multnomah Falls and the lodge, maybe ten or twelve miles in all. That way I made myself too tired for sex.

"After one of my Columbia Gorge hikes I was cooling out in the parking lot when up walked this good-looking lady in a pink sweatsuit and Coke-bottle glasses. She told me she wanted to hike to the Falls, but she was a little nervous since it was getting dark. I offered to get my flashlight and guide her. When we were coming back down the narrow trail, I thought about taking her to my truck and enjoying her company for a while—just a little diversion, nothing too heavy. I tried to figure out how to ask her in a nice polite way. The worst she could do was turn me down.

"But as we got closer to the parking lot, I started to fantasize. That other no-good mean part of my personality thought how easy it would be to take her. For starters I could yank off her thick glasses and grab her breasts. If she freaked, I might back off—and I might not.

"I made a mental list of everything that could go wrong. She could scream and attract other hikers. She could report me to the cops. She could kick me in the nuts.

"Then I thought, *After I fuck her, I can throw her over the edge. She'll fall six hundred feet. Who could prove she didn't slip?* By the time they found her body, I'd be back home playing with my kids.

"I planned every step in my head, but in the end I chickened out. Over coffee in the lodge I asked, 'How did you know I wouldn't take advantage of you up there?'

"She said, 'I could see in your eyes that you're a nice man. You would never do something like that.' Before she left, she gave me her phone number in Pasco, Washington. I never called. I was a married man."

8 | "She's Ashes Now."

Serial murderers are frequently found to have unusual or unnatural relationships with their mothers.

—Steven Egger, *The Killers Among Us*

Keith returned from a long haul to learn that his mother's lymph-node cancer had metastasized. Mother and son hadn't been close since he was small, but the prospect of losing her made him shudder. "Mom was the glue that held us together while Dad was working or hanging out with his cronies and I was struggling to make a living and all my brothers and sisters were marrying and moving away. Without Mom we wouldn't have had any family at all. When things were at their worst between me and Rose or between me and Dad or my brothers, she was the one who smoothed things over. We couldn't lose Mom."

Just after Keith's thirtieth birthday, in April 1985, his father called with bad news. "Mom and Dad were living in the Alps Mobile Home Park in Moxee, and he told us to come right over. When Rose and I got there, he was running the show. He says, 'Well, Keith, you'd better go in there and kiss your mom good-bye.' It was like a slap in the mouth. I wasn't raised to kiss my mom, and it made me uncomfortable.

"I sat on the bed and said, 'Mom, I find it hard to kiss you good-bye because I never kissed you before. All my life we never hugged or kissed.' Maybe she hugged me when I was a baby, but I didn't remember. I said, 'Mom, this is kinda like breaking the mold now. The only reason I'm gonna kiss you is because you're dying.'

"I crawled into bed and hugged her, but we never really kissed. We talked for maybe twenty minutes. She said, 'Keith, don't raise your kids the way we raised you. Never, never hit 'em.'

"I said, 'Mom, I'll raise 'em with love and understanding.'

"She said, 'It's good you took off some weight, son. I hope you keep it off.' I told her I would. She said, 'Try to get along with Rose and Dad.' I promised.

"When I left the bedroom, Dad grabbed me and said, 'What'd she say?' It was like he was worried that she'd blurt out a family secret. I just turned away. Mom was on her deathbed and Dad was still trying to control the world.

"Mom died two weeks later. I was relieved that she wasn't in pain, but I didn't feel too bad otherwise. Maybe that was a sign there was something wrong with my emotions—I don't know about things like that. Brad cried at the funeral—mama's boy. We had a memorial service at the funeral home in Yakima. Everybody commented that I didn't show my feelings. Well, the truth was that I didn't have any special feelings. It struck me as funny that the others were bawling. I said, 'What's the big deal? She's ashes now.'

"A month later Dad told me he was going on a trip to Canada with Betty Clasen, like he was asking if it was okay. I said, 'Since when have you asked us for permission to do anything? When you want to do something, you do it anyway.' Within a year they were married."

• • •

Keith's trucking job with Jerry's Steel ended in November 1986, when he was displaced by a rookie driver: his boss's son. "I called in from Seattle and was told that I was finished at the end of the day. Three years of faithful service and no apologies. No 'thank you, Keith.' Just 'You're outa here!' "

He fell behind on mortgage payments, lost the equity in the mobile home to the bank, and relocated his family to a seedy little house. He blamed Rose for poor money management. One of his complaints was that she fed the three children at McDonald's too often. Rose argued that he wasted money at truck-stop restaurants and should look for a job that kept him near home. That way he could economize with a lunch bucket and thermos.

Keith disagreed but tried to be understanding. "I knew what was eating Rose. She was tired of being alone with the kids and always being in debt. Now I was out of a job. I collected unemployment for a few months, then ran a punch press and went to work for the Yakima Holiday Inn as security officer and bouncer. In February '87 I got a job running heavy equipment from 6:30 A.M. to 6:30 P.M., so I was juggling three jobs. Caffeine pills and Jolt kept me going. The Holiday Inn paid five dollars an hour plus tips, and I made another twenty to sixty dollars a night by stealing door charges from the dance hall. I knew it was wrong, but I had to make our payments."

One night Keith caved in to the pressure. "Rose accidentally overdrew our bank account. I felt like hitting her, but I'd made up my mind to end the Jesperson family's cycle of violence, no matter what. So I slammed my fist into the front door and made a big hole. I yelled at her to never do that again. She left for a few hours to let me calm down. I never fixed the door. It was a reminder to both of us to make sure there was money in the account before we wrote checks."

• • •

Later Keith had to admit that he was no more adept at money-handling than his wife, and after a few more months they were floundering in debt. They went through credit counseling twice and finally had to declare bankruptcy.

9 | Threesome

Just before Christmas 1986, Keith was feeling frazzled and upset when he drove his son Jason to Yakima to pay a social call on old friends Billy and Ginny Smith. In eleven years of marriage, Keith had often fantasized about Ginny. "She was slim and had a very good-looking body and long brown hair, but I never made a move because she was married to my best friend. A short time after little Jason and I arrived at Billy's house, he told me he would take the kid to the store while I kept Ginny company. I thought this was a little strange because us men usually went to the store together.

"Jason and Bill were barely out of sight when Ginny gave me a tongue kiss. Here was my favorite fantasy coming true and I couldn't do anything about it. Billy would shoot me dead on the spot. He was that kind of guy.

"Ginny went into the bedroom, and I just sat there and tried to act like it was a joke. When she came back out and grabbed my crotch, I said, 'I can't do this! I've never been unfaithful to Rose. Billy will catch us and I'll lose my best friend.' "

"When they got back from the store, I took Bill aside and told him that Ginny made a pass. He didn't even flinch. He said it was all planned. They were swingers and Ginny told him she wanted me for Christmas. He said, 'Hey, man, get in there and give her a good fuck.'

"When I realized he was serious, I kind of staggered into the bedroom. At first I didn't know how to start, but then I thought I might as well pretend to be her lover. She took off her clothes and unzipped my fly. She was very playful, gave head and loved receiving it all ways. What a difference between her and Rose!

"Just as I finished my first orgasm, Billy came into the bedroom and got into the act as well. I asked him what my son was doing and he said he was watching TV in the living room. A good hour passed before I got dressed and took him home.

"The next night I couldn't get back there fast enough. Billy and I took turns on Ginny. After that, I didn't want to share her. Maybe Bill read my mind, because he warned me not to go near the place when she was home alone. That made me want her more. I would ride my bicycle and meet her while the kids were at school. She said she liked my thick size because it filled her up. We'd have sex in the shower, then in bed and on the floor.

"We did all the things that would have made Rose call 911. Then I'd go back home and wait for Billy to call up for a threesome. For the first time in my life I was getting all the sex I needed. Then he got a job in another town, and they moved away."

During 1987, his thirty-second year, Keith reverted to fantasy sex again, often involving force, plus an occasional uninspiring session with Rose. His truck-stop flirting accelerated, and he seldom passed a stranded female motorist without pulling over. "It opened up my conscious mind to think about having sex with them. My fantasies ran wild."

Late in the year he met two teenagers from the Yakima Valley. "They got into my truck to check it out, and all of a sudden I had a couple of horny young girls on my hands. I did my best to satisfy them. I saw them often, and we had an understanding that I was married and if they wanted to party, we'd party—no love or long-term relationship. Mary was gorgeous in height and weight, and her body fit my body nicely. We enjoyed each other on several trips south as I smuggled her along for our steamy experiences.

"Sometimes one of them was busy and I screwed the other. But then they began to fight over me, and it freaked me out since they only lived four miles from my house. To avoid another *Fatal Attraction,* I tried to find a girlfriend further away. I realized that the head between my legs was controlling my actions, but I couldn't stop.

"It was unnerving at times. Rose got suspicious calls, and I had to make up excuses. Trucking allowed me too much freedom, I guess. I began to find girls everywhere. I even bedded our baby-sitter after driving her home. I had the sex drive of a stallion, and I could perform all night and half the next day.

"I would park in rest areas and watch the lot lizards making their moves. It was tempting, but I stuck to my rule of not paying for it. I avoided my fellow drivers, refused to play follow-the-leader in our mini-convoys—three to six trucks headed in the same direction and stopping together. I didn't want any strings on where I went or what I did.

"One night I was in the restaurant at the Texaco truck stop at Exit 161 off I-5 in Oregon when I noticed a woman in her late thirties or early forties. We talked, I bought her dinner, and she got into my truck. Her name was Nancy Flowers, divorced, living alone between Gold Hill and Rogue River. We kissed and my hands found her breasts, and we were just about down to the bare skin when she said no at the last minute. With Nancy no meant no. I still wasn't into taking women against their will, although I did it every night in my fantasies. We just steamed up the windows for a while. I got her number and told her I'd call.

"On my way back from California, I phoned her from Gold Hill and she picked me up and took me to her place. She had an octagon-style house in the woods. After we had sex she woke me at 7:00 A.M. so that I could make my delivery in Seattle on time. From then on I slept with her whenever I was in the neighborhood. She was forty-four, and I was thirty-three. I never told her I was married, but I think she kind of knew."

10 | Les in the Driver's Seat

For a few months Keith's extracurricular activities were inhibited by the presence of an unwanted codriver who insisted that driving truck couldn't be too complicated if Keith could do it. "Dad always tried to integrate himself into my jobs, but I never expected to see him in my truck. Believe me, it wasn't my idea. He went out and got himself a commercial license, which meant he could drive anything up to eighteen-wheelers. Then he went to my boss and said he wanted to start a business hauling produce, but first he had to learn to drive truck, and what better way than with his own son?

"I was leaving Seattle when I was ordered to return to the main office and pick up a loaded trailer going south. The boss said, 'You'll have a helper. His name is Les Jesperson.' Was I pissed!"

In an odd reversal of their relationship, father and son drove together for two months, Keith as teacher and Les as student. Their situation provided frequent opportunities for the son to feel superior, and Keith took full advantage. "The first time Dad drove, he was grinding the gears something awful. I tried explaining to him, 'Dad, the rpms of the motor has to match the rpms of the gearbox. If one's running faster than the other, it's not gonna work right.'

" 'No, no,' he says, 'it's not my fault—it's this goddamn

truck.' Etcetera, etcetera. Just like Dad—he was never wrong.

"I told him what to do over and over, and he still didn't get it. I said, '*Goddamn it, Dad,* you're grinding my gears to pieces!' "

"He tried again, and it's clank clank, clunk clunk, grind and grind. You could smell the smoking plates. I was thinking how glad I was that I didn't own this truck. It was a dark umber-and-bronze 1984 Freightliner conventional, with a four-hundred horsepower Cummins motor and a thirteen-speed gearbox—too nice a truck to be headed for the junkyard.

"Dad kept making things worse with every shift. I finally blew up and said, 'Pull this truck over right now!'

"He said, 'You're mad, aren'tcha?'

"I said, 'Dad, I'm *way* beyond mad. Now pull over and get out!'

"It's nighttime, we walk to the back of the truck, and he says, 'Are you pissed, Keith?' He's ready for me to jump down his throat.

"I said, 'Dad, stand there. Just take a few breaths.' Then I said, 'Are you all nice and rested, now? Relaxed? Comfy? You're just fine?'

" 'Yeah.'

"I said, 'Now Dad, you're gonna get in the truck, climb into the sleeper, and go to sleep.'

" 'You're not mad, Son?'

"I started laughing. I couldn't help myself. He says, 'What's funny?'

"I says, 'Think about it, Dad. Remember when you used to say, How many times do I have to tell you something, Keith?—and now I'm telling you the same damn thing.'

"He got into the sleeper, and every once in a while I'd hear grumbling. I said, 'Don't get too cozy back there, Dad. We'll try again in a while. If you keep grinding those gears, I'll dump you at the next truck stop. It's a long walk home.' That felt good. He shut up after that."

• • •

The next day the wrestling bears pulled into loading docks in Watsonville, California, and Keith instructed his father to back the big semi into Door 6. "I went inside and took a leak, and when I came out, the guys on the docks were laughing their asses off. Dad was all cockeyed with the truck. One of the lumpers asked me, 'Where'd that dude learn to drive?'

"I got in the cab. Dad's face was beet red, and he was cussing a blue streak. I said, 'Move over!' I said, 'You're making it more complicated than it is.' I spent a half hour showing him how to park the rig in the dock. He still didn't get it. He said, 'Son, I'll never be able to drive a truck like you. You act like this is a sports car!'

"I said, 'Dad, it *is* a sports car—a seventy-two-foot sports car. You can't let it drive you. You gotta be boss.'

"He finally gave up. Last thing he said was, 'That goddamn transmission must have a hundred gears, and I bet I stripped every one of 'em.'

"I was so happy to get rid of him. Driving with him was like driving with women. They enjoy the scenery and I do the work. Now I was free to do as I pleased."

11 | First Hookers

Solo again, Keith was driving on Highway 97 near Gold-endale, Washington, when the headlights on his Peterbilt silhouetted a female walking her bicycle in the rain. "She was shivering, and I stopped to give her a lift. I gave her my coat to get warm. I noticed that she was Indian, maybe fifteen years old, but stacked. Something about Indian girls always turned me on—maybe it went back to the ones I knew in Chilliwack. My rape fantasies were running wild even before I stowed her bike in the load of scrap steel.

"I decided to take this girl on the spot. My heart was pounding in my shirt as I parked at a wide spot on top of Maryhill. She must have read my mind. The second I reached for her, she opened the door to get out. I grabbed at my coat and off came her sweater, exposing her bra. She ran like an antelope. I had the sickening feeling that the situation was getting out of hand and I was headed for deep shit.

"After she ran about fifty feet, she turned around and yelled for her bike and sweater. I said, 'Come back! I was just trying to get my coat.' By this time I was really scared. I handed over her sweater, reached into the load and pulled out her bike. Then I took off at top speed.

"I kept thinking about all the ways I could be caught. The name on the truck. A load that could be traced. My log. There weren't many drivers as big as me. I'd tried to take a minor against her will, and that was a penitentiary offense. I figured she'd go home and tell her sob story to Daddy and I'd be on my way to prison.

"I didn't sleep for a week. I kept listening for a knock. Every birdcall sounded like a siren. When I was on the road, I looked in my rearview mirrors more than my windshield. Whenever I spotted a police car in a truck stop or a rest stop, I rushed off to the next one.

"But nothing ever came of it. Everybody knows that most rape victims don't go to the cops. I kept reminding myself what a close call I'd had. I swore I'd *never* try anything like that again. I would still chase women, but on their terms only. If they wanted sex, okay. If they didn't, bye-bye. The Maryhill moment haunted me. I knew that from now on I had to control my fantasies. If I wanted sex, I had to get it from Rose. Or masturbate. There was no other choice."

Within a few months of the near miss, Keith had to conclude that he would never be able to satisfy his sexual needs at home. For a while he vented his frustration on familiar targets. "I hit a cat with a rock while my son Jason was with me. He began to cry as I kept stoning the cat. I threw the carcass in a ditch down the roadway. When I was by myself, I caught a neighbor's dog and killed it in steps, holding its head underwater and then letting it breathe, then up and down till it drowned. It was an early version of the death game that I played later. The technique made it last longer and gave me a hard-on.

"I couldn't hide my attitude about animals from my family. My children knew that their father would kill a cat or dog if he caught it. I would corner cats and agitate them with a pole till they struck back, and then I'd wring their necks. In winter I'd douse them in cold water and put them out in zero weather. I'd splash them with gasoline and light 'em up. I beat my own kids' dog to death. He had bad hemorrhoids and I had no patience with problems like that. I took him out back and smashed his head. My kids cried for days. Nothing I did would console them."

With the incident at Maryhill still fresh in his memory, Keith decided to give professionals a try. "My first real hooker experience came when I drove into the Oceanside rest area on I-5 between San Diego and Los Angeles. Linda was petite, had little titties, and wore a long peasant dress and glasses. She looked more like somebody's kid sister than a truckers' whore. She was very energetic and I spent three hours getting my twenty bucks' worth.

"She liked my loving so much that she gave me her home phone number, and I called her whenever I was near. Great sex, and free! I fantasized about her and requested loads to San Diego just to see her. Every encounter was the same as the first. We kissed like lovers, and for an hour or two we *were* lovers.

"On a trip to Denver I sat three days waiting to get loaded. I took a waitress named Dee Dee into my truck and screwed her. Turned out she was a kiss-and-tell gal. Pretty soon the other girls were sniffing around to see if I was as good as she said. I decided I didn't need the publicity and dumped Dee Dee for good.

"By now I was getting pretty good at sex, and one of the reasons was because I could never arouse my wife. That made me work extra hard on the others. I treated every screw the same. First, I would hold them to feel the warmth of their skin against mine. Then I would use foreplay to get to know them better. To me, the ejaculation part was almost an afterthought. Hookers knew they could get more out of me than just sex.

"A whore named Sharon told me to slow down and fuck her till she came. I did what she asked. We went at it a second and a third time before she let me go. She put out the word that I was big and patient, and other hookers wanted to do me for free. It reached the point where I was almost annoyed if they asked for money.

"On my truck routes I had whores from eighteen to fifty-five. When I got home I'd try to have sex with Rose, but it was never anything to scream about. By this stage of our marriage, once a week was too often for her. I needed it every day, two or three times if I could get it. I was masturbating more than ever."

12 | Terminal Warfare

Now and then Keith took another wild stab at being a family man. In the summer of 1987 he drove his six-year-old son to southern California on a produce run. "Jason had a blast. A couple of weeks later Rose asked to ride. We drove to Phoenix with a load of Washington apples and picked up tomatoes in Nogales, Arizona. She thought it would be a holiday, but she found out that trucking was hard work. When she wasn't sleeping, she was griping. At the end of a week she said she would never ride in a truck again. That suited me fine."

Family members heard a different version of Rose's disenchantment. One said, "They got to Phoenix, and Keith took her out to dinner. On the way back to their hotel they walked past a black limousine with two guys who looked like pimps. Keith shoved her toward them. He said, 'Here! You can have my wife.' Then he laughed.

"When they got back home, he went out to the irrigation canal and strangled a cat. He dropped the carcass on the ground to show his kids. At the time they were six, five and two. Rose told me he had a glazed look in his eyes. He explained that the cat didn't get out of his way. It must've fought for its life because he had deep scratches up and down his arms. Rose got angry and brought the kids in the house. That's when the rest of us began to wonder about his sanity. Rose had wondered for years."

Keith remembered the Arizona trip as the start of terminal warfare with his unhappy wife. They'd been married for twelve years and agreed on few subjects other than the well-being of their children. "When I felt like hitting Rose, I took long walks or bike rides to cool down. It reached the point where I wasn't home even when I was home—my head was at some truck stop or in my sleeper. I found excuses to get away, killed the odd animal, set a few fires, shoplifted. I got in fights with strangers for the first time in my life.

"On the road I pushed myself even harder. I guess I was running from something, but I didn't know what. I chased NoDoz with coffee and Jolt and Dr. Pepper. I tore up my stomach with chocolate-covered coffee beans. Sometimes I slapped my face to stay awake. I did crazy things like driving from Washington to Florida without sleeping. I'd switch on cruise control and start to nod over the steering wheel or hear an air horn and discover I was crossing the center line.

"I had the shortest fuse on the highway. I caused accidents and wrecked four or five trucks, including one of my own. I lost a couple of jobs that way. Once I was driving at sixty miles an hour near Four Corners, California, when a trucker tried to ease past me in the face of oncoming traffic. When he got alongside, he yelled on his radio for me to let him in—quick.

"I told him to back off. 'Try again when you got enough speed!'

"He screamed like a maniac—'You're supposed to yield! It's the unwritten law of truckers,' blah blah blah. I lost my temper and ran him off the road. Never heard a word about it.

"I was driving south on Highway 97 in Oregon when an interstate trucker tried to pass me the same way. When he pulled alongside, he turned his signal on to claim the right-of-way. I didn't yield, and he gets on the CB and calls me crazy. I ran him onto the shoulder. I did that to a couple of other drivers, too. I'd become a one-man wrecking crew. There was an unwritten code among truckers, and it saved my ass. Nobody ever ratted me out."

13 | Enter Peggy

Still in his road-warrior mood, Keith added another set of grievances to his growing list of complaints against females. It was springtime, 1988, a year and a half before he would begin his murder spree with Taunja Bennett. "At a truck stop south of Weed, California, I met a skinny little brown-haired waitress named Peggy Jones. I flirted with her for a while and got her phone number. Then I had to leave for my run north.

"A few weeks later I stopped in Weed for a ten-hour layover and called Peggy's number in Dunsmuir. I dropped my trailer and ran bobtail to her place to pick her up. All I was looking for was a quick lay on the way back to Seattle. We went to a tavern in Weed and had a few drinks and played pool. Later we got into the back of my truck and had sex. Then I drove her to the truck stop and had sex again and drove her home and had sex one more time. Peggy was the only woman I ever met who could keep up with me and still want more. She asked, 'Will I ever see you again?' I said, 'In a few days,' and I kept my word.

"I told her I wasn't married. She said she was divorcing her husband and he had custody of their two kids. Since Dunsmuir and Weed were right in the middle of my north-south runs, I started spending my sleeping time with her. Pretty soon I was falling in lust with her and then in love. I was spending more time with her than with my wife and kids.

"After I took her on a couple of trips to Los Angeles, we began to think of ourselves as a couple. But what would I do about my family? Peggy forced the issue. She called information in Yakima and Selah and talked to several Jespersons, and they all told her that I was married. I explained that I was getting a divorce and considered myself single. She said she was in love with me and asked if I was in love with her—if I wasn't, I wasn't going to get laid that night. So I told her I loved her, too.

"Peggy told me to divorce Rose and get out from under Dad's thumb. She said she wanted to move to Yakima to make sure I went ahead with my divorce. At the moment I would agree with anything she asked to get into her panties.

"I knew I was gambling with my family's future, but I brought her back to Yakima and dropped her off by the Twin Bridges Tavern. I gave her money to look for a job and then drove home. I kept playing over in my mind what Peggy wanted. But what did *I* want? Same as always—I wanted my kids. I wondered if I'd ever been in love with Rose, or did I just use her to get away from Dad?

"I played with my kids that night and put them to bed. I laid next to Rose and said, 'I'm not happy with the way our lives are going. I want some major changes.' She asked what kind. I said, 'I want a divorce. I'm tired of coming home to problems.'

"She rolled on her side and went to sleep. I laid there thinking of what I'd just put on the table. Why didn't she argue? Why didn't she say that she loved me? She just accepted the idea of divorce and nodded off!

"In the morning I had more fun with the kids. Rose said nothing, just played her part as mom before I left on a run to Los Angeles. When I came back four days later, I found an empty house and a Dear John letter—she'd taken the kids to Spokane to live with her mother. She demanded everything except my golf clubs, bowling ball, bicycle and clothes. I read her letter and cried.

"I went over to Peggy's little apartment and told her to sit tight. Then I drove two hundred miles to Spokane. When I pulled into Rose's mother's driveway, my three kids met me with tears in their eyes. I wondered, *Is this what I really want? A separation might do our marriage good, but . . . a divorce?*

"I thought and thought and thought, and then I made my usual mistake—I let my crotch decide. Back in Yakima I had a willing piece of tail to satisfy me day and night, four or five times a day if I wanted. I couldn't walk away from that. I put a higher value on sex than on my family and friends. That's when my life went off the rails.

"When I thought about it, I realized that my troubles began the very first time I cheated on Rose. If I hadn't been seduced by Ginny Smith and learned that some women are better lays than others, I'd have stayed home and lived happily ever after. Instead, I was losing everything.

"I drove my kids to a restaurant and we had a good cry. I promised I would always support them and be a part of their lives. Then I rushed back to Peggy. She moved to White Pass Lodge and took a job as waitress. I moved into her room, and in a few days Dad and his second wife, Betty, showed up to have dinner and be waited on by Peggy. Afterwards they came over to our room to see how we lived. Dad didn't take to Peggy. He said she was 'tougher than banjo strings with turpentine sauce.' He never could handle strong women. Maybe that's why I stayed with Peggy so long, because it pissed him off to see us together. He would say, 'This affair is over, Keith. It's time for you to go back to Rose.' I got up the strength to say no. I was tired of being told what to do."

14 | Worst Mistake

In the summer of 1988 Keith decided to seek domestic counsel from his wise sister Jill. "I felt like she could help me talk it all out and maybe pick up the pieces of my life. Early in the evening I drove my number 45 truck up I-405 toward her place just north of Seattle. Running bobtail is a tough job in any traffic. I should have taken it easy, but my mind was on my problems and I pushed it.

"Traffic was moving along at sixty and sixty-five when suddenly the whole line stopped. I drove into the median to avoid rear-ending the guy in front. My truck flipped end to end and I ended up in a meat wagon. When I healed up, I was fired. I swore to myself I'd never have another accident in a big rig."

On Peggy's days off from waitressing, she began to accompany Keith on short hauls. "She became undependable on her waitressing job because she *loved* being in my truck. The restaurant manager told me to find a new girlfriend. He said he'd seen her flirt with truckers and almost ride off with one. I just passed it off as her usual flirting.

"Peggy and I moved into a one-bedroom mobile home in a trailer park and she went to work as a truck-stop waitress in Union Gap, just south of Yakima. Sex was great, but everything else was bad. Rose and the kids were out of sight and I began to fall behind in my child support. I was on my way to being a deadbeat dad, all because of Peggy. We were getting poorer and poorer and I got pissed off and thought about leaving.

"My father was still sticking his nose into my business. If he would have butted out, I might've gone back to Rose and my kids. But he kept yammering about Peggy and what a terrible thing I was doing and no decent man would leave his own kids and blah blah blah. I sued for divorce just to spite him, just to shut him up.

"I cried when I filed the papers. The divorce was final on our thirteenth anniversary. Rose was a good mother and housekeeper and a fine woman. Maybe marrying her just out of high school was a mistake, but getting involved with Peggy was a worse mistake. And losing my wife and kids was the worst mistake of all."

15 | Rape Impromptu

After Keith and Peggy had been together for a year, he decided that it might improve their finances if she became his permanent driving partner. "That way we could rack up a lot more miles and I'd get a good piece of ass every time we stopped."

Peggy quickly earned a combination truck-auto driving license, but an abrupt change of mood came over Keith before they hit the road together. "Every time I saw Dad, he would drill me about dumping Peggy. Every time I called my kids, they begged me to come back. I felt whipsawed. Sometimes I'd be on the verge of dumping Peggy, but then we'd have some more great sex and I'd change my mind. I didn't realize that I was being pussy-whipped.

"After three months without seeing Rose or the kids, I couldn't take it anymore. I was having nightmares about letting my kids down. I decided to go back. I told Peggy she might as well head for California.

"We had a good-bye drink before I started to move my stuff out. I left our mobile home for a few hours and when I got back, she'd smashed the TV. She was passed out on the bed in her blue jeans and loose top and tennis shoes. It turned me on to see her like that. It made me want to have her one more time. I decided to leave her some sperm as a memento.

"I pulled off her shoes and size-three jeans and gently entered her. After I got off, I laid inside her and waited for my penis to get hard again. I kept screwing her until I got sore on the fourth try.

"When she finally woke up, she couldn't remember taking off her clothes and I didn't tell her what I'd done. She was still groggy. When she passed out again, I laid down with her and kissed her and fondled her breasts for the last time. Then I drove to Dad's house to spend the night.

"The next morning she showed up in her Pinto and asked me if I'd had sex with her last night. I told her yeah, I did. She said, 'And you still want me to leave?' I said, 'Yep.' She said, *You're gonna miss me, you son of a bitch!*'

"For the next two to three weeks I stayed with Rose and the kids even though it meant no sex. I realized how much I'd missed them. I'd been with Rose for fourteen years, and most of that time I was faithful. So we had something together, no matter how bad things got. But the rape of Peggy kept playing in my mind. I missed her hot sexy ways. I tried to do the right thing by Rose and the kids, but . . . I had to go back."

Keith called his trucking boss and got an okay to enlist Peggy Jones as his codriver. It took him a few days to locate her. She'd hitched a ride to Los Angeles with another trucker—"an old guy," as she described him to Keith.

The reconciled lovers became trucking partners. There was trouble from the first trip. "Peggy let her emotions steer her driving. She would drive four to six hours a day and then say she'd had enough, she wasn't in the mood anymore. I had to drive all the mountain miles and snow miles while she played games with other male truckers over the CB radio. She would promise to meet some guy for sex, then wouldn't show up. She thought that was fun. I thought it was childish."

• • •

Christmas was an ordeal. Les and his wife, Betty, a pleasant middle-aged woman from an old Yakima Valley apple-packing family, invited Keith for dinner, but conspicuously omitted Peggy. "When I walked in the door, the first thing I saw was Rose and the kids. The old control artist planned to push us back together. It made my blood boil. At dinner he gave a little lecture about how unnatural it was to live without a wife and family. I told him that I knew somebody who could live without a family just fine—*'Just watch me, Dad!'*

"I left early and broke my children's hearts again. I told Peggy about Dad's meddling. I took her advice and didn't talk to him for six months."

It didn't take long for Keith's trucking boss to decide that Peggy was a liability and order her out of his cab. He sneaked her back into the jade-green Kenworth conventional but regretted his move. "She never developed a sense of direction or any road smarts, and all she thought about was men. On one trip I was so exhausted as we drove out of Yuma, I showed her the route to Bakersfield and slid into the sleeper to take a nap. She yelled at me that she wasn't stupid and she already knew the route. I just tuned her out and fell asleep.

"When I woke up, we were parked in a truck stop on I-40 at Exit 76 in Kingman, Arizona. I put a towel over the steering wheel—that's the trucker's sign that nobody's in the sleeper—and I went into the restaurant. There she sat with a bunch of other drivers, drinking coffee and bullshitting. One guy had his hand on her knee, and I heard him say something about driving with her. They'd met on the CB and she'd followed him here.

"I pulled up a chair and put my arm around her. I looked straight at the guy and said, 'Why are we in Kingman, Peggy?'

"She got all wide-eyed and said, 'Isn't this where we're supposed to be?'

"I asked the other driver, 'Do you *really* want this girl as your codriver?' He nodded yes. I said, 'When you go to sleep and wake up two hundred miles off course, just remember what I'm telling you. We're supposed to be in Seattle by midnight tonight, and instead of being on our way in Bakersfield or Santa Nella, here I am looking at your ugly face in Kingman. You want her? *You can have her!*'

"I got my thermos filled with coffee and headed back to the truck. Peggy was dogging my steps, crying and whining—'I'm sorry, I'm so sorry.' What a sorry bitch! Before we left Kingman she gave me a quickie in the sleeper."

Through 1988 and 1989 the odd couple stayed together, with indifferent commercial success. Keith was drained from sex and overwork. "We made a good team in good weather. In bad weather it was hell on wheels. I had to drive 80 percent of the time. And when she was driving I had to stay awake to make sure she didn't follow some other trucker to Dallas when we were en route to Chicago. On the good side, we had sex two or three times a day in the sleeper. In rest areas we kept that semi rocking, and when we were waiting for loads, sex occupied our time. Sometimes I wished our arrangement would never end. But it did. It ended and started and ended and started more times than I can remember."

The Jesperson-Ellis driving team was laid off in April 1989 and moved in with Peggy's mother in her crazy little haunted house in northeast Portland. While Keith was recovering from an injury to his arm, he drew unemployment and then went from job to job—excavating, plumbing, sewage, construction, heavy labor. "My friends kept telling me to get rid of Peggy. They saw what I couldn't see. It took me a long time to realize that she was dragging me down.

"Our worst times came when I was hurt and she started driving with other guys. One night she called me from California and told me she'd lost her codriver and wanted me to meet her in Tigard, Oregon, just south of Portland. She took four hours longer than normal for the run. When she unloaded she couldn't handle the three-hundred-pound tarps and had to sweet-talk other truckers and lumpers into helping. I could only imagine how she paid them back. When she finally showed up that night, it turned out that the only reason she wanted to see me was because she needed money to finish her run. I went back to our little house with an empty wallet and a hard-on."

16 | Alone and Restless

By 1990 Keith's relationship with Peggy Jones was nearly over. "One night she came home and said she was pregnant and the baby was mine. Then I got a letter from a mutual friend telling me that she cheated on me every time my back was turned. The friend had evidence and phone numbers. When I told Peggy that I didn't want a damn thing to do with the baby unless she proved it was mine with blood tests, she got defensive.

"By then I'd had enough, so I moved in with a great cribbage player from Spokane. He was a retired military man with multiple sclerosis, and he lived his life in a wheelchair. A mutual friend told me that he needed help. Eldon introduced me to tournament cribbage. He had a little block of wood with an arrow to show whose crib it was. You had to shuffle the cards for him and put them in his hand. I'd even pick him up and put him on the toilet. For a while it made me feel good, made me feel I was on earth for a purpose.

"But after a few months I began to feel a little *too* sorry for him. During a crib game one night he began gasping and moaning. It took him an hour to recover. I figured he didn't have long on earth. What good was he to himself or anybody else? I could put a pillow over his face and put him out of his misery.

"I finally decided it was too dangerous. People knew I

was living with him, and the cops would nail me fast. Otherwise, I'd have killed him for sure—a public service. I decided to go back to Peggy."

After more unsettled months Keith's bedmate stopped returning to her mother's little house in Portland and seldom called unless she was out of money. When he dropped into local truck stops, he heard tales about her liaisons, past and current. Fellow drivers tried to set him straight. "Why follow that little piece of ass around?" "That whore takes your money and goes after every guy she sees." "She'll work you for your last dime, man. . . ."

A friend informed Keith that Peggy had consorted with men in Yakima and Spokane while they were living together. Not only had she cheated, but she'd done it openly, brazenly. It was the third time he'd heard the same message.

He still wasn't sure he was hearing the whole truth. Just because he was being true to Peggy didn't mean she was being true to him—that was obvious. But he'd never caught her in the act, so how could he be sure? *I can't confront her while she's on the road*, he told himself, *so why torture myself?*

Temporarily unemployed because of his poor driving record, he spent his days watching TV, visiting bars, playing pool and reading. He'd had a job from the age of twelve, sometimes two or three. Working was as ingrained as breathing. Idleness gave him ideas, and drinking made him nasty and antisocial.

He was feeling restless when Sunday, January 21, 1990, arrived chilly and damp in the Rose City of Portland. Taunja Bennett was saying good-bye to her mother for the last time. Peggy Jones was somewhere in the East, trucking with her new partner. *It was the kind of winter day that always got me down—windy, gray, nothing happening. I was in a bad mood before I even rolled out of bed. . . .*

7

KEITH

HUNTER

JESPERSON 4

1 | The Trap

The morning after I killed Julie Winningham, my eighth victim, I drove to Vancouver, Washington, to get my driver's license renewed. My fortieth birthday was coming up, and I didn't want the license to expire. I called the office and got a load of lumber going to Pennsylvania from Corvallis, Oregon. I loaded at noon, got tarped by one o'clock, and headed east.

On my way I thought about moving Julie's body farther from the road, but I decided it was too much bother. I drove straight through to Baker City, Oregon, and played a little cribbage. I made a few bucks and hit on some of the women. I gave a couple of Julie's old coats to a cute girl from Boise. Not smart.

By Monday, March 13, three days after the killing, I was in Ogden, Utah. Late the next day I reached Pennsylvania, thanks to a couple boxes of NoDoz. I unloaded and picked up some stainless steel for a mine north of Deming, New Mexico.

Every time I crossed a state line or pulled into a rest stop I expected a swarm of cop cars with blue lights to order me out at gunpoint. But now that I'd been on the road for a few days, I began to relax. Maybe they weren't onto me yet. Each mile took me farther from Julie's body.

My little girl Carrie's twelfth birthday was March 17, and I called her from the parking lot at Jimmy Polen's dance club in Little Rock. She thanked me for the hundred dollars I sent her. I told her I loved her and wished her a happy birthday and hung up with both of us crying. That's the way it always was when I called home.

At Texarkana, the Arkansas-Texas border town, I began to feel on edge again. My gut told me that cops were around. I called my dispatch boss in Spokane and told him I was sick but would deliver to the mine in a day or so. When he told me to take my time, I wondered if something was up. That guy *never* told a trucker to take his time. It was always faster, faster, *faster*. I asked if anybody was looking for me and he said no. I had the feeling he was jerking me off.

I met two women in Texarkana, but I couldn't trust myself with them—they could be undercover cops, and I might give something away. I had a crazy idea that I should kill again for more fantasy material.

I met a female trucker named Karen, and we struck up a conversation about both of us wearing leather. I bought her coffee and walked her back to her semi. She reminded me of Peggy and I thought about keeping her, but we ended up saying good night. I laid back in my sleeper and listened to the CB radio—hookers and sluts arranging their dates. I thought about killing. When the urge got too strong, I climbed out and took a walk.

"Hey!" a male voice shouted.

I turned and saw the truck-stop security guy beckoning. I stopped and waited for him to say, "You're under arrest!" But he just turned out to be a lonely old dude who wanted to talk.

I went back to my truck and rehearsed the lies I planned to tell when I was arrested. I took myself back to when I killed Taunja and tried to figure out what made me cross the line into murder. Was it the things I read about in the detective magazines—arson, animal abuse?[6] Did I kill to make up for a wasted life, for my own fuckups? Was it Dad's fault, my brothers', my mother's? It was too easy to blame the rest of the family. Maybe I was just a no-good son of a bitch that got off on killing women. Maybe it was my nature. I decided to stop thinking about it and kill another one before they put me away for good.

The next morning I had breakfast with Karen. She told me she had to visit her family. That saved her life. I found a woman wanting a ride to DeKalb, Texas. We spent the day drinking beer, playing stink-finger and necking. I figured I would kill her on the way to DeKalb, but she backed out of the trip. Two lucky girls.

In Dallas I stopped at the Petro Truck Stop and bought a gold necklace for sixty-five dollars. Maybe it would come in handy. I hung it around my neck even though I didn't wear ornaments.

I drove all night and pulled into a Unocal 76 Truck Stop in El Paso at 6:30 A.M. I stood at the magazine rack reading a detective magazine with the story of Susan Smith in it. She was the woman who drowned her two sons in a lake and blamed it on a black carjacker. I thought about my own kids and felt a little sick. How could a mother be so cruel?

I had some money, but I shoplifted the magazine just to keep in practice. On the way out I tripped the exit sensor. I told them it must be defective and they let me go, but they knew damn well I had something I hadn't paid for.

Walking across the parking lot, I passed a couple of drivers from my trucking company. As soon as they saw me, they turned away. Normally they would want to buddy up and talk my ears off. Something was wrong.

I called my dispatcher and said I needed forty-four dol-

---

[6]The so-called homicidal triad, believed by some behaviorists to be a childhood indicator of future violent criminal behavior, consists of arson, bed-wetting and cruelty to animals.

lars for a permit to get the truck into New Mexico to deliver to the copper mine. I drank some coffee but didn't see any bitches in the restaurant. They were still sleeping off their drugs from the night before.

After I got the money for the permits, I drove on I-10 to the New Mexico port of entry. They looked over my paperwork, and one cop asked my full name. This had *never* happened before. I was sure I was being tracked. I thought about disappearing, walking off in the purple sage like Clint Eastwood. But how long would it take the law to find a guy my size? I had to brazen things out, act normal and hope to slip through the cracks somehow. What other choice did I have?

On two-lane Highway 22 between Deming and the mine, I spotted two white cars on a side road. I checked my mirrors and they didn't follow.

At the mine a crew bent over backwards to unload me and get me on my way. Another first! Their usual attitude is "Fuck you, man—we got other work ahead of you." The desert wind was up and I couldn't fold my tarps in the open. I rolled them on the deck and strapped them down in the unfolded pile.

I called Dispatch and they told me to check in later for another load. As I drove toward town, two police cars pulled in behind. On the outskirts of town they passed me and slowed down. Then they drove out of sight.

At the truck stop in Deming I called my office again, and the dispatcher said he'd have something lined up for me the next day, March 22. He said, "Keith, don't go anywhere!"

That made no sense. They'd had three days to find a load for my truck. There was nothing a truck dispatcher hated more than downtime. So I knew he'd been reached by the cops. I still couldn't run. That would have been like signing a confession.

I dropped off to sleep thinking of *Little Cotto,* my grandpa Bellamy's fishing boat. In my mind I saw myself steering and my son Jason fishing. I don't think we caught anything.

2 | Suits with Guns

After a few hours in my coffin, I decided to wash the old blue Pete while I was waiting to hear from the dispatch office. When I drove up to the truck wash, the "open" light blinked off. A red-and-black Ford Bronco four-by-four was parked to one side, and the driver was looking me over.

The wind was calm, so I folded up my tarps, strapped them down and called the truck stop on the CB radio. "Is the truck wash open?" I asked.

"It's always open," they said. I didn't argue. I figured that the cops didn't want me washing evidence off the truck. Everything was hanging together. I was in a trap, and there was no way out. The whole damn world was onto me—that old feeling again. And there was nothing I could do about it.

Dispatch finally ordered me to pick up at the Las Cruces Fairgrounds. I asked what the load was and was told they didn't know. *Didn't know?* That was crazy. I asked again and they said it was possibly machinery and had to be loaded at noon.

I drove back to Las Cruces and parked at the hilltop truck stop a mile down the frontal roadway, east of the Fairgrounds. That gave me a good view of the pickup site. It looked deserted. What kind of a load could I be picking up? I waited till just before noon and put my rig in gear.

That same red-and-black Bronco pulled up to the front gate just as I arrived. A chunky guy in a black suit got out to meet me. He held his arms out from his sides like Matt Dillon getting ready to draw. He told me my load was at a dumpster next to a Quonset shed in the center of the grounds. He said he didn't have the keys to the front gate and told me to drive through the gate on the side. He said, "Do you think you can get through that opening?"

I took that as a challenge. "Sure," I said.

I backed up and swung wide in an "S" pattern to thread the needle. Once I was inside, I noticed how cramped the space was for a tractor trailer seventy feet long. Did they really expect me to load there? I'd been in tough spots before—if I could drive into an area, I could drive out. I was a super trucker. I consistently outperformed everyone else.

I got out and followed the guy toward the Quonset. He led me around to the rear. I said, "Where's the load?"

Two suits stepped out from the wall and aimed guns at me. One said, "Face the wall! Spread 'em!" They patted me down for weapons.

I tried to act surprised and bluff it out. "Are you serious?" I said. "What's this all about?"

"You're wanted for questioning in an ongoing investigation," they said. I'm thinking, *What kind of investigation? Arson? Killing?*

They put me in a New Mexico county sheriff's car. I was relieved. I hadn't killed anybody in New Mexico. I'd set a few fires, yes, but that was chippy stuff.

They waited till we were almost to the sheriff's office in Las Cruces before one of them said, "We're investigating the death of your fiancée, Julie Winningham."

I said, "Oh, really?" I tried to look shocked that she was dead.

"Yeah," he said. "They found her body on March eleven. A Sunday."

So she'd been found the day after I killed her. I realized

that I should have acted on my gut feeling and dragged her body further away.

One of the detectives commented that I didn't seem surprised. I said, "Hey, nothing surprises me about Julie. She was into drugs and everything."

"How come you didn't ask how she died?"

"Okay. How'd she die?"

"Strangulation."

"Oh," I said. "That's interesting."

3 | Accused

When we reached the sheriff's office in downtown Las Cruces, the two suits told me they were from Clark County, Washington. That was where I killed Julie. The big honcho was Detective Rick Buckner. The name rang a bell.

He told me I was a suspect in an ongoing investigation and asked for a complete confession. I told him that I had nothing to confess. I lied like I always lie when I'm in trouble. I learned that as a kid, and I was good at it. They might have a lot of people from Clark County claiming they'd seen me with Julie, but they needed my confession. If they didn't show me proof of my guilt, I didn't intend to give up anything.

Buckner asked if I'd been arrested before. I thought, *Surely he knows about Corning and Shasta? And my shoplifting back home in Selah?* So I told him about the woman named Jean who nursed her baby in front of me and how all the charges were dropped. My honesty seemed to score some points. Then, very abruptly, he asked when I'd last seen Julie.

I told him how we met the first time and how we met up again on the fifth of March and had an argument over her two DWIs before she got out of the truck and left. I said I hadn't seen or heard from her since then.

• • •

For about five hours the two detectives told me over and over that I killed her. They let me use the bathroom to wash the dirt from my hands and arms. When I was finished, they told me that Julie's body had been dirty too and asked where the dirt on my arms came from. I told them the truth—it was from folding tarps that morning. They said they were sure I'd rolled her body in those same tarps and carried her down the hill off Highway 14. I told them they were wrong. I kept thinking, *When do I get arrested? When do I hear my Miranda rights?* The longer they dicked around with me, the more I realized that they were still short on evidence.

They finally showed their hand and promised to turn me loose if I passed a lie-detector test. When I said okay, they dropped that bluff and didn't mention it again.

They had me photoed and fingerprinted and took me to a doctor's office for blood and hair samples. As I watched the tube turn red, I realized that DNA evidence would nail my ass sooner or later. I'd left too much of Keith behind. All I could do was to try to stay free till the last possible hour.

They escorted me back to my truck, and Buckner invited me to dinner. He said, "We screwed up your day, and we'd like to make it up to you."

I said, "No, thanks. I got my Slim Fast in the cab."

He says, "You eat that stuff?"

I was thinking, *I'd rather eat Slim Fast by myself than a New York cut steak with a guy that's trying to get me executed.* I said, "Yeah. I eat it all the time. I'm on a diet. I like all the flavors. Especially the orange pineapple. The chocolate malt's pretty good, too. And the French vanilla."

He gave me a funny look and said, "Come on, Keith. Lighten up. Clark County can spare you a steak."

For Chrisakes, just let me out of here! I said, "I'm sorry, but I have to decline your offer."

• • •

At the Fairgrounds Buckner said, "One more time, Keith. Tell us why you killed her."

I said, "I didn't kill anybody. You're wrong. Tell you what—after you let me go, I'll keep in touch and help you find out who did it. I loved Julie. I was gonna marry her. Why would I kill somebody I was gonna marry?"

"You tell us."

"All her friends were dopeheads. Probably one of them did it. These drug deals go wrong all the time."

When we reached my truck they grabbed my tarps as evidence. It took the two of them to pick up each tarp. They confiscated my logbooks.

I climbed in the cab, and Buckner reached through the window and handed me a copy of the affidavit he'd filed for the search warrant. "I'll give you one last chance, Keith," he said. "Why'd you kill her?"

I said, "I didn't kill anybody," and started the motor. Fuck him. I just wanted to haul ass. I figured I had two or three more days of freedom, and I had to make some final plans.

4 | Suicide by Sudafed

I drove to a truck stop in Las Cruces and read the affidavit over coffee. What a shocker! Every one of those crackheads in Clark County had fingered me to take the heat off themselves. I saw my life pass in front of me—my children, my family. I thought of how they would suffer when I was arrested. Dad would be pissed. My kids would be ashamed.

I considered running for British Columbia. I was still a Canadian citizen, and Canada didn't have the death penalty. But I knew I couldn't trust my dispatchers to find me a load that would take me that far north. They were working with the cops.

I thought about taking the Greyhound, but that would give the cops three or four days to intercept the bus and grab the only guy that was six-foot-six.

I looked through the window and saw a uniform in a sheriff's car monitoring the truck stop. I knew why he was there. I had the same feeling as when I murdered Taunja Bennett. I was marked as a murderer.

I went into the shop and looked for a quick poison. They had some strong stuff for flushing radiators, but I wanted to die, not just burn out my throat. I got a package of twelve-hour Contac and sixteen Extra Strength Tylenols. I already had Sudafed and a bottle of Anacin in the truck—maybe forty pills altogether. I bought a bottle of mineral water to wash them down.

As I walked back in my truck, I noticed that the deputy was still there. I was afraid he'd revive me and pump my stomach. I had to do this right, and not act suspicious.

I crawled into the sleeper, pulled off my boots and closed the curtain. I started to write a suicide note but changed my mind. What would I say? That I was a poor misunderstood kid who never had a chance? *At forty?* I thought, *Who gives a shit anyway?*

I shook the pills on the bed and stared at them for a long time. I thought of the good times I'd had in my life. But the bad stuff kept getting in the way.

I knew I had to swallow the pills fast or I might chicken out and end up dying by electrocution or hanging or rotting away in a prison cell for the rest of my life. I gulped the pills and laid back on my pillow. After a few minutes my head began to swell and my eyes felt like they were popping out of my skull. Then I dropped off.

When I woke up it was still nighttime. I pulled on one boot and opened the window. I stuck my hand out and felt a cool rain. If I could feel rain, I wasn't dead.

I made it across the parking lot and stumbled into the men's room. I looked like something that crawled out of a septic tank. After I took a leak, I went back to the truck. As I started to climb in, a fist reached through the sleeper curtain and punched me in the face!

I'd gotten into the wrong truck. It was a Prime Trucking semi, parked for the night. A shaggy-looking driver dragged me toward the office by the arm.

I nearly fell on my face when we got inside. I couldn't think straight. A couple of deputies came and asked me to identify myself. I wasn't even sure of my name. After a while I explained that I took a couple of sleeping pills and that the next thing I remembered I was getting punched. In my confusion I'd climbed into the wrong truck.

The deputy asked to see my logbook. I told him that I'd spent six hours talking to detectives on a bum rap and they'd taken all my stuff. I said I was fed up with answering questions.

The Prime driver was a good guy and declined to press charges. The deputy took my keys and told me to sober up. He said I could collect them in the morning at the truck-stop security office. The subject of suicide never came up.

It must've been 3:00 or 4:00 A.M. when I swallowed the rest of my pills and passed out again. This time I slept till noon. The parking lot was nearly empty. The Prime driver had gone. There was a smelly whitish mess on my comforter and I realized that I must've been upchucking the whole night. My dad was right. I couldn't do anything right.

After a few cups of coffee I checked in with my boss. He said the cops had released their hold on me. I reamed him good for setting me up at the Fairgrounds. I told him the cops had taken the tarps and it was his own fault—don't bother billing me for the loss. He gave me a half-ass apology and told me to head for Phoenix for another load.

As I drove west, I thought how hard it is to kill a human being. I snapped that Shasta woman's neck three times and she was still alive to lie about me. I had to use all my muscle to finish off some of the others. Now I couldn't even kill myself.

I swore I wouldn't botch it again. What went wrong? My stomach must've got too much too soon and threw it all up. *Tonight I'll cut back a little on the dose. Just enough to go bye-bye.*

At the last truck stop in New Mexico, I ordered a steak and asked my waitress if she liked necklaces. She showed me a cheap little thing around her neck. I gave her my new sixty-five-dollar gold necklace as a tip.

She said, "Why are you doing this? You don't even know me."

I said, "Where I'm going I won't need this."

The other waitresses clustered around. I said, "I'm on my way to jail. I'm facing eight life sentences. Or maybe the gas chamber." When I drove away, they were watching my truck.

At a truck stop at Exit 378 in Arizona I bought three bottles of nonprescription sleeping pills. I climbed into my coffin and swallowed them all. I was upset and forgot my own advice not to take too many or I'd throw them up.

The next morning I woke up groggy and angry at myself for still being alive. I didn't find out till later that you need prescription stuff like Seconal and Amytal to do the job. I always hated drugs. I didn't know the subject.

In the distance I saw Chiricahua Peak, ten thousand feet high. I could climb up to the snow line and let hypothermia do the rest. Death by freezing was like going to sleep.

But first I wrote a letter to my brother:

> *3-24-95*
>   *Hi Brad—*
>   *Seems like my luck has run out. I will never be able to enjoy life on the outside again. I got into a bad situation and got caught up with emotion. I killed a woman in my truck during an argument. With all the evidence against me, it looks like I truly am a black sheep. The court will appoint me a lawyer and there will be a trial. I am sure they will kill me for this. I am sorry that I turned out this way. I have been a killer for 5 yrs. And have killed 8 people. Assaulted more. I guess I haven't learned anything.*
>   *Dad always worried about me. Because of what I have gone through in the divorce finances, etc. I have been taking it out on different people.*

> *We pay so much of child support. As I saw it I was*
> *hoping they would catch me. I took 48 sleeping*
> *pills last night and I woke up well rested. The*
> *night before I took two bottles of pills to no avail.*
> *They will arrest me today. Keith*

I walked up to a mailbox at the next truck stop and stopped
dead in my tracks. I felt the hair on the back of my neck
stand up. If I mailed that letter there would be no turning
back. My gut told me to rip it up.

I dropped the letter in the slot.

5 | Horse and Rider

After I mailed my letter, I called my voice mail and told my boss that I didn't trust him anymore and I wouldn't be driving to Phoenix. The way my voice sounded, he probably thought I'd lost it. I was sure on the verge.

I looked at the map and found a side road toward the Chiricahua National Monument. I parked in the foothills and set my keys on top of the front tire to see if anybody moved it while I was gone. These are the crazy things you do when you're not thinking straight. I never intended to come back, so what difference did it make?

I hiked up a faint trail and kept looking around for cops. Nothing moved, not even a roadrunner or a jackrabbit. It didn't take me long to make the climb, but it turned out to be a false summit. I had to double back down to a creek and climb up the other side. I finally reached the snow line about 3:00 P.M. I sat on a rock, looked down the trail and saw something move.

It was headed in my direction. At first it was just a speck. Then it turned into a horse and rider.

There was no doubt in my mind that the guy was following me. He pulled up for a few seconds, then nudged his horse into the brush. I was sure he was the local law.

But after a few minutes I realized that he was working some stray cows. I figured it would be just my luck to go to sleep for the last time and wake up in front of a campfire that this cowpoke had built to thaw me out. I was beginning to wonder if God wanted me to die. I thought about Selah and wondered if I would ever see it again. In a month or so the trees would start to bloom—miles of red and golden Delicious apples, Fuji, Braeburn, Bosc pears, Tilton apricots, bing cherries. Selah farmers said if you dropped a peach pit, you better stand back.

A few more breaths of cool mountain air cleared my head. I decided to act like a man for a change. Let the police and the state kill me if they wanted to. They could only do it once.

I jogged back to my truck, drove to Exit 378 and placed a collect call to Detective Rick Buckner in Vancouver, Washington. I halfway hoped he would refuse to accept the charges—that would be another friendly sign from God. But he answered right away and told me he'd call me right back. He wanted to get to a phone with a tape recorder.

When we spoke, I told him I was ready to confess killing Julie Winningham. I described it as a "passion killing" after an argument in my truck. I left out that I raped her, and I didn't mention my other victims. One murder sentence would be bad enough.

He told me to wait in the restaurant till he could find somebody to pick me up. I didn't want to make a scene in front of a dozen customers, so I wrote my name on a piece of paper. When the Arizona deputies arrived, I handed them the paper. They handcuffed me in front—very courteous—and drove me to the sheriff's office at Willcox. On the way they asked if I'd ever tried suicide.

"Sure," I said. "Three or four times in the last two days. But I'm over that now. That's why I'm here instead of the morgue."

They put me on suicide watch.

The next morning I was shuttled with other debris to the county jail in Bisbee. I wondered if it had been a mistake to turn myself in. I was chained at my ankles, hobbled like a horse, shuffling along in little mini-steps. The waist belts that held my arms to my side were cinched so tight that they cut my skin, and the ankle chains dug into my ankles. I was issued a bedroll and led to a cell.

Suicide watch meant that the light would stay on all night. The shouting and screaming never stopped. Most of the county inmates were Hispanics. We had no TV or radio, just a few ratty paperback books to pass the time. I tried to read, but I couldn't concentrate.

I thought a lot about driving truck and how I'd messed up my life. I worried about not being able to see my children. Without me sending child support, how would Rose and the kids make it? I got mad and punched the wall. With no one to talk to or hear the other side of the argument, I ganged up on myself. It made me wish I'd done a better job with the pills.

When the county shrink asked how I was doing, I lied and told him I was fine. So they moved me to a pod with other jailbirds. I knew enough to keep my mouth shut in jail. But at my extradition hearing in downtown Bisbee, some of the inmates overheard the charges: rape, kidnapping, murder. I wondered where they came up with kidnapping and rape. I certainly hadn't confessed to anything like that. I was getting a look at the unfairness of the justice system.

On the way back to jail, the other inmates cut me dead. When I asked what was going on, they told me they didn't talk to rapers. The kidnapping charge didn't bother them. Murder didn't bother them. But they didn't approve of rape.

I was moved to a one-man cell. Every time I was let out, I heard the yells of "rape-o" and "freak." But I thought we were all innocent till proven guilty! Why were these guys against me? It wasn't fair.

My size intimidated the guards, and they chained me up whenever I was moved. I explained that I wasn't going to harm anyone, but they'd heard that story before. It didn't matter how nice and polite I acted, I was assumed to be a cold-blooded killer who would murder anyone he could get his hands on. This took some time to get used to. But after I became accustomed to my reputation in jail, I learned to live with it. I put out word that I'd beaten a man to death. After that I got respect.

I decided to use my jail time to better myself. I watched my food intake and began to exercise again. If anybody made a move on me, I would be ready.

6 | Return

Three days went by before Rick Buckner and another detective arrived to take me back to Washington. At first Buckner treated me like a decent guy for turning myself in. He went to great lengths to tell me that the justice system wasn't as harsh as I thought, that I might be able to serve my time and still have a bit of life outside of prison after twenty or thirty years.

My mind was on another tangent. I thought about those Happy Face letters and my letter to Brad. If I could just get him to burn it, the cops wouldn't have anything on me except Julie, and no way that was first-degree murder. I would be spared a lengthy prison sentence. I could fish with my kids someday or take them for hikes. But if the cops saw my letter, I might never get out.

I barely listened as Buckner changed his tone and talked about being my enforcer. He tried to get me to admit to other crimes, but I didn't bite. His style was to talk down to me, to patronize me with goo-goo talk like I was his little son. He told me about the badasses he'd had in the same handcuffs I was wearing, like I should be honored.

"Westley Allan Dodd once wore those cuffs," he said.[7] When he mentioned being Dodd's detective, I remembered

---

[7] Hanged after pleading guilty to the 1989 murders of three young boys.

being in Portland at the time Dodd was caught. I thought, *If you knew what I've done, man, you'd faint.* But I kept quiet. My court-appointed attorney in Arizona had told me to shut up till I had a chance to confer with a lawyer up in Clark County, Washington.

The two detectives drove me to the Tucson airport in a Cadillac. For some reason airport security ordered them to remove my cuffs before we boarded the plane. We had a two-hour layover in Phoenix before we were scheduled to catch a nonstop ride to Portland. I sat in the empty plane under airport security guard while Buckner and the other detective got out and stretched their legs. I thought about making a move but gave it up fast. I just wanted to go back home and get it over with. I was resigned to the idea that I was going to prison no matter what. So why make a fuss?

On the Phoenix-Portland leg Buckner didn't bother to cuff me. He acted friendly and told me that I might get off with five to ten years because of the nature of the offense. It looked like he believed my lie that the killing resulted from an argument. That would make it manslaughter or second-degree murder. Maybe a five-to-ten-year sentence—out in three or four years with good behavior.

I couldn't stop thinking about my letter to Brad. It wasn't bad enough that I'd admitted to being a serial killer, but now the forensic guys could compare the handwriting to the Happy Face letters and verify my confession. I decided to call him the first chance I got. Brad and I had our problems while we were growing up, but I knew I could trust him. After Dad he was the smartest of all the Jespersons. He once lent me fifty thousand dollars on a truck-leasing deal that didn't work out. When we were little, he helped the other kids to tease me, but he grew up to be an okay guy.

• • •

At Portland International Airport I was surprised that no film crews met us. I thought there might be coverage because of the notoriety. But to the press I wasn't a big-time story. Just another sleazebag sex-murderer.

I absorbed every detail of the car ride across the Columbia River to Vancouver and the Clark County jail. As we drove up the interstate, I missed being in my own semi, maybe my purple Pete or that umber-and-bronze Freightliner that Dad and I drove. I was just a passenger now and someone else was in control. I never liked that. It gave me an uncomfortable feeling, like the time I got a ride with a drunk and he played chicken with the telephone poles and I closed my eyes so I wouldn't see the pole that would finally kill us. Sitting in the Clark County police car, I closed my eyes again, but even with my eyes closed I could feel all the familiar bumps and potholes that I knew so well from driving truck. It made me want to grab the wheel.

As we passed other drivers, they stared as though to say, "There goes a no-good murdering son of a bitch." I tried to look the other way so they couldn't see my face. I felt they knew all about me.

At the Clark County jail they put me in the rape pod, C-1. I heard that the newspapers already had convicted me, but— of what? I tried to remember how Washington executed killers. Electric chair? Gas chamber? They hanged Westley Dodd. I thought, *My God, can they hang a guy six-foot-six?*

They finally let me call Brad. I told him to be sure to destroy my letter. His response was so shocking that I thought I'd heard wrong. He repeated that Dad made him turn the letter over to the Selah police.

I was stunned. I guessed it was more important to suck up to his cop pals than it was to save his brother's life. He said Dad's reasoning was that he could go to jail for withholding evidence. I told him it wouldn't be evidence if he destroyed it. I was his big brother, slept in the same room with him. He should have done what I said. I wonder if he has any regrets over that.

Back in my cell I was pissed at myself for getting into this situation. My fifteen-year-old son Jason and fourteen-year-old daughter Melissa visited me through glass, and it only made things worse. The phone connection was bad and the guards rushed me away before we really started talking.

I cried as they led me off. I felt sorry that my kids had to see me this way. I couldn't even tell them I loved them. I had a feeling I wouldn't see them again.

8

JUSTICE

1 | Father vs. Son

From his first days behind bars in Clark County, Washington, where he was charged with the first-degree murder of his girlfriend Julie Winningham, Keith Hunter Jesperson seemed intent on a personal crusade to embarrass the justice system. Thrust onto a public stage for the first time in his life, he began strutting in the limelight like the villain in a silent movie.

To reporters he issued a pious statement that he had no interest in saving his own skin but was determined to free the two innocent Oregonians who were now in their fifth year of imprisonment for the murder of Taunja Bennett. "That takes priority over everything else," he proclaimed. "Those people have suffered long enough." He also expressed annoyance that no one in the justice system had taken his earlier graffiti and Happy Face letters seriously.

Journalists and behaviorists jumped in to explain why he seemed so eager to be in the public eye, but no two seemed to agree. His sister Jill thought there was a simple answer: "Keith is just trying to get attention. He never got a whole lot when he was growing up."

Others suspected a darker motivation. By trying to prove himself superior to authority figures, Keith seemed to be repeating his lifelong pattern with his father. It seemed to be an echo of events like the mutual trucking adventure: the experienced, skilled son versus the neophyte dad.

Leslie Samuel Jesperson, burdened in his advancing years by his son's claims of child abuse, didn't see the situation quite the same way. From his first stunned awareness that Keith was a confessed killer, the alpha-male groped for an explanation. "The morning I found out, I couldn't think straight. I'd walked into my son Brad's office to say good morning and talk business. He looked awful—eyes red, downcast. The last time he looked that bad was in 1985, when I had to tell him we'd lost his mother. He handed me a sheet of paper. 'Here, Dad,' he said. 'Read this.'

"He sat behind his desk with his face in his hands. When I read Keith's letter, I understood why. Brad and his brother shared the same bedroom for sixteen years. I had to read the letter twice to absorb it. When I realized that Keith had confessed to serial murder, the walls closed in. I cried and shook all over. In my mind I saw my little curly-haired son coming home from Sunday school in Chilliwack, dressed in the short pants and shirt his mother made for him.

"Of course I told Brad he had to give the letter to the police or he might go to jail himself. I was so upset I had to go to the doctor. I couldn't stop shaking, couldn't stand up or support my own weight. Doc gave me a shot and diagnosed a nervous breakdown."

2 | Streak of Lunacy

On a menu of tranquilizers and antidepressants, Les recovered in a few weeks and began an intense study program in an effort to understand his middle son's behavior. "There had to be an answer. Keith was raised just like our other four children. There were no signs that he was in trouble. He wasn't on dope, seldom drank and didn't act like he had problems. He was a healthy physical specimen who enjoyed a normal childhood, fresh air, rural and small-town environments, vacations in the north woods, plenty of pets, fine schools, good friends. Keith had it all. If he could become a serial murderer, anybody could."

Les went to the library and took out every book he could find on the subject, including Lionel Dahmer's *A Father's Story,* a poignant work about the cannibalistic Jeffrey Dahmer. In his opinion it shed little light. He wrote to the elder Dahmer but received no reply. To Les it seemed that the chemical engineer from Milwaukee had taken too much of the blame himself. It was Jeffrey Dahmer who killed and pickled all those people, not his father. Wasn't it obvious that the young man was simply insane?

• • •

Les wondered if there might be a streak of lunacy far back in the family tree. As a child he'd heard gossip that his uncle Charlie, his blacksmith father's brother, had died in a Canadian mental hospital, but no one in the closemouthed clan had ever discussed details. He checked with relatives and learned that the uncle had been committed for incessant masturbation and death threats against his physician. Les thought he might be onto something and kept digging.

A request under the Canadian Freedom of Information Act turned up documents. A death certificate verified that Charles Edward Jesperson, a thirty-two-year-old laborer from Chilliwack, British Columbia, had died on May 19, 1934. The cause of death was listed as "suicide—by driving a 3½ inch nail into his skull." Only a half-inch of the spike had been visible when he was discovered by an attendant. Charlie Jesperson had been locked in a provincial mental hospital for eight years. The general diagnosis was "dementia praecox," a catchall label popular in the 1930s. A clinical note on the commitment papers observed, "Patient says whole family are of neurasthenic types."

Les noted some resonances between his suicidal uncle and his homicidal son. In addition to abnormally strong sex drives and violent impulses, they seemed to share other characteristics. He read on: ". . . The patient's ideas are disconnected . . . his actions are restless . . . rather foolish and erratic in his actions and speech . . . erotic ideas strongly evident . . . he has no insight . . . foolish . . . inclined to be seclusive and does not mix very much. . . ."

To Les the medical report went a long way toward explicating the inexplicable. He realized that it was possible that no one was responsible for what Keith had done—not his parents, not his brothers and sisters, not his wife, Rose, not his victims, and certainly not Keith himself. Like Uncle Charlie he might simply have a screw loose.

Les reported his conclusions to his son in an excited letter. "I read the approximately two hundred pages of text carefully and could see a distinct resemblance to some of your actions. The doctors in this text state that this disease, dementia praecox, is hereditary." He pointed out "a distinct resemblance to Uncle Charlie in some of your actions."

Keith ridiculed the idea. He showed no interest in being certified as a member of a long line of neurasthenics and the lunatic nephew of a lunatic uncle. His vehement disagreement made Les doubt his own conclusions. "I guess you're not crazy, Son," he wrote. "You just let yourself get led around by your pecker."

Les told a friend, "I think Keith kept some of the bodies around to screw them after they were dead." Later he wrote:

> I am predicting that Keith will eventually confess to some killings on the Green River case and to many others all over the United States of America before long. He has mentioned many times that he will be known as the most prolific killer in America. . . . I asked him how many people he actually killed. He looked me square in the eye and said, "Dad, it is in the three figures. . . ."
>
> All these latest developments have left me . . . to take a good look at my life and face realism. Like all the advice my friends have been giving me: distance yourself from your son, go on with your life. I have lost a son. The son I knew has ceased to exist. The man in prison is a sick serial killer. He has turned and bit the one that loved him the most. Even his brothers and sisters have given up on him as he continues to try to drag the Jesperson name through the mud.
>
> How many other fathers and mothers have gone through this same anguish and pain? What have they done? They say that out of everything that is bad something good comes out of it. It has turned my life around and led me to Jesus Christ, who has helped me carry this heavy burden. . . .

Les worried that his imprisoned son might be in mortal danger, especially since he refused protective custody. "I expected to get a phone call someday and find out he's in the morgue. He was locked in with a bunch of thugs. They killed on the outside, and they killed on the inside. I don't care how if you're six-foot-six-or eight-foot-six—a blade is a blade. If Keith didn't end his own life, someone might do it for him. That was my greatest fear."

3 | Media Campaign

From his cell near the mouth of the Columbia River in Vancouver, Washington, the confessed lady-killer issued a drumbeat of claims that he was indeed the murderer of Taunja Bennett and hinted that he might have killed others. From their cells in downstate Oregon, convicted killers John Sosnovske and Laverne Pavlinac chimed in with renewed claims of innocence.

No one in the criminal justice system rose to the bait. The case had been closed for four years, and neither police nor prosecutors showed an interest in proving that they'd locked up the wrong people. In offering "proofs" of the pair's guilt, prosecutors asked how Pavlinac could have led them straight to the murder scene unless she'd been involved, and how she'd known so many inside details about the killing. If Sosnovske was innocent, they asked, why did he cop a plea? The Jesperson scenario was a joke.

Thus rebuffed, Keith smuggled out a succession of press releases in defiance of a gag order. After several newsbreaks he managed to apply enough pressure to force Portland detectives to take him to the venues of the crime to prove his claims. "It was early in October 1995, and they drove me past the little brown house where I killed Taunja. They didn't even slow down. I said, 'Hey, there's bloodstains in there! I'll show you where she peed the floor. It's soaked into the wood. You can bring it out with Luminol. *There's DNA in there, mine and Taunja's.'*

"One of the detectives said, 'Hey, man, it don't make no difference.'

"We drove past the B&I Tavern without going in. On the way out the Scenic Highway, one of the detectives covered the odometer with his hand. The papers had all said that the body was found ten miles from my house.

"I couldn't be sure of the exact place. It was raining hard, and everything was green and grown over. I'd dumped the body five and a half years earlier at one o'clock in the morning—pitch black. All I'd seen was shadows. I told the cops, 'I think it's this canyon here. It's down past that tree branch that looks like a hand. I can remember looking back up from the body and seeing a hand against the silhouette of the moon.' I was in handcuffs and leg irons and asked if I could go down the slope to find the spot. They said no.

"They drove us to the place on the Sandy River where I got rid of Taunja's purse and Walkman. On the way I said, 'You guys don't want to find this stuff. You're gonna bury it. You don't want this thing solved.' They asked me what Taunja was listening to on her Walkman the day I killed her, and I said, 'How the hell should I know?'

"By the time we reached the river, I was convinced that they didn't believe me and would never give me a fair chance to prove my story. So I deliberately pointed to the wrong spot. I didn't want to give them a chance to mess with the evidence. That night I smuggled a diagram to Phil Stanford, a reporter I'd talked to before I was arrested. A crew of Explorer Scouts took the diagram and hacked through the bushes and weeds. Phil and some other journalists were on hand as witnesses. They found the purse exactly where I said they would. Taunja's laminated driver's license was in perfect shape."

41 | Another Liar

Even with the finding of the purse, Oregon authorities doggedly refused to admit that they had prosecuted an innocent man and woman. The comic opera continued for nearly a year before justice finally limped onstage and Laverne Pavlinac and John Sosnovske were freed.

The question of how the hapless couple had managed to get themselves convicted in the first place was answered in bits and pieces. The grandmotherly Pavlinac explained that her pickled paramour's amorous techniques had escalated from blackening her eyes and beating her bloody to threatening murder. After complaints to police produced no action, she set about putting Sosnovske behind bars by implicating him in various crimes and misdemeanors, including a bank robbery that she reported to the FBI. Veteran lawmen put her down as an enabler and crank and continued to ignore her claims.

When Pavlinac heard the news about the Bennett killing on TV, she saw an opportunity. She told police that she'd overheard her bearded boyfriend talking about strangling a girl in the Columbia Gorge. To lend verisimilitude she added a few original touches of her own. She said that she'd helped Sosnovske to dispose of the body and backed up her claim by producing the fly front that she claimed she'd sliced from the victim's jeans.

After the swatch failed to match up with the evidence,

Pavlinac cried and admitted that she'd cut the swatch from her daughter's pants.

A few days later she produced a second swatch that came closer but still didn't match. Then she broke down and admitted that she'd been creating false evidence to "make sure that the son of a bitch is convicted." Her position made a degree of sense to police and prosecutors after she claimed that Sosnovske had threatened her and her four children with death. "It's terrible to live your life in jeopardy," she said through tears. "I want him caught. He's guilty anyway."

Investigators chauffeured her to the old Scenic Highway and asked her to point out where Taunja Bennett's body had been dumped. After a fifteen-minute ride in the police car, the blue-eyed woman peered into the brush and said, "Here!" She was thirty yards off but claimed later, "The cops said I was close enough."

Some of the homicide detectives believed her story, but an assistant D.A. felt that the case was too weak. Plans were made to release Laverne and her mean-drunk boyfriend. She was terrified that Sosnovske would go straight to the nearest bar, drink himself into a rage and exact his revenge. In desperation she committed the ultimate act of self-preservation. She claimed that she'd held Taunja Bennett down while Sosnovske committed rape and murder.

After she was booked on homicide charges, Pavlinac hugged the arresting detectives. Out of her own mouth she'd made herself an accomplice to a capital crime, but she'd also convinced the most cynical investigators of her truthfulness. With the ragged edges of her tale neatly rounded off, she was led into an interrogation room to make a full confession into a tape recorder.

But in the lonely hours in her cell before her trial, the confused woman lost her taste for confinement. She confessed that every word of her story was false. Detectives asked how she'd been able to take them to the spot where the body was found. At first she explained that she'd peeked at the car's odometer till it showed that they were exactly 1.5 miles from Vista House as they approached Latourell Falls, a location that had been described on TV and in the newspapers. When detectives expressed their doubts, the sweet-faced woman admitted that she'd spotted a red splotch of crime-scene spray paint along with broken branches and tire tracks.

None of the investigators believed her latest revised scenario. In the district attorney's theory of the case, she knew the location of the retarded woman's body because she'd helped to dump it there. John Sosnovske was a frail drunk with weak knees. He wouldn't have been able to carry a dead weight down a steep slope without assistance.

At Pavlinac's trial the prosecutor had wasted no time in playing her confession for the jury—"I didn't plan to kill her. . . . I didn't mean to. . . . I feel like it's my fault." As jurors frowned, the courtroom walls resounded with tape-recorded sobs and cries. It was at once the dramatic high point and low point of the trial.

After the woman's lawyer sawed the air in a seven-hour closing argument ("It's not logical to assume that this fifty-eight-year-old grandmother strangled a girl to death. . . ."), the prosecutor calmly replayed the tape. He allowed a suitable pause for his client's Biblical weeping and wailing to have its effect, then said, "You listen to those words and that emotion, and you will look at Laverne Pavlinac and see the face of a murderer."

She was found guilty of murder. Nine of the twelve jurors had voted for aggravated murder, a crime that carried the death sentence. The judge sentenced her to fifteen years to life.

• • •

A week before his own trial, John Sosnovske and his lawyers suddenly realized that he was at risk of the death penalty. He'd already flunked a second lie-detector test—not unusual in suspects under high stress. Prosecutors had found scribbling on a half-sheet of paper in his possession: "T. Bennett: A Good Piece" (apparently planted by Pavlinac).

The defenseless boyfriend realized that his own jury would soon hear his old girlfriend's hysterical voice implicating him in a vicious rape-murder. If the tape recording had convicted her, it might convict him. Hours before his trial was set to open, his lawyers plea-bargained a life sentence.

5 | Rotting Remnants

From his county jail cell, his curly brownish mane shorn by an inmate barber, Keith Jesperson continued his campaign to muddy the legal waters. Most of his confessional letters were sent after his own lawyer told him to shut up. The notes were uniformly upbeat—"Have a nice day, from Happy Face."

He wrote to the *Columbian* in Vancouver, Washington:

> *First of all, you probably want to know why I am doing this? Well, it has robbed me of sleep for five years. . . . I am in fact the Happy Face Killer that Phil Stanford has talked about in his editorials. I created that man because I wanted to be stopped but it is hard to just come out and say it.*

Another letter ended: "I am sane! I know what I want. I want to save everybody a lot of taxpayers money. I want justice to be served."

He buttressed his credibility by using a fellow prisoner to leak information that helped California police to clear three open cases: the strangulation murders of Cynthia Lynn Rose near Turlock, an unidentified woman named Cindy near Corning, and the woman he'd known as Claudia in Blythe. He also confessed to the Laurie Pentland killing in Salem, Oregon, and the murder of Angela May Subrize.

In his cell he drew complex diagrams showing the final resting places of his victims. Bodies found by police search crews turned out to be decomposed beyond recognition, but enough rotting remnants appeared to substantiate his claims.

Whenever he was moved, Keith was surprised by the security measures. "They put me in handcuffs and leg irons. I had to take baby steps. Outside the jail people stared at me in my bright jumpsuit. The cops had a neck leash in case I started to thrash around. We were on I-5 when four police cars shut down a rest area so I could use the toilet. I shuffled up to the urinal with cops on my left and right. I said 'Well, guys, who has the biggest one?'

"A laugh came from one of the shitters, and the cops covered the stall and wouldn't let the guy out till we'd cleared. When he finally came out, he gave me a thumbs-up. Later his truck passed us on the highway and he pointed to his CB mike. He was telling the world how Happy Face made the cops turn red."

As always Keith seemed to enjoy the attention.

6 | Worst Face Forward

The psychopath makes a mockery not only of the truth but also of all authority and institutions.
—Arnold Buss, M.D., *Psychopathology*

As his revelations mounted, the killer turned to the Internet for more attention and notoriety. Members of America Online were inundated with tasteless examples of his lack of empathy, balance and taste.

Through a pen pal with a computer, he opened a Web site and offered a "Self-Start Serial Killer Kit—Now you can be the only serial killer on your block"—and a life-size blowup doll of a murdered woman. In articles that began "Hello my Internet Fans!" he referred to his victims as "my piles of garbage," and made other emetic comments in the process of soliciting donations for his legal defense.

AOL, prodded by outraged members, shut down his Web site, but outrageous and contradictory statements continued to emanate from his jail cell, most of them in interviews with the media: "I actually killed 166 people in five states over twelve or thirteen years." "I didn't only kill women. I beat a man to death at the mines in Canada." "I never said I killed 166. It was much less." "Sosnovske and Pavlinac paid me twenty thousand dollars to lie for them." "I only ever killed one person in my life." "I'm innocent."

"I'm the victim of a fix." "I'm guilty as hell. Now let 'em prove it."

He informed a TV reporter that he didn't kill Taunja Bennett and "now you know the truth." To his most egregious lies he routinely added, "I swear all this to be true as God is my witness."

He explained later that he'd been deliberately sowing doubts about his reliability and sanity. The resulting headlines reflected confusion: "Ringmaster to His Own Media Circus." "Happy Face Killer Denies Wyoming Slaying." "Serial Killer's Cyberspace Forays Push Limits," "Jesperson Offers Another Confession," "Murder Admissions Were Lies," "Man Who Claims to Be Killer Still an Enigma."

As plea-bargaining overtures began, a veteran Wyoming public defender expressed doubt about the Jesperson strategy: "It's a terminal illness to go around confessing to murders. . . . He is literally pissing in the wind—and, I might add, pissing all over himself in the process."

The party of the first part disagreed. "I'm still alive," he said. "I haven't been executed. So is my strategy right or wrong?"

In an open letter to Wyoming prosecutors, he said, "Boy, have I got a deal for you!" He promised to waive extradition and stand trial for the Angela Subrize murder provided he was assigned a court-appointed lawyer at public expense. He promised that if he was sentenced to death, he would draw the case out for so long that taxpayers would be outraged at the expense and demand to know "the name of the idiot that forced the death sentence on me." He promised to bankrupt any state that dared to try him for a capital offense.

• • •

Annoying as his manic arrogance seemed to be, there proved to be some method in his loudness. After early consultations with his lawyers, he'd realized that the main evidence against him was his own words. "That's really all they had. By the time they got to the bodies, they couldn't even determine the cause of death. The Florida woman was bones. Angela Subrize was destroyed under my truck. Claudia's body was eaten on by animals. Cindy laid behind boulders for months. In all those cases they had my confession and nothing else. And a confession without corroborating evidence can't be used as evidence. I knew *that* much about the law."

He was firmly on record that he'd strangled Angela Subrize in Wyoming and ripped up her body on a freeway in Nebraska, but he revised the scenario after Wyoming governor Jim Geringer extradited him to stand trial for capital murder. The U.S. marshal's plane had hardly landed in Cheyenne before the accused man began explaining that he'd lied about the murder site because he wanted to draw Gerry Spence into his defense.

The Cowboy State's famous defense lawyer declined the invitation, and when the Subrize case slid from the front pages and into the cold reality of the courtroom, Wyoming prosecutors began to see the enormity of their task. Now that Jesperson had advertised himself to thousands of possible jurors as a pathological liar whose statements and confessions were as variable as the Rocky Mountain weather, a first-degree murder conviction was unlikely and the death penalty clearly beyond reach.

"I outsmarted them," Jesperson gloated. "I knew that if I threw enough crap to the media, the more I'd lose my credibility, and eventually the authorities would just want to get me off their hands. The minute I'm not in the news, I could die in my cell that night. The police wanted to kill me so bad, I thought there'd be a setup and they'd say it was a suicide. With a little help from the media and the Internet, I made a mockery of the system. I convinced the whole damn jury pool that I was a liar and my confessions were worthless."

He referred to his new archenemy, Wyoming governor Geringer, as "the flounder who bit the hook and refused to let go as I reeled him in" and "has sucked the wrong pepper-flavored egg this time." He derided the Oregon and Washington prosecutors. "They didn't want confessions. They wanted to prove my guilt in court. They wanted the glory of solving the mystery known as Keith Jesperson. They wanted a big public conviction. I took that away from them."

As the killer escalated from excess to bombast, some began to perceive him as a narcissistic, immature man-child, obsessed with getting his way, even if it meant destroying his family's good name and making a public fool of himself. He seemed proud of his chicanery and often repeated his signature claim: "I'm a liar and a damn good one."

Producers from the Fox Network issued a challenge of their own. They offered to hook him up to a lie detector and hire former O.J. Simpson prosecutor Marcia Clark to ask the questions. "Bring it on," Jesperson said. "This time I'll tell the truth."

Privately he said, "I never failed a polygraph test in my life. If you lie all the time, it's easy." Fox dropped the idea.

After the bumptious prisoner had been held in a Laramie jail for five months, the frustrated Wyoming officials gave up and returned him to the Northwest.

7 | Crocodile Tears

The grandiosity and pomposity of some psychopaths often emerges in dramatic fashion in the courtroom.

—Robert D. Hare, *Without Conscience: The Disturbing World of the Psychopaths Among Us*

At a hearing in the Julie Winningham murder case in Vancouver, Washington, Keith continued to show his contempt for authority. Addressing the bearded judge, Robert Harris, the confessed serial murderer said, "Your Honor, I was kinda hoping for a week's furlough for Christmas. But I don't believe Santa Claus will give it to me." He grinned at the judge and added, "Well, Santa, reach into your bag of goodies and give me what I've got coming, sir."

Judge Harris sentenced him to thirty-four years and four months.

Julie Winningham's sister, Joanie Faria, told reporters that she would try to withhold tears for her sister until the killer was put to death. "No matter what my sister did in life, there was no reason for what he did. This monster makes a joke out of murdering somebody. He shows no remorse."

• • •

After the "monster" was sentenced to life without parole in the other murder cases, the *Wall Street Journal* observed that he spoke in the "anodyne voice of an accountant" and suggested that hell would be "an appropriate place for him." Once again psychologists pointed out that such flat affect and failure to feel remorse were the classical signs of antisocial personality disorder, also known as ASPD, psychopathy or sociopathy. To professionals in the field of behaviorism, Keith had never been much of a mystery.

Ever protective of his image, the lady-killer offered a different spin. "Of course I feel remorse. But victims' families don't want to hear about it. Remorse isn't gonna bring anybody back. What good does it do to apologize? It's a waste of everybody's time."

In jail awaiting transport to the state penitentiary, he continued to play the lead role in his own dramatic production, autographing shirts with a Happy Face, sitting for self-important interviews, firing broadsides to the media and offering generous legal advice to his fellow inmates.

On the day that John Sosnovske and Laverne Pavlinac were freed for good, he described his reaction to the Associated Press: "I started crying. I couldn't help myself for about ten minutes. I lost total composure. I was just very overjoyed. Basically my feeling is God bless them."

He didn't explain why he'd allowed them to serve four years for his crimes.[8]

• • •

---

[8]Eventually the legal fandango was transformed into a cable TV presentation titled *Happy Face Murders,* described by a newspaper critic as "a repellent little documentary." The Showtime movie featured Ann-Margret as the aging Pavlinac and opened with a written disclaimer: "Most of what you are about to see is true. The stuff that isn't true is the stuff that's most believable. Go figure." To insiders the glib wording was almost understatement.

The Happy Face Killer was scheduled to began serving his stacked-up sentences in February 1996 as inmate number 11620304. His file showed him to be forty years old and in good physical health. He was rated a "moderate" escape risk with anger, aggression and cognition problems. He would become eligible for parole on March 1, 2063, a month before his 108th birthday.

9

KEITH

HUNTER

JESPERSON 5

1 | Life Inside

When it was time for me to start my life sentence, two guards dressed in black chained me up and put a metal box between my wrists so I couldn't get out of the cuffs—not that I would've tried. The big guy said he would shoot me if I made a move to escape.

Most of the cops and detectives who'd worked the case were pissed that I'd gotten two people out of prison and beat the death penalty myself. But some of them still had a morbid interest in Happy Face. When we pulled into the Intake Center in Clackamas, one guard asked if I would pose with him for a picture.

I was put in solitary confinement in "D" block to keep me safe from other prisoners. Lady-killers and rapists ranked near the bottom of the food chain in the prison system, barely above child molesters and crooked cops. I was allowed one hour of yard time a day—no books, no cards, no nothing. Wherever I went, the pointy fingers came out. Everyone wanted a piece of the celebrity.

On my way to the showers, I had to pass in front of ten other cells. Those little fellows acted pretty tough behind their bars, but if you opened their doors they'd piss their pants. They feared me for what I was, a serial killer who enjoyed it and said so. They didn't know how to handle somebody like me. Who did? I didn't know how to handle myself.

• • •

After eight days in the processing center, I was strip-searched and loaded into a van with other traveling cons. At Oregon State Penitentiary in Salem, I was searched again and issued jeans, T-shirt and tennis shoes by an inmate who'd had the same job for ten years. He said, "You're Happy Face?" He looked nervous. It didn't take him long to spread the word.

Now I was a "FISH": "Fresh Inmate Stopping Here." They put me in the tank. The place was scary—so many hard-asses with cold stares. I expected more of a welcome. Didn't I give myself up to free two other convicts? Shouldn't the other inmates at least respect me for that?

Instead they began to spread gossip that I cannibalized my victims or had sex with dead bodies. They didn't understand that the death game ended when life ended. I had the same revulsion about dead people as everybody else.

When the bell rang for dinner, the doors clanged open and a couple of dozen men shuffled toward the chow hall. At first I stuck out like a neon light.

A con in the chow line asked if I was Jesperson. I nodded. A buzz began. After I collected my meal, I tried to find a place to sit, but they kept saying, "Not here. . . . Keep walking. . . . Move on, man. . . ."

At last I found a guy who didn't reject me. I ate in silence. I could hear whispering behind my back, "That's him!" "That's Happy Face!" "That's the mother-fucker! . . ."

I was assigned to Delta Block and celled in with another inmate. First thing he said was, "You better not be no rapist or pedophile. I don't want to live with no freak. What're you in for?"

I told him I killed eight women, but I wasn't a freak. I

found out later he was a child molester. He hated himself and didn't want to associate with other sickos. He claimed to be born again but found no forgiveness for my crimes. A hypocrite, in other words. The prison was full of them.

The first night we were together I came back from the chow hall to find him all pissed off. My bunk was soaking wet. Someone had thrown coffee through the bars—maybe another inmate, maybe a guard. I got coffeed every night for a week. I thought to myself, *What a bunch of cowards. Don't have the guts to take me on.*

The situation made my counselor offer to put me in protective custody. I was still a little shook, but I said no. I was told that some of the inmates planned to shank me in the yard. I told the security guard I didn't intend to give up any yard time. If they wanted to shank me, tell them to stick it deep. They won't get a second chance.

After that, I was put in a one-man cell. It was five-and-a-half-by-six feet, with a bed and a toilet. The walls were steel and the front was made of one-inch hexagonal bars on four-inch centers. I had a steel desk, a chair and a lockbox for my personal material.

Once a day I was allowed to go to the yard, and it was still the most dangerous place. There's nothing meaner than a crowd of yellowbelly cowards. You didn't dare show any fear. If those piranhas found out you were scared, you were finished, especially somebody as notorious as me. I had to take my fears head-on if I was ever to be accepted. So when I went to the yard, I walked the track like I owned it.

One day a bunch of inmates encircled me. A loudmouth little shit did all the talking. "Hold it right there, motherfucker." "You don't look so tough." "Who you think you are, big man?"

I stopped in the middle of the track and waited. The guy said, "Did your mommy spank you when you were little? Is that why you had to kill women? You look like a pussy, man."

I stared hard into his eyes, and after a while he moved off with the other cowards.

On the track a couple of nights later, I heard two guys talking loud enough for me to hear. "I'd love to hit that prick one time!"

I whirled around and said, "Why not right now?" They couldn't get away fast enough.

A few weeks later five gangbangers stopped me in the yard. One got in my face and told me he was Taunja Bennett's cousin. I said, "Okay, I'm sorry it happened. Now what do you want to do about it?"

He says, "I'm broke, man. You gotta help me out."

I says, "Not gonna happen." I was nervous about being surrounded, but I didn't show it.

One of the sucks says, "He's crazy. He'd probably fight back."

I said, "Bet your ass I'll fight back. I'm not taking extortion lying down. I'll take you out one by one."

My nose and the leader's nose were a few inches apart. He was a Hispanic or Indian type, tattoos on the back of his neck, a toque on his head to make him look tough. I said, "You'll be the first to go, man." He backed off. I was six-six and he was five-nothing.

In the shower I was confronted again—forty or fifty naked guys jacking around and making smart remarks. One thing was for sure—nobody in the shower had a shiv. If there was a fight, it would be bare fist against bare fist.

I yelled, "I'll take as many of you on as I can. Who's gonna be first?" Nobody moved.

When I got back to my cell I tried to figure things out,

but I couldn't make any sense. *I barely got here, and they're cutting me in the chow hall and coffeeing my bed and busting my chops in the yard.* I'm starting to think that nobody likes me. Back in Clark County Jail an old con told me that when I got to the state pen the inmates would shake my hand and buy me Cokes and want my autograph. He was full of shit, like most convicts. These guys don't wind up in prison by being bright.

As I wiped more coffee off my bunk, I thought, *Well, hell, I don't like my jacket either! I wouldn't like me any more than the other guys do. I'll be in here for the rest of my life to deal with what I've become—a self-admitted serial killer. Everybody hates me, and I hate myself. And we're all right!*

In those first few months the only good thing was that Dad wasn't here. Maybe I killed people because I wanted to be sent where he couldn't find me. Alone at night I had more peace than I ever had on the outside. None of the other guys could understand that, but they hadn't been raised by Dad.

2 | Outcast

Everything went the same for three or four months—same scene in the chow hall, same cracks in the yard, same rumors. I got goddamn sick and tired of being coffeed, so one night I skipped my evening meal and waited in my cell. The guy was starting to toss the coffee when he spotted me. He turned six shades of white when I jumped up and told him he was a dead man.

Talk about me being a freak—*this guy was the freak!* A longhaired hippie, a castoff of the sixties and seventies. To me all drug users were freaks. Dad taught us that the worst thing a kid could do was to take drugs like those longhaired hippies. The freak gave me a wide berth after that, and the coffeeing stopped.

Weeks went by and I still couldn't figure out how to be accepted in the chow hall. There were forty tables. The drug dealers ate together, and so did the blacks, Hispanics, Aryan Brotherhood and other cliques. Back when I drove truck I refused to join up in our company caravans, and I kept the same attitude in prison.

Mostly I ate by myself. When I'd start to sit with others, some guy would always get up and leave. He thought he was better than me because he was in for cocaine or pot or thievery and I was in for killing women. I'd wave and say

"Bye-bye," and dig in. Otherwise I avoided all eye contact.

One guy said, "How many girls did you kill?" I said eight. He said, "Me, I only killed one."

I said, *"What?* You didn't have the balls to do it again?" That kind of comment didn't help my popularity.

Another guy says, "I don't want you sitting next to me."

I said, "You're a Christian, right? Aren't you supposed to forgive?"

He says, "What's your problem?"

I said, "I don't have a problem, man. I forgive you for being upset that I'm in the same joint with you."

He sat there stewing. Then he says, "Yeah, I'm a Christian. But you're a stone killer. Jesus would never forgive a guy like you."

I said, "Are you a jailhouse Christian or a real Christian? If you're a real Christian, when are you gonna start learning the Bible?" I showed him up as a hypocrite and he went to another table.

If you did make friends in the chow hall, they'd give you heartburn with their stories. It's like they were all turned out on the same printing press. Every one of those guys was misunderstood. Somebody else fired the shot. It wasn't meth, it was aspirin. The cops planted the coke. *It wasn't my gun.* . . . Two thousand men, and they were all railroaded.

Well, I wasn't. A man couldn't possibly be *more* guilty. I was caught fair, tried fair, convicted fair, and sentenced fair. I was a self-admitted degenerate killer. The other guys couldn't handle that kind of talk. It was too hard on their hypocrisy level.

3 | Linebacker

I knew that sooner or later I'd have to defend myself in a real fight, and it happened in April 1996, two months after I arrived. I was watching a volleyball game in the yard when a guy sucker-punched me in the nose. I didn't go down, only bent over a little. He was another longhaired freak, and he was running away. At least twenty men saw what happened. But when I looked up, they were all looking elsewhere.

I sat on a bench till the bleeding stopped. Somebody asked who hit me, and I told them to mind their own fucking business. I waited by the gate where everybody had to pass. The longhaired freak showed up and I hit him flush in the left eye—lifted his ass right off of the ground. Then I body-slammed him. Before I could finish him off, a guard tackled me and I was cuffed and led away.

For the next three weeks I learned to deal with life in Cell 105 of the Disciplinary Segregation Unit. I liked the hole. We were locked down twenty-three hours a day, but at least they supplied reading matter. With no distractions I could read a book a day. Breakfast was served on trays in our cells—a lot better than having to go to the dining hall and worry about getting a shiv up your ass.

My stomach started to balloon up on the veggie trays

they served, so I just ate breakfast. It was a nice, quiet life—nobody to bother me, nobody to argue with. We could shower every day. On the way I'd hear the other guys yelling at me—how I was a piece of shit and they would fuck me up good when they caught me out in the yard. It was all talk.

General population seemed more peaceful when I got back. I'd proved that if somebody challenges me, I will put him down. A friend said that when I swung at that hippie, prisoners ran in all directions. They knew I had nothing to lose by killing again.

From then on nobody challenged me directly. But they kept on circulating rumors. I got a cushy kitchen job as "linebacker," keeping the food boxes filled up and the line moving. I was the best linebacker they ever had—did the work of two men. But somebody put out word that I intended to poison the population. From then on I was barred from the kitchen jobs. Too bad. I liked that job.

After a while they let me have my own TV and AM-FM radio. That meant I didn't have to go to the card room to watch the big-screen TV and take the chance that some punk would try to make a name for himself. I would do my assigned work and take my shower, and the rest of the time I'd stay in my cell.

In prison danger comes from all directions, especially if you're high-profile. You can never prepare for it. You have no privacy. My whole world revolved around what went on in front of my cell. My view was of a walkway enclosed in wire mesh. When I was sitting on my toilet, anyone could watch. Sometimes it would be a female guard trying to make me uncomfortable. I tried to put on a good show.

One day an inmate came up to me in the yard and started asking a long list of questions. Some of my answers were true and some not. The next day I was called into the security offices. The dude had put a hit on me. He thought he could sell my answers to a crime author, and if I was dead, the information would be worth more. That's the way their pea-brains worked! This taught me not to give out personal information. And it reminded me to watch my mouth.

The next threat came from cigarettes, which I never touched. OSP was a nonsmoking joint, but that didn't mean there was no smoking. The guards would break a cigarette into three and sell each section for three bucks. For your money you got a couple of drags. I was happy that I didn't smoke.

One numbnuts sent a kite to the security unit saying that he would start killing guards if they didn't restore our smoking rights. He signed my name and added a Happy Face. Lucky for me that he left his greasy fingerprints on the kite. Like I said, they wouldn't be in prison if they were smart. He wound up in the hole. I wondered if this kind of crap would ever end. It never did. That's the price of fame.

4 | The Regular Visitor

Now that I was all alone in Keith's World again, I began to have anxiety attacks. I couldn't explain them and I didn't know what brought them on. When they hit, I wanted to smash things, even my own. I would get this overwhelming contempt for personal property, hate it, be repulsed by it. If something of mine was too nice, it made me anxious and had to be destroyed.

I tried to fight off the attacks so I wouldn't end up wrecking everything I owned. The pattern went back to my earliest years. When a puzzle was too hard, I trashed it. If something malfunctioned, I got rid of it. When I got bored with my toys, I wouldn't put them aside or give them away, I'd smash them. I never figured this out.

For a long time I couldn't keep pictures of myself and my family. I knew I would never see my kids again, and the pictures panicked me. I'd cut them up or send them off in the mail. Memories were not for me. My brothers apparently felt the same way. My kids wrote once in a while, and Sharon and Jill kept in touch, but Bruce and Brad cut me dead. Never visited, never wrote.

Dad became my only regular visitor, twice a year, rain or shine. At first I didn't know whether to be mad, glad or sad. It was nice to have one last little contact with my family, but most of the time he seemed to be trying to aggravate me. He couldn't wait to tell me that Brad and Bruce ripped up my letters without reading them. He said I'd made their lives too hard and they never wanted to hear my name again.

I laughed when he said that. He said, "What's so funny, Son?"

I said, "Aw, gee whiz, Dad, Bruce and Brad tormented me all my life. Now they're getting payback, and they don't like it. You don't think that's funny?"

He didn't. He said that old friends in the Yakima Valley had stopped talking to my brothers, and their kids got taunted in school—"Happy Face! Happy Face!" I knew damn well that if my nephews grew up to be serial killers, I'd get the blame. That's the way it was in our family. Whatever went wrong, it was Keith's fault.

My sex life didn't change all that much when I first went to prison. I'd always had to masturbate, and I just picked up my schedule a little. I tried to relive those special moments I shared with my victims and some moments I wished we'd shared. My penis remembered every detail of the Death Game and what each woman did to try to make me stop.

Most of my fantasies were still about Taunja Bennett. I would dream of having her in the shower and then throwing her on the mattress and screwing and beating her to death all over again.

In my fantasies about Jean, the nursing mother in Corning, I'd throw her over the hood of my car and screw her hard instead of dicking around half the night and letting her get away.

I brought Julie Winningham back to mind so vividly that she might as well be have been in my cell while I masturbated. She was almost a living presence. Made me almost sorry I'd killed her.

• • •

After my first year inside some of my sex fantasies began to fade. I could still see aspects of my victims—Taunja's black eyebrows, Claudia's round little ass, Angela's Tweety Bird tattoo bobbing up and down as she rode my cock. But I couldn't revive the feeling of killing them. I guess you have to keep up on the Death Game, or your mind drifts off to other things.

I started seeing myself in my dreams, like watching home movies. I'd see Dad stand over me and take off his belt. I'd try to say it wasn't my fault—and no words would come out. I'd yell, "I didn't do it. *I didn't do it!* STOP!" Then I'd wake up. I could never challenge my dad, not even in dreams. Other inmates cut out their parents' hearts at night.

One night I escaped from prison, bought a lottery ticket, and cashed in $100 million before I woke up. I think they call that wish fulfillment.

All my life I used to get teary eyed when I read about personal tragedies, survival stories, rescues. I liked to read about heroes in the *Reader's Digest* or see them on TV. In my dreams I became the hero who saved lives instead of taking them. Those were the sweetest dreams of all.

10

FATHER

AND SON

1 Bigger Than O.J.

An Oregon detective annoyed Les Jesperson with a series of pointed questions about Keith's claims. First the interviewer warned, "Some of my questions are personal and might hurt you." Then he asked permission to tape-record the interview.

Permission granted, the detective asked the anguished father if he'd ever beaten his wife. "We had arguments," Les responded, "like any married couple." But he'd never used physical force.

The detective wanted to know if Les had ever used Keith "as a punching bag."

Les replied with heat that he hadn't. Well, had he ever used his belt? "Yes," Les replied, "as did my father, grandfather, and the schools in those days." He explained that he didn't hit hard enough to produce cuts but might have left the odd mark on the boy's skin.

The detective asked if Les had seen Keith torture or kill animals. "No," the father responded. "I never did." If he'd witnessed such an act, he said, he would have done something about it.

Les didn't tell his interviewer how distressed he was by his son's behavior, but he explained to a friend: "Keith will do anything for publicity. He wants to be up on that pedestal where everybody sees him. He doesn't care if they applaud or throw rocks, as long as he's noticed. He keeps telling me he'll be bigger than O. J. He argues with judges like they're a couple of high school debaters—no respect, no sense of where he is and how he should behave. Why, he called the governor of Wyoming an asshole! What does that say about his mind?"

As though to confirm his father's charges, Keith appeared on the network news program *Dateline* and admitted that he was contemptuous of the justice system—"It's humorous at times to see the craziness."

His voice took on a sepulchral tone as he parried his interviewer's comments.

"People don't know whether you're telling the truth, whether you're lying, whether you've killed these people, whether you killed 5 people, 8 people, or 166 people."

"That's right."

"Why should we believe anything you say here today?"

"Because I'm telling the truth. . . . But, see, am I telling the truth this time, or am I lying to you?"

He was asked if it made him feel powerful to embarrass prosecutors. "At times," he answered. "It makes me feel like I have some type of control on it."

A chilling exchange near the end of the interview sounded as though it originated in a mausoleum:

Q.   *How many murders have you committed?*
A.   *I've told the number as up to around 166 people.*
Q.   *A hundred sixty-six people?*
A.   *Yes.*
Q.   *You must have been killing a person a month, almost.*
A.   *Yeah, that's normal.*
Q.   *Normal to you.*
A.   *I'd kill 2 or 3 a week.*

Q.   *How could you have killed 166 people and not get caught?*

A.   *It's easy. . . .*

After the interview aired, there was a short truce between father and son while they made plans to cash in on the national publicity by coauthoring a book. Keith did the math: "Ten percent of a $6.00 book is 60 cents times 100,000 copies = $60,000—a million copies, $600,000."

Keith agreed to supply the raw information, and Les, in his late sixties but still busy with poetry and other writings, would cobble up the text. As he explained to a reporter on the Chilliwack *Progress:* "I have four other children who are good. I write as a hobby . . . and as therapy. My doctor said writing about Keith would help. Of course, the story is as well a history of the family."

He told the reporter that he'd written an earlier book about his own life and printed up fifty copies for his family. He'd written a work about life as a snowbird, living in an RV. "I also wrote a prize-winning poem. I write a lot of poems and try to put humor and living into them."

The first eighty pages of raw autobiographical material arrived in Les Jesperson's mail, and the old polymath was shocked to read in wordy detail how he'd beaten his son with his belt, punched him in the face, overworked him, cheated him in business dealings, sabotaged his plans for college, and in general transformed a good little boy into a serial killer.

Keith recalled the ensuing blowup. "Dad wrote back right away and complained that I blamed it all on him. Then he burned my manuscript. I told him to write the damn book himself, any way he wanted. He said he couldn't write it without my input. He wrote, 'You can trust me to handle it right. I'm your dad.'

"I sent him more stuff about his style of punishment,

and he didn't like that, either. He told me I needed to write the truth. I said, 'Dad, this *is* the truth.' I told him if we published a book that left out what made me a killer, nobody would read it. And he said nobody would read it if I blamed everything on him and his belt."

Members of the extended Jesperson family were dismayed by news of the work-in-progress. The consensus was that the family scandal had been sufficiently publicized.

Les seemed oblivious to his relatives' unease and set to work on *My Son, a Serial Killer?* He decided on a frank, semi-apologetic tone:

> *I know you have not enjoyed reading some of the gory details of this story, but it has served its purpose in helping me cope with my depression. Time heals with a death and in a lot of ways this is a death. I have lost a son. The only thing wrong here is that there is no positive ending. He will always be in prison and in my mind as a blemish and as a sad spot. He has dragged the proud name of Jesperson through the mud. . . . Maybe some day he will repent. May the Lord have mercy on his soul!*

The manuscript had reached some sixty thousand words before he yielded to family pressure and gave up.

2 | Apologia

Inside Oregon State Penitentiary the serial killer penned a book-length counter-draft of his own in the classical protagonist-antagonist form. He wrote about the deaths of cats, alcoholism, his father's belt, dead dogs and horses, electric shocks, family favoritism. He sent the hand-printed text to his father, who demanded an immediate denial in writing.

Keith stewed for a few weeks before he concluded that his father was only trying to save face and probably intended to flash the exculpatory document before old and new cronies, his banker, his barber, and the other members of his family. No harm done. At last Keith complied with the request:

> *A lot of times I've wanted to sit and write to you and tell everything, to let you know how I feel and to let you know the whole truth. Sometimes I would write it all and just flush it. So much has happened in my life I have been ashamed of. To blame my father for my childhood is crazy. He is a good father. . . .*

The long letter again posited the existence of two Keith Hunter Jespersons, one normal and law-abiding, the other a work of the devil:

> *This man that rides along with me carries out the evil deeds. I try to keep him under control but at times he protects me the only way he knows how.*

In any case, he stressed, his childhood was not to blame.

Swept up by his conciliatory mood, Keith then wrote to his old mine bosses in Elkford, B.C., and apologized for stealing the leather pants and other items. He also reached out to old childhood and family friends. At Christmastime he wrote:

> *I remember the good times I had with Dad and Mother and the fun we shared. It wasn't always hardships. And I want to make up to my ex-wife Rose. I want to go back to the day we separated and swallow hard. If I had just sat and talked it out instead of rushing out the door to drive another load. . . .*
>
> *Regrets? Damn right. I regret ever leaving my family and not having the balls to swallow my pride and admit I was wrong.*

A similar mea culpa arrived at two of Keith's home newspapers, the *Selah Optimist* and *Yakima Herald*:

> *I wish to apologize to the Selah community and the Yakima Valley, along with my friends, coworkers and family for my actions in my crime that brought everyone undue hardships and criticism in their lives.*
>
> *The problems in my life that caused me to be a serial killer were problems that I brought on myself, not from my childhood. My brothers and sisters are not murderers and yet they had the same parents and lived in the same community as I had.*

*I am not the Green River killer like some people
want to believe. All of my crimes happened after I
left the Yakima Valley.*

*All of my friends and relatives are not respon-
sible for my actions. But many people act like they
are. I have lied to everyone at one time or another. So please people of Yakima and the surrounding area, don't punish them for my crimes.
It is bad enough to lose me to what I've done
without dragging everyone I have known through
the mud as well.*

Sincerely,

*Keith Hunter Jesperson, the so-called by the
Press 'Happy Face Killer.'*

A scribbled addendum instructed the editors to "please
print this letter in its entirety in your paper." His letter was
ignored.

When there was no public reaction to his apologies, Keith
threatened suicide. He wrote his father:

*I miss my kids and . . . if they visit me in the next
five years then we can still come to love each
other. If not I will overdose on something to end
the misery or stretch my neck to get it over with. I
have thrown my life away. . . . I will not prolong
it. . . . Death will be a comfort to me.*

He still had accounts to settle with Les. He wrote:

*Dealing with your antics all of my life it isn't hard
to see how I turned out the way I have. . . . You
are up to your old tricks again in that thing you
call a brain. . . . Thank God for that letter you
begged me for. Thank God for the apology you de-*

manded from me. You know why you wanted it and it wasn't to give you peace of mind like you said. It was to discredit me as telling anyone of abusive behavior I was dealt by your hands. Hell Dad! . . . It only shows the world how desperate you are to save face.

Sure we had some good times, but we also had some bad times too. I have always been afraid of you and treated you as my friend to only watch out for the games you were playing on us kids . . . always for control. . . .

You're screwing with the wrong people Dad. . . . At least now you admit you used the strap. . . . You might as well stop writing me and visiting me. I feel like the boy named Sue. I look at you as in the end of that song. You are my Dad because of the gravel in my gut and the spit in my eyes. . . . You created me to be like you. If you don't like what you see, then leave me and never come back. I can live without you and sometimes I feel better for it. With you, everything is a price tag, well I'm tired of paying you. . . .

Forget I exist. . . . I do love you Dad! Because you are my Dad.

The patriarch of the Jesperson family wrote a friend that he was "floored" by the outburst.

I now realized I had a very sick son in that prison. I called Brad and read him some of the letter. I felt so depressed that I had to talk to someone. I did not and never have felt guilt for Keith's crimes. I did feel however that by talking to my other son, my grief would be relieved somewhat.

Brad confirmed without hesitation that what Keith wrote was straight bullshit, to put it in his own terms. He advised me to drop the whole thing and forget Keith. He said that Keith was just dis-

turbing the whole family and life was not worth the hassle.

I looked back in my correspondence file and dug out the letter in which Keith told of a normal life as a child. . . . I took that letter along with the hate letter and had copies made. . . . I wanted all to know the truth as Keith was actively spreading this propaganda around in an effort to blame someone for his crimes. This is a hard pill to swallow with all the love I still have for my son.

3 | The Letter Wars

Father and son settled into a year of epistolary combat, with the heaviest salvos muffled by pro forma protestations of love. The love-hate messages made fascinating reading in the prison censors' office:

> *Son, I am feeling numb and like a zomby. I keep thinking back when you were a kid running behind the trailer, hanging onto the endgate going into the Blackwater. Then the tears come and I can't stop them. . . . I can imagine you dressed in a Mountie uniform, Son, instead of prison garb. What a waste of a good person. I will never get after you for your vicious deeds as those were performed by a Keith Jesperson that I do not know.*

> *Your poems always leave a bad taste in my mouth, Dad. . . . I'm tired of having poor, poor, pitiful me rolling over and over thru the lines. Please when you write poetry to me again leave out the pity. I don't need it. . . .*

> *Well, Son, I guess if you are in a cell for 22 hours every day for a long time you have a right to think a little different. . . . I am sure that if your mother*

was alive you would not say that she wants pity. She would be so torn apart that it would bring about her demise.

You want to throw my mother's death at me, too? . . . Nobody tells the truth anymore, Dad. . . . I wasn't born this way! I was created by all of my experiences, before I killed . . . I have nothing really to live for. . . . Last week a man with 104 years to do left the only way he could. He hanged himself with his own shoelaces.

Keith, I wrote a poem about my feelings. . . . It's called "Oh God Be With Me." I submitted it in a poem contest sponsored by a large book store and won first prize. . . . I guess you forgot it was my birthday on the 14th of March.

. . . . If you do not make out our [book] contract as I want, then you can suck eggs till you are blue in the face and still not get anything more out of me. If you threaten me, then it is over before it gets started. . . . Have a nice day.

Received your letter yesterday, Keith, and was shocked at your sucking eggs bit. There are other ways of being firm without being rude. . . .

Dad, you don't follow directions very well, do you? I will not write a contract with you, ever! . . . Don't give me threats of our trust. I quit trusting you a long time ago in business. . . . Dad will do what Dad wants to do, no matter what anybody else has to say. I love you.

The last letter you sent was full of bitterness and resentment. It left me with a feeling that it was not my son that was writing that letter. . . . I have *never reprimanded you for your terrible crimes. . . . I have forgiven you and have asked the Lord to forgive you also. . . . You have to admit you have put your family through one hell of a mess. People don't know where I live so have missed most of the harassment.*

Your brothers and sisters have not been so lucky. Brad has had life threatening phone calls and verbal harassment. . . . Your nieces and nephews have had slanderous remarks thrown at them at school. Sharon's been bitter over the whole thing, expressing disgust at your desire for publicity. I think it would be nice for you to send us all a letter of apology. . . .

Dad, I do two hours in the morning of classes so if I get out of prison I won't do this again. The class is called anger management, deals with the way I was raised and the punishment dished out to me as a child. We talk openly about the belt and wooden spoon and the fist and backhand and the verbal abuse. . . . Under the program we have the prison pointing into your corner on why I am here and why I turned out to be a serial killer. But that is alright, Dad. I still love you, anyway. . . .

In reading your and Sharon's letter, Son, it seems that I am the worst father that you could of had. I beat you and don't know when your birthdays are. I have no love or compassion and am interested only in money. I was always drunk and thought only of myself. I don't keep in contact with the grandchildren, and Betty and I spend too much. I haven't worked in years and spend all my time down in Yuma.

Just read that paragraph over again and sit back and think. You two have hurt me beyond description. . . . The modern shrink is good at blam-

ing one's problems on what happened as a child. . . . I remember using the belt but it never was applied without justification. I got it when I was a kid and also it was applied in school. I remember that real good. . . .

Yes, Keith, I was, and I say was, an alcoholic. It is true that I always had a bottle with me under the seat or in the pack saddle. This is all over with! I quit on my own and never had a drink since. You should be proud of me for that. . . .

In reading your letters and story I see there is a lot more I am to learn about your activities. I am getting immune to the hurt but the feelings of a father who has a son like you cannot be minimized. I was completely unaware of you killing dogs or shoplifting. . . .

You must have a hell of a sex drive to do what you did. That thing in your pants controlled your mind. Just take what this letter says as fatherly advice. . . .

Dad, we must both understand what goes on in our own heads are fact. I do respect you and love you very much and do not want to hurt you at all with this anymore. I am very aware of the discipline that we all got as kids and what I got, I very well probably deserved it. . . .

The reason I sent Sharon your letters and you Sharon's letters is to show you both what I am hearing. . . . There is something that causes us to be bitter towards you and vice versa. . . . Let's bury the hatchet and pick up and go on.

I was so pleased to receive your last letter, especially the last line. . . . I was watching the Montel Show yesterday and he states that his dad used the belt on him. He also stated that he deserved the licking. He said that if the same lickings were

*given today it would be called child abuse. . . .
You can not lay a guilt trip on me for your childhood. I am proud of our family, even you, Keith.
You showed some courage in setting those two
people free from jail. It shows there's some good
in you. . . .*

*Please do not blame me for your problems as I
am not a killer and have had a lot more lickings
than you have had. I love dogs and while I do not
want a cat around, I would not kill them for the
fun of it. . . . I look forward to your letters each
and every day.*

*It is your son that writes the letters, Dad. . . . I
just wrote some of the beatings I had gotten at the
times. Also wrote of the good times on our life.
Yes, you used your fists on several accounts. Of
course you don't remember them because you
were drunk at the time! . . .*

*Your apology is accepted and I am sorry for
what pain I may have caused you in referring to
spanking as beatings and to insinuate the outcome of a harsh and obsessive upbringing. I had
wanted you to see it as I saw it through my eyes
and that was a mistake to assume that you could
see it that way, not looking at it through the eyes
of a young boy growing up. I apologize for the
problems I have caused. I love you. . . .*

*Keith, Betty and I have sent you $250.00 via
money order so you can buy a TV. We can not
imagine spending all the time you have to in your
cell without this entertainment. . . .*

*Dad, there were problems at times with the justifi-
cation of an ass whipping when I had gotten it at
school as well. . . . I never remembered Bruce*

getting it and only a couple of times that Brad did. When I was a child, I felt that I was the one you picked to get mad at and to use your belt on. . . .

I was living in fear. . . . I was scared and frightened of getting into trouble. . . . Then I decided to change the outcome of your rages and brought you close to me. . . . getting into the pleasing mode. To do everything to please you, to give you gifts that you wanted. I was different from my brothers and sisters. Birthdays came and they gave you pennies and I gave you the wind machine you hinted for. Paid for it myself. Then when it was completed and the glow in your eyes was seen by all, they jumped in and took the credit and paid me nothing for their share of it. What about that square clock by your bed and with the large numbers and radio? The same happened there.

. . . . And when you asked for payment of room and board, who was the only person to pay it? Me! All I had given was kept and they had not paid a cent. I did not want to make waves. I needed you to be mellow toward me for the fear of the belt. . . .

Then I looked at what positives that you were in my life and realized that it was me that controlled my destiny and you had only been there to help guide me along. You held the reins and gave me a kick in the right direction and hopefully I would follow your lead. All you did for us kids was to try to make us grow up with respect for ourselves and for you as well. I began to really see you as you were. Not perfect, but my father that tried to do us right with the best he could do. . . .

By seeing the passing away of mother and the coming of Betty and the spark in your eyes and also the tears, reminded me that you are only hu-

*man and that I do love you. Each time I drove to
see you I couldn't wait to hold you and stroke
your hand and play cribbage and beat you at it.
Sometimes I would let you win. . . .*

*I appreciate your effort at frankness, Keith, found
it hard to believe how you could do such things,
especially drag the victim under the truck, and
being so quick to take a life. . . . In every case the
crime was entered into because of a sexual desire. . . . I had another poem of mine published in
the Church bulletin in Yakima. I called it Living In
God's House. . . .*

*As on the phone, Dad, didn't you realize that we
really do not have much to say to each other? The
phone conversation seemed strenuous at best. Yes,
it was good to hear your voices. . . . Come and
visit me sometime if you can stand being in prison
with me. The visitation room has no glass to hide
behind.*

*Be honest with your Dad and tell me the truth. I
don't think you better yourself by stringing anyone along. Thank you, Keith, in advance, for being honest with me. . . .*

*You are in self denial, Dad. To you, you are an an-
gel! One without sin. <u>Hear Me Out!</u> You admit to
drinking steady and yet you don't believe you
were a drunk or an alcoholic. Then why did you
quit? . . . You remember being drunk three times.
How many times don't you remember anything at
all? Please describe drunk to me. . . . What impression did you give me while you <u>drank all the
time?</u> . . . You have been a king bullshitter for a
long time. . . .*

   What is remorse? Saying sorry for what you

have done? Well, I've done that. What do you want me to do? Cry every day? Bullshit! It doesn't sound as if you want to bury the hatchet on this. . . . This is a reality check. I do love you and care for you. But wake up. . . .

Two months ago you begged for the right to visit me. May 31st the clearance came and still with only one hundred miles between us you have not come to visit. What is wrong? Are you afraid? . . . Well screw you too, Dad. . . . Just stay away! . . . Love, Keith

Keith, I am through with blaming each other for everything. . . . As each of us believe that we are telling the truth, lets both ask forgiveness to each other and go on with life. I now ask your forgiveness for anything I have done to hurt you or make you angry at me. . . .

Dad, when are you going to visit me? Are you planning it soon? . . . I have sent letters to Bruce and Brad and asked for forgiveness. . . .

The visit to see you was enjoyed by Betty and I both. It was nice to give you a hug and hand shake. I still have trouble when I look at the picture we had taken at the prison. It is hard to think that your stay in that place is permanent, period. . . .

Dad, I guess I should be thankful to have a father around when I grew up and still now, as everyone else wants to wish I wasn't born. You are not going to live forever and there will be a day in the not-so-long future that I will be told of your passing. What do you want said over your body as they lower it into the ground or roast it into ashes? I would like to say that I loved you very

*much and only regret to tell you before you died
that you mean so much to me.*

*Keith, the last letter I got from you was dated Feb
5th, over one month ago. I have written you two
times since and have had no replies. I am worried
to what has happened. I hope I have not done
anything that has caused you to not write. What
gives? . . .*

*[A detective] questioned me about brutality
with my children. Thank God you sent me a letter
telling the truth about your childhood where we
had fun fishing etc. and did not blame me for your
crimes. The lickings were the norm, and your
killings were your own idea. I sent him a copy of
that letter.*

*. . . . The other night I had a realistic and heart
rendering dream. I was looking at you standing in
front of me along with Brad. You were about ten
years old. In my mind I knew what I know now,
that you turned out to be a serial killer, even
though you were only ten and had not done anything bad yet. You were wearing those short
brown pants and the brown and white striped
shirt your mother made for you. I reached over to
you and hugged you. I cried as I asked you why
are you going to kill when you grow up.*

*It was so real that it woke me up. I had tears
from my eyes running down my face. I still ask
you why. You just don't know the pain I have suffered.*

4 The Visit

Despite the flareups in the letters, Les and his second wife Betty continued to be Keith's only visitors, arriving twice a year in their thirty-five-foot "fifth-wheel" trailer pulled by a Dodge Ram diesel that cruised smoothly at sixty-five, as the old man proudly told his son.

Keith noticed that whenever Les took his seat on one of the hard metal seats in the open visiting room, his eyes began darting toward the exit, and he usually left before the scheduled visiting period was over. The son observed this behavior with bemusement. He looked forward to the visits, but he reminded himself that he and his father would always be out of sync. He wrote about one of the visits:

> I learn that Dad and his wife are here when I come back from lunch. I get into my good clothes and make it down to the visitors' room. Even before he comes in, I know what to expect. He's begging me to see his side. We make eye contact, and I can see tears in his eyes—not tears of joy to see me again, but tears of knowing his son is in prison for life and he has to come to visit. They're tears of self-sympathy, as if what I've done has affected his own retirement and motivation. I kind of laugh to myself at how pathetic this is.
>
> We hug each other, and I feel the mass of flexed

muscle he tightens up to show me his power. He holds a white piece of paper in his left hand. It is the questions he wants to cover in the visit. Very businesslike.

I've gained weight, but he doesn't show any negative response, only that I look better, my color is better than the last time. He's buttering me up for the kill. "Do you want anything, Son? Pop? Candy?" I get a Snickers bar and a coffee. Betty keeps the Snickers coming, more coffee and some jelly beans. They remind me of the jelly beans Mom used to put on top of our birthday cakes.

Dad covers the bad news and good news first— then on to the real purpose of his visit. "I almost didn't come this time, Keith," he says. "I cried at how you still are blaming me for what you did. But no! I came in here to see my son. I have to love my son no matter what he's done."

He says, "Keith, when you wrote about me shocking you in the greenhouse, you made it sound as if you were seriously hurt. Son, it was in fun! You got it all wrong. It wasn't 220 volts, it was 12, the same voltage we used in the lighting."

We both know better, but I won't argue. The 220 was for the three big exhaust fans. I helped to wire them in. Dad says he shocked us kids with 12 volts, just for a joke, and nobody complained because they could hardly feel it. I just let him talk. If it made him feel better. . . .

It's a typical day in the big open room. These visits are life and death to some of the inmates. A black guy is talking nasty to his white visitor. He leans into her face and spits, and the guard on duty picks up the phone. Two other guards grab a guy who's talking with a little old lady—his mother, I guess. They must suspect her of passing dope. That means this visit is over, he'll have a *full body-cavity search, and the next time mom sees her son, it'll be through glass.*

Dad is fidgeting around, taking it all in, but there are other things on his mind. After a while he says, "Son, let's get something straight once and for all. You have a bad memory. Why did you blame me when you were arrested? Why did you do that?"

I tell him, "Well, Dad, it was real easy to just say you're an alcoholic and you really couldn't help yourself."

He says, "You didn't have to say that, god-damn it! Sure, I drank when I was younger, but I was never an alcoholic."

I say, "Dad, you were drunk every day by noon."

I'm watching him squirm, like he's thinking, Goddamn it, I wish I could just stand up and pop this punk and teach him a fucking lesson. *That's what I've been waiting for. One day he'll snap. He'll take off his belt one more time. And I'll drop him.*

He's so upset about being called an alcoholic, he's shaking. I'm thinking he's really in a bad po-sition. He's lost control of me and everybody else in our family. . . .

He says, "Son, I still have a hard time believ-ing what you've done. You must have been on drugs."

I deny this, but it doesn't satisfy him. I tell him, "The consensus of opinion about serial killers is that it comes from their parents."

This is not what he wants to hear. He says, "Didn't you write me a long time ago that I was a good father and it wasn't my fault?" I tell him that I sent him the letter he requested so he could show it around. He tells me to stick with that story because it was the truth.

He says, "It wasn't your mom's fault, and it wasn't my fault. It was that thing between your legs. Thank God your mom isn't around to see you in here. What would she think of you now, Keith?"

I say, "Mom isn't with us anymore. She's dead."

He asks what the state will do with my body when I die. I tell him I think they'll incinerate me with the rest of the trash, or hang me up in the yard for a piñata. Dad doesn't get the joke— death is a serious subject for him since his prostate cancer.

I tell him to spread my ashes along Interstate 90 from the flatbed of a 379-Series Pete conventional tractor with plum paint and a Vari-shield and ten grand worth of chrome. Make sure it's washed and waxed. Then I wonder, Is he worried about my dead body or does he just want control of my ashes?

I wolf down another Snickers bar and the rest of the jelly beans. He has a couple of questions about driving truck, and I can see he still feels competitive. He starts talking about shifting gears, and I have to tell him he's got it wrong— "It's basically a five-speed, Dad. . . . Then you come back to second instead of first. . . . That knob in the center position, you shift it like a super-eight. . . . Then bring the other knob up, 1 2 3 4 5 6 7 8 9 10. That one's like a super-ten, but you have a double under. . . ."

He's barely listening, pretending he already knows the shift sequence. When he's finally reached the last question on his list, he tells me he has to leave because some friends are waiting outside. I'm thinking, Friends outside? You got a son inside, you son of a bitch! Which is more important? There's still thirty minutes left!

To keep him around, I point out Randy Wood-field, "the I-5 killer." He's talking to a gorgeous young woman with big tits. Randy is a handsome guy, a star jock, drafted by the Green Bay Packers. It seems like he has a different female visitor every week, and they all have big tits.

I say, "Dad, look over there. That's Jerome Brudos, the lust killer. He made lampshades out of his victims' skin."

I point out a couple of thrill killers, Price and Bradbury. Dad keeps saying they look like ordinary people. Well, what the hell does he think we are? Hannibal Lecter? We are ordinary people. We don't have horns.

This visit ends like all the others. We hug and say good-bye, and he whispers, "You need a good licking for what you put me through." He can never leave without saying that. He says, "I wish I could just put you over my knee."

Whenever he leaves, I make sure to tell him I love him. It might be my last chance. And he tells me the same. Tears well up in his eyes. Not me—I never show tears. Tears are a sign of weakness. When you cry, you're always crying about yourself. It's self-pity.

As he heads toward the exit with Betty, I remind myself that he's got cancer and other medical problems. All those years of breathing tobacco smoke and welding gases and black-smithing fumes ruined his lungs. Every time he gets a cold he's at risk of pneumonia. He's never far from his oxygen tank. He's on antidepressants.

Sometimes after the visits I feel worse than when he stays away. Maybe I'm in here to force everyone in my heritage to shape up, to take heed of being a good parent and show love to one another. I am the person in the family that created the most impact on everyone else, so much that it

shook up the foundation of everyone named Jes-
person and they will only have to mention my
name to bring in the reality that being selfish and
doing anything illegal will destroy their way of
life. My terror is now their hidden terror. Never
will they outrun the horror of my story. I will be
ever etched in the back of their minds for all of the
generations to come.

   I feel power in their pain.

5 | The League of Serial Killers

With the last threads to his family broken or under strain, Keith thought about making new connections. But how? And with whom? He certainly didn't want more contact with his fellow inmates. There were too many crosscurrents, feuds, racial divisions, too many snitches, opportunists, angle-players. And there was too much resentment of him and his notoriety.

He tried to decide what type of person might want to correspond with a serial killer. Bleeding heart social workers? Teenagers looking for kicks? He'd had enough of that kind of attention.

The answer came to him with a jolt—why, other serial killers, of course! Maybe they strangled and stabbed and shot innocent people, but that doesn't mean they're unfeeling monsters. *Just look at me!*

They could exchange advice and information, discuss mutual problems, pass along their artwork and photos, share their fears, hopes, news, legalese, holiday cheer, and their courthouse smarts and savvy. He reckoned himself the ultimate arbiter on issues of crime and punishment. "When I went down, I had ignorance of the law. I was flying blind. I had to sit in my cell and analyze things before I wised up. Now I could help other lifers. And by figuring them out, maybe I could learn a little more about myself."

Most of his correspondents were on death row, and he

prided himself on being the rare exception. He seldom
tired of explaining how he'd outmaneuvered the authorities. "A feat in itself!" he wrote to an admirer. "A serial
killer that does not get executed. *Unheard of!"*

His first attempt to establish contact with a marquee murderer had taken place early in 1996, while he was still juggling legal problems in Oregon, Washington and
Wyoming. He'd written a friendly letter to Danny Rolling,
facing execution in Florida for the massacre of five college
students. Jesperson's letter to "the Gainesville Slasher"
congratulated Rolling on finding a new girlfriend—"she
sounds like a neat and great person." The letter had a whiff
of sycophancy. "Hope all will go well with you, my friend
in Christ," wrote the lifelong agnostic. "God bless you. No
response is needed."

None was received. While Keith was awaiting a reply,
the fastidious Rolling was telling a third party that he
found the Self-start Serial Killer Kit and Keith's other at-
tempts at Internet gallows humor in atrocious taste. "That
kind of humor doesn't impress me," said the man who'd
slashed four victims to death and decapitated a fifth.
"There is NOTHING, absolutely nothing about KILLING
that is humorous."

After the rebuff Keith waited a year before contacting
other killers. Then he started a correspondence with Jeff
Shapiro, a triple-murderer who was being held in a super-
max prison in Colorado. Shapiro's approach to cruelty and
violence seemed as lighthearted as his own. "You must
have an encyclopedia of different pen pals and the like,"
Shapiro wrote admiringly.

The correspondence was short-lived. "Shapiro began to
act annoyed that I got so much media coverage. He's a foot
shorter than me and I guess it made him jealous. I wrote,
'If you want some press, go out and get it, man! It's not

hard. Just stick your nose where it doesn't belong. Act arrogant. Do something weird. The media will make you famous.' Then the silly son of a bitch hinted to me that he was the Green River Killer. His stupidity meant that from now on the prison would be studying every word we exchanged. I didn't need that kind of attention. I cut him off."

An enthusiastic "Greetings from Paris!" opened an exchange with Nicolas Claux, "the Vampire of Paris," a former mortuary assistant serving life for cannibalism. Claux enclosed a photograph of himself in his cell, working on drawings that were eerily similar to the pictures that Keith was just beginning to turn out for his friends. Also known as "the Ghoul," the Gallic gourmand was pleased to share his own expertise:

> *I personnaly think that any kind of spiced sauce will spoil the naturally sweet taste of human flesh and blood—human meat is a gift from the Gods, and it is a shame to ruin its delightful taste with seasonings and spices. . . . Bon appetit!.*

A less-inspired correspondence began after Keith saw the serial killer Arthur Shawcross on the TV program *Justice Files* and sent off a letter: "Instead of writing groupies, why don't you write to another convict?"

Shawcross, murderer of two children and eleven women, was an avid artist like Claux and had auctioned some of his primitive paintings on the Internet before being sent to the hole for violating prison policy. His letters were barely literate and full of whiny complaints. Keith offered the child killer some unsolicited advice on doing time, but Shawcross, nearing his twentieth year in custody, failed to respond.

• • •

Keith wrote Pierre Navelot, a French citizen serving thirty years for decapitating a woman, and Javed Iqbal of Pakistan, the confessed murderer of a hundred children, but there was no response from either. Patrick Kearney, a homophobe who had left thirty butchered bodies alongside California highways, proved friendlier. Kearney wrote in an upbeat letter:

> *Keith, you and I have corresponded with some of the same people. This building has birds in it. They come right up to you and beg for food. No fear! I even saw a guy walking around with one sitting on his shoulder.*

Kearney, "the Garbage Bag Killer," was full of gossip about other imprisoned murderers ("Bobby Beausoleil of the Manson clan was in Oregon for awhile but has been moved elsewhere"). He complained about being transferred so often—"we call it 'bus therapy.'"

Tommy Lynn Sells, "the Coast to Coast Killer," a carnival roustabout who had conducted a twenty-year murder spree, agreed to join the letter-writers on receipt of "a little good faith." Keith lost interest when he read that "$100 would be a good start."

Charles DeFrates, a Washington serial murderer and cop killer, sent erudite letters from the penitentiary at Monroe, Washington. A killer from Kansas called himself "Slavemaster." A seventeen-year-old Oregon prisoner claimed that "voices" made him murder a seven-year-old girl and hide her body under his parents' floorboards. The boy wrote, "I have my problems but I can get well don't you think dreams can come true?" Keith dispatched several pages of solicitude and advice.

• • •

Angel Maturino Resendez, "the Railway Killer," proved to be the most bizarre member of the group, writing letters that seemed to have originated in a rubber room on a psychiatric ward. Once the FBI's Public Enemy Number One, Resendez awaited lethal injection in Texas for murdering three dozen victims while riding the rails. His envelopes came festooned with slogans, cryptic messages and irrelevancies: "Viva la France," "9-16-1999 Mexican Independente from Spain," "Do not purchase anything made in China. . . ." He referred to himself as "the angel of death" and wrote letters almost as long as Keith's.

The pen pals endured a rocky period when one of the Jesperson letters was made public. Resendez had sent it to a third party who posted it on the Internet, resulting in newspaper articles about how easy it was to kill and avoid the death penalty, plus five pages on the fine art of defeating the justice system. When Keith learned of his worldwide exposure, he fired off a message:

> *Please don't give my letters away . . . when the pricks get letters I sent you, do you know that he now can sell the rights to copies? . . . If I cannot trust you to keep the material I sent to you, then I will no longer write you.*

A chastened Resendez replied: "Man I fuck-it-up for you. I was especting something good out of this. I do not blame medication, I did not try to reach into my mind to see what could happen. . . . I did you bad my Friend."

The Hispanic killer promised to avoid future problems by returning Keith's letters after he read them. He wrote:

> *The day I get Kill many will be kill also. I have so many followers, and I must die to show that I did not fear to die in order to truely serve God and my Lord Jesus. I will be more dangerous when I die.*

Like his fellow correspondent, the Railway Killer was
given to exposition and exegesis, often for pages on end.
He explained that John F. Kennedy, Jr., died because of "a
Radra Round antena as the one use to deteck military air-
craft." He described abortion clinics as "temples of Baall
and Moleck and must be destroy." He quoted religious ad-
monitions about homosexuals and reeled off pages of Biblical references that Keith ignored. He sent his "shortest
poem":

> No!
> No! No!! No!!!
> No!

It was signed, "par Angel." Les Jesperson, the only
prizewinning poet of Keith's acquaintance, read the poem
and observed that it needed work.

By the turn of the millennium, Keith's serial killer network
was taking up most of his time, but he doggedly answered
every letter. "These were my people. When they first got
arrested, they were naive, stupid, didn't know how to handle the legal system. I would tell them guilt or innocence
makes no difference—it's what the cops can prove that
counts. I'd teach them how to get second-degree murder
instead of first. I'd teach them about alcohol, drugs, prison
medications. The smart ones realized it was a good idea to
keep in touch, even some of the old cons.

"Charles Manson was always after new followers. If
you wrote and said you'd like to join his family, you'd get
a letter that looked like it went through a blender. Most of
the time, other prisoners would answer his mail for him,
and they used a signature stamp. Another easy one was the
Night Stalker, Richard Ramirez. Promise to worship him
and his demons and Satan and you were in like Flynt.
Henry Lee Lucas used to write to anyone who sent him ten
dollars. And John Wayne Gacy loved young men. All you

had to do was pretend to be gay or bisexual and he would start reeling off his sexual exploits. He even sent money to his young lovers so they'd visit him in the prison. Nobody went into mourning when he was executed."

6 | Author, Author

To supplement his contacts with butchers and maniacs, Keith stayed in touch with criminologists, journalists, TV producers, detectives, high school students, lawyers, teachers, researchers, distant relatives, doctoral candidates, celebrities, "jailhouse Annies" and other aficionados of bloody murder. On the phone it never took him long to launch into his well-worn accounts of resentments, angers, slights, injustices, favors unreciprocated, justice denied, paydays when he was shorted, undeserved punishments, grasping females, males who cheated him or let him down.

He answered all letters in a free-flowing artistic hand with rounded Os and Cs and his trademark Happy Face symbols to verify authenticity. He generously volunteered suggestions to investigators who were working to solve murders, and he often corrected experts in the voodoo art of profiling.

He was careful to alter his tone to suit his audience. To a teenaged gunman in Georgia, he wrote: "Now it is your duty to tell the public why you went to school to shoot it out. Thank God you didn't kill anyone!"

He had no hesitancy in offering advice about such matters as habeas corpus, Miranda, rules of procedure, courtroom style and decorum. As though he were running for national office, he prepared position papers on capital punishment, religion, law enforcement, the psychology of crime, and fired them off to the media under catchy titles: "From Being to Prison and Beyond," "The Fears of Murder," "The Gimmes of Law," "Who Really Are They? Morons?," "The True Power of Confessions," "The Glove of Justice That Covers the Hand of Deceit," "A Tale of Two Tails. . . ."

Certain privileged correspondents were treated to book-length versions of his life and hard times. Since Oregon prisoners were denied access to copying machines, he had to handwrite each new version. A manuscript to journalist Robert Ironside was scrawled across two thousand pages, which were soon followed by a scathing twelve-hundred-page satire titled "The Adventures of King Pin Trisani and Johnny Foreskin Forwood" (variations on the names of Wyoming prosecutors who had sought his execution).

He provided a 900-page version of his life story to a fellow prisoner who immediately put it up for sale but found no takers.

He sent a 60,000-word "novel" to his father, explaining that the fictional form provided more latitude for the real truth about his life. Besides, the novel might be a commercial success and he could use the money. The tone was tasteless and lurid:

> *A dim light in one of the sleepers allows me a view of two bodies fucking. . . . I hope to see naked skin. . . . She positions herself to suck me off. . . . She slides up and straddles my penis and guides it up in her. Moans of false pleasure purr from her lips. . . . My limp penis falls into the cool air. I lean down to kiss her, but she refuses to be kissed. This was about sex. Not love! Sex and money! Murder! I feel excitement as I ponder the thought. . . .*

• • •

One book-length manuscript after another kept the prison censors busy. Keith explained that he intended to continue committing his insights and discoveries to paper "till I get it right." In a version written in mid-2001, he summed up his most recent conclusions about his favorite subject:

> *My motivation wasn't to get off. It was to kill these women. The killing itself wasn't a sexual turn-on. When they were alive, I had sex with them, but the killing was simply for killing's sake. It wasn't for the rush of power or to get even with women in general. I like women. I just didn't like these women. Something just simply caught me wrong with them to have me decide when and where I'd kill them, like putting them out of their misery.*
>
> *Taunja Bennett reminded me of Peggy and her partying ways. Claudia called herself a throw- away woman, so I threw her away. Cynthia died before I got any sex. Laurie Pentland died be- cause I decided to pay her for sex and then kill her. Cindy died because I knew I would kill her af- ter I got her in my truck. Susanna died because I picked her up knowing she would die. Angela Subrize pissed me off with her lies. Julie Winning- ham was a doper.*

Much of his incoming mail came from social scientists with a professional interest in his case, but some letters were simply exercises in bad taste. He tended to laugh off threats and seldom took unsolicited criticism to heart.

An angry woman sent an oddly punctuated inquiry about his fourth victim, Laurie Pentland:

> *Did you know that Laurie was a very abused child? She had been raped by old men all of her childhood and then she was raped by her brother that she did not even know. Then she came to live*

with me and she had a baby his name is Chris you took his mother away from him and he will never get to know her. . . . Could you please tell me for sure what day Laurie died and what time it was. What was her last words and what did you do to her . . . and did she suffer how long did it take her to die? . . . Did Laurie fight for her life or did she just let you kill her?

Keith told a friend: "The woman who wrote that letter was Laurie's pimp. I knew her very well. When Laurie wasn't around, she used to blow me in the truck-stop parking lot. She was as big a whore as Laurie. She has a hell of a nerve criticizing me." His attitude seemed to be that pimps and prostitutes deserved what they got.

7 | Survival

On most days he spent his yard time on the phone, endlessly reciting the minutiae of his life to anyone who would accept his collect calls. Like his father he was his own font of knowledge and wisdom, offering detailed ruminations about family relations, parenting, marriage, "driving truck," education and his all-time favorite subject: how he outwitted his prosecutors and cheated the executioner. Some of his contacts listened with interest and even egged him on, but by 2001 most were declining his dollar-a-minute calls.

Journalist Robert Ironside maintained the relationship longer than most. "Keith seemed so needy of notoriety and attention. He sent me interminable letters and phoned me four or five times a week. I honestly felt a strong rapport with him. But sometimes he made me feel odd, offbeat, as if I'd touched something evil. He liked to mock the last sounds of his victims, gurgling and blubbering with their last breaths. He cried once, reverting into a little girl's voice, imitating a victim begging for her life. It reminded me of one of our politicians mimicking the voice of a woman he was about to execute. One night he said in this very flat voice, 'You know, Rob, it's harder to kill people than you think.' He sounded like he was talking about stepping on a roach."

• • •

Keith logged his mail in a notebook—a habit left over from his truck driving days. In 1999, he sent 372 letters. After tightening his stamp budget so he could buy art supplies, he mailed only 242 letters in 2000 but received 465. Some of the letters were to and from his three children and two sisters. He had no contact with his brothers.

He estimated that he made five hundred collect calls a year. His father was steadfast in his semiyearly visits, and his older sister, Sharon, made three trips to the penitentiary. Keith kept a long list of names on his official visiting list, including every member of his family, but no one except Les and Betty showed up after 1997.

He often had to fight off black moods. "My nighttimes in prison are spent dreaming of seeing my kids one more time. Would I escape if I was let out by accident? Damn right I would. Back to Canada, to Chilliwack. I should have gone there thirty years ago. Dad never should have made us leave.

"Now my life is over. Sometimes I hope for death. If the state had offered the death sentence, I might've taken it—*if* I could have been executed the same day. But I didn't want to sit in a cell for twelve or fifteen years waiting to die.

"I often think of my attempted suicides. Maybe I succeeded! Maybe this prison is the hell where I was supposed to go! Think about it. Nobody's ever come back to describe hell. How can I be sure I didn't die when I took those pills?

"My future is to survive, that's all. To die an old man inside these walls. I keep trying to feel better. I polish my story. I write letters to vampire friends like Nicolas and crazy friends like Angel. I draw with colored pencils. I watch TV or take long walks on the track or lift weights or play miniature golf on our putt-putt course. I work, I visit, I play cards. There aren't many inmates who play crib-

bage, though. I do miss crib. Dad and I used to have some
hot games."

At forty-seven Keith told a counselor that he'd stopped
thinking of suicide and was beginning to feel at home with
his surroundings. In his one-man cell the sharp geometric
edges of the outside world began to blur and fade in his
mind. Like other lifers, he stopped watching newscasts.
"None of the news on that screen will ever have the slightest effect on our lives."

In the prison society he no longer felt excluded, exiled,
an object of snickers and ridicule. Nor did he tremble in
fear. His size had always made him feel different, but it
also afforded protection. Prison personnel reported that his
inner rage seemed diminished, or under better control. He
spent less time feeling sorry for himself and attacking his
detractors. In some ways he seemed to be living the best
years of his life.

Since he would never be returned to society, he was offered
only token psychotherapy, but he tried to gain insights on
his own. "People say I killed for no reason. I think there
was a reason, but I'm not sure what it was. I keep trying to
figure it out."

He still refused to trace his sexual sadism to his great-
uncle Charlie or other genetic factors. He realized that he
lacked feeling for his fellow humans and regarded this as a
moral defect. He was curiously impersonal about matters
like sociopathy and narcissism, empathy, bonding, attach-
ment. When he discussed such subjects, it was in terms of
others, never himself. He expressed a rote sort of remorse
about his victims, but only when prompted. He seemed to
view the eight murdered women as minor supporting ac-
tors in the drama of his life.

•   •   •

The conflict with his father appeared immutable. In correspondence and conversation, he continued to refer to Les as "that prick" and "that son of a bitch." But kinder comments revealed his ambivalence. "I still love my dad," he said. "I love him for his talents, his sense of humor, for all the things he taught me." He quickly added, "Dad is a fuckup to the family. I really didn't want to be like him."

On rare occasions he seemed willing to accept some blame for his crimes. Early in 2001 he wrote a friend:

> *Ever since I was arrested in Arizona, I've been denying responsibility for what I did. I blamed everybody else. Now I'm beginning to realize I had choices, and I chose wrong. Me: not others.*
> *I guess I'm where I belong.*

INDEX